Critical Acclaim for other books from PC Learning Labs

PC Learning Labs Teaches DOS 6

" ...if you can follow a cake recipe you should manage it [the book]."

"The hands-on approach is very effective in reinforcing and clarifying the information presented. This is a good book for beginners, especially for people who want a clear path to follow, with the assurance that at the end of the road they'll know a lot more about DOS 6.0."

—Neale Morison, *PC User*

"With graphics and illustrations and lots of background snippets, you get the 'ah-so' exhilaration when puzzling jargons suddenly become clear."

—Francis Chin, *Straits Times*

"For the beginner who really wants to make the best use of DOS, this is an excellent...highly recommended...learning tool."

—Hugh Bayless, *Monterey Bay Users Group Personal Computer Newsletter*

"Step-by-step instructions in the book are used with the disk's data files to provide readers with hands-on practice they need to advance to more sophisticated computing. The book is organized into easy to follow lessons allowing readers to work at their own speed."

—Emery Jeffreys, *Dayton Beach News Journal*

" ...will take a novice and move him/her up to speed quickly."

—Barry Mishkind, *Radio World*

PC Learning Labs Teaches DOS 5

"This book from an organization with 10 years of classroom teaching of personal-computer operation under its belt makes the learning process both easier and organized. It's like having a personal teacher...you will emerge a confident user of personal computers..."

—Hugh Anderson, *Gazette*

"[This] book is designed to help you attain a high level of DOS 5 fluency in as short a time as possible.…a solid foundation of skills in DOS file management…"

—Woody Liswood, *MicroTimes Magazine*

PC Learning Labs Teaches Microsoft Access

"The book is written in a very clear style with numbered, step-by-step instructions throughout. The layout, choice of fonts, and screen dumps are excellent and very appealing."

—Richard King, *PC Update*

" …uses a friendly, straight-forward style to take a new user by the hand through Access. New users should get the PC Learning Labs offering…highly recommended."

—Andrew Cameron, *PC User*

PC Learning Labs Teaches WordPerfect 5.1

" …a tightly focused book that doesn't stray from its purpose…it concentrates on the beginner, and it stays with the beginner."

—William J. Lynott, *Online Today*

"Excellent keystroke-by-keystroke instruction is provided by this handsome book."

—*Computer Book Review*

PC LEARNING LABS TEACHES WORDPERFECT 6.0 FOR WINDOWS

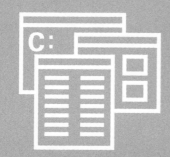

PC LEARNING LABS TEACHES
TEACHES
WORDPERFECT 6.0
FOR WINDOWS

LOGICAL OPERATIONS

Ziff-Davis Press
Emeryville, California

Writer	Susan L. Reber
Curriculum Development	Logical Operations
Editor	Jan Jue
Technical Reviewer	Dick Hol
Project Coordinator	B. Dahl
Proofreader	Cort Day
Production Coordinator, Logical Operations	Marie Boyers
Cover Illustration	Carrie English
Cover Design	Ken Roberts
Book Design	Laura Lamar/MAX, San Francisco
Screen Graphics Editor	Cat Haglund
Technical Illustration	Steph Bradshaw
Word Processing	Howard Blechman, Cat Haglund, and Allison Levin
Page Layout	Bruce Lundquist
Indexer	Valerie Perry

Ziff-Davis Press books are produced on a Macintosh computer system with the following applications: FrameMaker®, Microsoft® Word, QuarkXPress®, Adobe Illustrator®, Adobe Photoshop®, Adobe Streamline™, MacLink®Plus, Aldus® FreeHand™, Collage Plus™.

Ziff-Davis Press
5903 Christie Avenue
Emeryville, CA 94608

ISBN 1-56276-020-3

Manufactured in the United States of America
10 9 8 7 6 5 4 3 2 1

CONTENTS AT A GLANCE

TABLE OF CONTENTS

INTRODUCTION

Welcome to *PC Learning Labs Teaches WordPerfect 6.0 for Windows*, a hands-on instruction book that will help you attain a high level of Word-Perfect fluency in the shortest time possible. And congratulations on choosing WordPerfect 6.0 for Windows, an easy-to-use, feature-packed word processing program that will enable you to create professional-quality documents with a minimum amount of training.

We at PC Learning Labs believe this book to be a unique and welcome addition to the ranks of how-to computer publications. Our instructional approach stems directly from a decade of successful teaching in a hands-on classroom environment. Throughout the book, we mix theory with practice by presenting new techniques and then applying them in hands-on activities. These activities use specially prepared sample WordPerfect files, which are stored on the enclosed Data Disk.

Unlike a class, this book allows you to proceed at your own pace. And we'll be right there to guide you along every step of the way, providing landmarks to help you chart your progress and hold to a steady course.

When you're done working your way through this book, you'll have a solid foundation of skills in

- Creating, editing, enhancing, saving, and printing documents

- Working with tables, columns, templates, and styles

- Building mail merges

- Creating and customizing a button bar

This foundation will enable you to quickly and easily create sophisti-cated, professional-quality documents (such as letters and reports).

READ THIS BEFORE YOU PROCEED!

We strongly recommend that you read through the rest of this Introduction before beginning Chapter 1. If, however, you just can't wait to dive in, make sure that you first work through the section "Creating Your Work Directory," which appears later in this Introduction. You must create a work directory in order to perform the hands-on activities that appear throughout the book.

WHO THIS BOOK IS FOR

This book was written with the beginner in mind. Although experience with word processing and personal computers is certainly helpful, little or none is required. You should know how to turn on your computer and use your keyboard. We explain everything beyond that.

HOW TO USE THIS BOOK

You can use this book as a learning guide, a review tool, and a quick reference.

 AS A LEARNING GUIDE

Each chapter covers one broad topic or set of related topics. Chapters are arranged in order of increasing proficiency; skills you acquire in one chapter are used and elaborated on in later chapters. For this reason, you should work through the chapters in sequence.

Each chapter is organized into explanatory topics and step-by-step activities. Topics provide the theory you need to master WordPerfect; activities allow you to apply this theory to practical, hands-on examples.

 You get to try out each new skill on a specially prepared sample Word-Perfect file stored on the enclosed Data Disk. This saves you typing time and allows you to concentrate on the technique at hand. Through the use of sample files, hands-on activities, illustrations that give you feed-back at crucial steps, and supporting background information, this book provides you with the foundation and structure to learn WordPerfect 6.0 for Windows quickly and easily.

 ## AS A REVIEW TOOL

Any method of instruction is only as effective as the time and effort you are willing to invest in it. For this reason, we encourage you to spend some time reviewing the book's more challenging topics and activities.

 ## AS A QUICK REFERENCE

General procedures such as opening a new document or changing a doc-ument's margins are presented as a series of bulleted steps; you can find these bullets (•) easily by skimming through the book. These procedures can serve as a handy reference.

At the end of every chapter, you'll find a quick reference that lists the mouse or keyboard actions needed to perform the techniques introduced in that chapter.

WHAT THIS BOOK CONTAINS

This book is divided into the following 11 chapters and 4 appendices:

Chapter 1	WordPerfect for Windows Basics
Chapter 2	Navigating in WordPerfect
Chapter 3	Editing Text
Chapter 4	Character Formatting
Chapter 5	Line Formatting

To attain full WordPerfect fluency, you should work through all 11 chapters. The appendices are optional.

 SPECIAL LEARNING FEATURES

The following features of this book will facilitate your learning:

- Carefully sequenced topics that build on the knowledge you've acquired from previous topics

- Frequent hands-on activities that sharpen your WordPerfect skills

- Numerous illustrations that show how your screen should look at key points during these activities

- The Data Disk, which contains all the files you will need to complete the activities (as explained in the next section)

- Easy-to-spot, bulleted procedures that provide the general, step-by-step instructions you'll need to perform WordPerfect tasks

- A quick reference at the end of each chapter, listing the mouse or keyboard actions needed to perform the techniques introduced in the chapter

 THE DATA DISK

 One of the most important learning features of this book is the *Data Disk*, the 3½-inch floppy disk that accompanies the book. This disk contains the sample WordPerfect files you'll retrieve and work on throughout the book.

To perform the activities in this book, you will first need to create a work directory on your hard disk (as explained in the upcoming section "Creating Your Work Directory"). You'll then copy the sample files from the Data Disk to your work directory. This directory will also hold all the WordPerfect files that you will be creating, editing, and saving during the course of this book.

WHAT YOU NEED TO USE THIS BOOK

To run WordPerfect 6.0 for Windows and complete this book, you need a computer with a hard disk and at least one floppy-disk drive, a monitor, a keyboard, and a mouse (or compatible tracking device). Although you don't absolutely need a printer, we strongly recommend that you have one.

 COMPUTER AND MONITOR

You need an IBM or IBM-compatible personal computer and monitor that are capable of running Microsoft Windows (version 3.1 or higher). A 386-based system is technically sufficient, but both Windows and WordPerfect may run somewhat slowly on it; we recommend that you use a 486 or higher computer.

You need a hard disk with at least 31 megabytes (31 million bytes) of free storage space (if WordPerfect 6.0 for Windows is not yet installed) or 1 megabyte of free space (if WordPerfect 6.0 for Windows is installed) and at least 4 megabytes of RAM (random access memory).

Finally, you need an EGA or higher (VGA, SVGA, and so on) graphics card and monitor to display Windows and WordPerfect at their intended screen resolution. (**Note:** The WordPerfect screens shown in this book are taken from a VGA monitor. Depending on your monitor type, your screens may look slightly different.)

Windows must be installed on your computer; if it is not, see your Windows reference manuals for instructions. WordPerfect 6.0 for Windows must also be installed; for help, see Appendix A.

 KEYBOARD

IBM-compatible computers come with various styles of keyboards; these keyboards function identically but have different layouts. Figures I.1, I.2, and I.3 show the three main keyboard styles and their key arrangements.

WordPerfect uses all main areas of the keyboard:

- The *function keys* enable you to access WordPerfect's special features. On the PC-, XT-, and AT-style keyboards, there are 10 function keys at the left end of the keyboard; on the 101-key Enhanced Keyboard there are 12 at the top of the keyboard.

- The *typing keys* enable you to enter letters, numbers, and punctuation marks. These keys include the Shift, Ctrl, and Alt keys, which you need to access several of WordPerfect's special features. The typing keys are located in the main body of all the keyboards.

Figure I.1   **IBM PC–style keyboard**

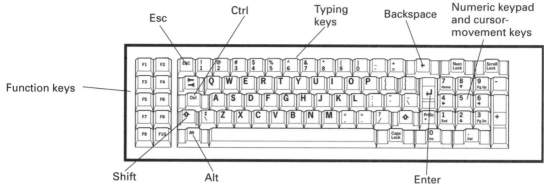

Figure I.2   **XT/AT–style keyboard**

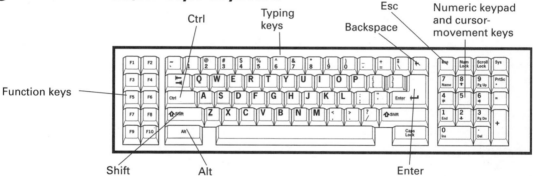

Figure I.3   **PS/2–style Enhanced Keyboard**

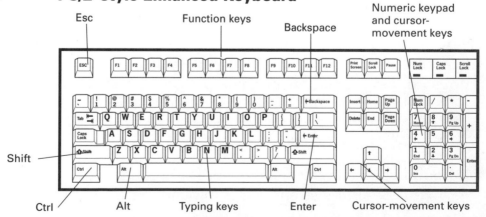

- The *numeric keypad* enables you either to enter numeric data or to navigate through a document. When *Num Lock* is turned on, you use the numeric keypad to enter numeric data, just as you would on a standard calculator keypad. When Num Lock is turned off, you use the numeric keypad to navigate through a document by using the cursor-movement keys: Up, Down, Left, and Right Arrows; Home, End, PgUp (Page Up), and PgDn (Page Down). To turn Num Lock on or off, simply press the Num Lock key. To enter numeric data when Num Lock is off, use the number keys in the top row of the typing area.

- The *cursor-movement keypad*, which is available only on the Enhanced Keyboard, enables you to navigate through a document by using the Home, End, Page Up, and Page Down keys. The cursor-movement keypad works the same when Num Lock is turned on or off. This enables you to use the numeric keypad for numeric data entry (that is, to keep Num Lock on) and still have access to cursor-movement keys.

 MOUSE OR TRACKING DEVICE

You need a mouse or other type of tracking device to work through the activities in this book. Any standard PC mouse or tracking device (a trackball, for example) will do.

Note: Throughout this book, we direct you to use a mouse. If you have a different tracking device, simply use your device to perform all the mousing tasks: pointing, clicking, dragging, and so on.

 PRINTER

Although you don't absolutely need a printer to work through the activities in this book, we strongly recommend that you have one. A laser printer is ideal, but an ink-jet or dot-matrix will do just fine. Your printer must be selected for use with WordPerfect; for help, see Appendix A.

CONVENTIONS USED IN THIS BOOK

The following conventions used in this book will help you learn Word-Perfect 6.0 for Windows easily and efficiently.

- Each chapter begins with a short introduction and ends with a summary that includes a quick-reference guide to the techniques introduced in the chapter.

- Main chapter topics (large, capitalized headings) and subtopics (headings preceded by a cube) explain WordPerfect features.

- Hands-on activities allow you to practice using these features. In these activities, keystrokes, menu choices, and anything you are asked to type are printed in boldface. Here's an example from Chapter 2:

    2. Choose **Edit, Find** to open the Find dialog box.

- Activities adhere to a cause-and-effect approach. Each step tells you what to do (cause) and then what will happen (effect). From the example above,

    Cause: Choose the menu command **Edit, Find**.

    Effect: The Find dialog box is opened.

- A plus sign (+) is used with the Shift, Ctrl, and Alt keys to indicate a multikey keystroke. For example, **press Ctrl+F10** means "Press and hold down the Ctrl key, then press the F10 key, and then release them both."

- To help you distinguish between steps presented for reference purposes (*general procedures*) and steps you should carry out at your computer as you read (*specific procedures*), we use the following system:

- A bulleted step, like this, is provided for your information and reference only.

1. A numbered step, like this, indicates one in a series of steps that you should carry out in sequence at your computer.

CREATING YOUR WORK DIRECTORY

Throughout this book you will be creating, editing, and saving several files. In order to keep these files together, you need to create a work directory for them on your hard disk. (A directory is like a folder in which a group of related files is stored.) Your work directory will also hold the sample files contained on the enclosed Data Disk.

Follow these steps to create your work directory. (**Note:** If WordPerfect 6.0 for Windows is not currently installed on your computer, please install it now, before you create your work directory. See Appendix A for instructions.)

1. Turn on your computer. After a brief internal self-check, your *operating environment* will load. If you are in Windows, go to step 2. If you are in DOS, skip to step 4. If you are in a non-Windows, non-DOS environment (GeoWorks, for example), exit to DOS and then skip to step 4; for help exiting to DOS, follow the on-screen instructions, or refer to your user's guide. If you don't know what operating system you are in, ask a colleague or technician for help.

2. Within Windows, locate the *Program Manager*. It can appear in two forms: as a window (rectangular box) with "Program Manager" in its overhead title bar; or as an *icon* (small picture) with "Program Manager" beneath it. If your Program Manager appears as a window, go to step 3. If your Program Manager

appears as an icon, use the mouse to move the on-screen pointer to this icon, and then double-click (press the left mouse button twice in rapid succession) to open it into a window.

3. Use the mouse to move the on-screen pointer to the Program Manager's *Control-menu button*, the small, square box in the upper-left corner of the Program Manager window. Double-click (press the left mouse button twice in rapid succession) on the dash within the Control-menu button. A box entitled "Exit Windows" will appear. Click the mouse pointer once on the **OK** within this box. You have now exited from Windows to DOS. Skip to step 10.

4. You may see this prompt:

```
Current date is Tue 02-18-1994
Enter new date (mm-dd-yy):
```

(Your current date will be different.) If you do not see a date prompt, skip to step 7.

5. If the current date on your screen is wrong, type the correct date. Use a dash (-) to separate the month, day, and year (for example, 6-19-94).

6. Press **Enter**. After you type a command, you must press the Enter key to submit your command to the computer.

7. You may see this prompt:

```
Current time is 0:25:32:56p
Enter new time:
```

(Your current time will be different.) If you do not see a time prompt, skip to step 10.

8. If the current time on your screen is wrong, type the correct time. Use the 24-hour format *hh:mm* (for example, 10:58 for 10:58 a.m., and 22:58 for 10:58 p.m.).

9. Press **Enter** to send the time you specified to the computer's internal clock.

10. The DOS prompt will appear:

```
C:\>
```

(Your DOS prompt may differ somewhat from this.)

11. Type **dir** and press **Enter**. The contents of the current disk directory are displayed, followed by a final line reporting the number of free bytes on your hard disk. If you have 1,000,000 or more free bytes, skip directly to step 12. If you have fewer than 1,000,000 free bytes, you will not be able to create your work directory and perform the hands-on activities in this book. Before you go any further, you must delete enough files from your hard disk to increase the free-byte total to at least 1,000,000. For help doing this, refer to your DOS reference manual. (**Note:** Make sure to back up all your important files before deleting them!)

12. Remove the Data Disk from its envelope at the back of this book. Insert the Data Disk (label up) into the appropriately sized disk drive. Determine whether this is drive A or drive B. (On a single floppy-disk system, the drive is generally designated as A. On a double floppy-disk system, the upper drive is generally designated as A and the lower as B.)

13. If the Data Disk is in drive A, type **a:** (type **b:** if the Data Disk is in drive B). Press **Enter** to change the current drive to that of the Data Disk.

14. Type **install c: wpwork** without pressing Enter (be sure to leave a space after the colon). To create your work directory on a hard-disk drive other than drive C, substitute your hard-disk drive letter for the "c" in this command. For example, to create your work directory on a drive-D hard disk, you would type *install d: wpwork*. WPWORK is the name of your work directory.

15. Press **Enter** to create your work directory. If all goes well, the message

```
Work directory under construction.
Please wait .....................
```

will appear. When the procedure is complete, the message

```
Work directory successfully completed!
```

will appear, followed by a line reporting the drive and name of your work directory (c:\wpwork, for example). If these two messages appear, go to the Important Note following this step.

If all does not go so well, one of two messages will appear. The first message is

```
Installation failed! c: drive does not exist.
Reenter the INSTALL command using the correct drive.
```

This message indicates that the hard drive you specified in your step 14 command does not exist on your computer. If you get this message, simply repeat steps 14 and 15, making sure to specify the correct letter of your hard drive.

The second message is

```
Installation failed! c:\wpwork directory already exists.
Reenter the INSTALL command using a different work directory name.
```

This message indicates that a directory with the same name as your proposed work directory (WPWORK) already exists on your specified hard disk. If this happens, repeat steps 14 and 15, specifying a new work directory name of your choice instead of wpwork. For example, you might type *install c: mywpwork* or *install c: wpfiles*, and so on. Your work directory name can be up to eight letters long. Do not use spaces, periods, or punctuation marks. Do not use the names wpwin60, or wpdocs as they are already used by the WordPerfect program.

Important Note: The hands-on activities in this book assume that your work directory is on drive C and is named WPWORK. If you specified a different hard-disk drive or a different directory name, please remember to substitute this drive and/or name whenever we mention drive C or WPWORK.

BEFORE YOU START

Each chapter's activities proceed sequentially. In many cases, you cannot perform an activity until you have performed one or more of the activities preceding it. For this reason, we recommend that you allot enough time to work through an entire chapter in one continuous session.

Feel free to take as many breaks as you need. Stand up, stretch, take a walk, drink some decaf. Don't try to absorb too much information at one time. Studies show that people assimilate and retain information most effectively when it is presented in digestible chunks and followed by a liberal amount of hands-on practice.

You are now ready to begin. Good learning and...*bon voyage!*

CHAPTER 1: WORDPERFECT FOR WINDOWS BASICS

If you've ever used a typewriter to create a document, you know that it's easy to make mistakes. Because characters you type are committed to paper as you compose the text, even simple typing changes like erasing a character can become difficult. More extensive corrections generally require that you retype the entire document.

A word processing *program*, or *application*, like WordPerfect for Windows provides a much more efficient way to create, revise, and save a document; you can edit it and even make major adjustments. (The terms *program* and *application* will be used interchangeably throughout this book.) For example, you can change the margins or page breaks in a single step or series of steps. Then, once you're satisfied with the appearance and content of your document, you can print it.

This chapter introduces the basic concepts essential to effective word processing. You will encounter most of these procedures each time you use WordPerfect for Windows. When you're done working through this chapter, you will know

- How to enter text
- How to insert, delete, and replace text
- How to save, name, and print a document
- How to close a document
- How to create a new document

A QUICK REVIEW OF MOUSING SKILLS

The *mouse* is a hand-held device that enables you to communicate with WordPerfect for Windows by manipulating (selecting, deselecting, moving, deleting, and so on) graphical and text objects that are displayed on your computer screen. When you move the mouse across the surface of your mouse pad, a symbol called the *mouse pointer* moves across the screen. You use this mouse pointer to point to the on-screen text that you want to manipulate. The mouse has one or more buttons. You use these buttons to communicate with WordPerfect for Windows in several ways, as detailed in Table 1.1. (**Note:** Read through the following table to familiarize yourself with standard WordPerfect for Windows mousing techniques. It's not necessary, however, to memorize every technique. Instead, think of this table as a quick-reference guide, and refer to it whenever you need to refresh your memory.)

Table 1.1	**Mousing Techniques**	
	Technique	**How to Do It**
	Point	Move the mouse until the tip of the mouse pointer is over the desired object. "Point to the word *File*" means "move the mouse until the tip of the mouse pointer is over the word *File*."

Table 1.1   **Mousing Techniques (Continued)**

Click	Press and release the left mouse button. "Click on the word *File*" means "point to the word *File* and then press and release the left mouse button."
Double-click	Press and release the left mouse button twice in rapid succession. "Double-click on the file name *SKILLS1.WPD*" means "point to the file name *SKILLS1.WPD,* and then press and release the left mouse button twice."
Triple-click	Press and release the left mouse button three times in rapid succession. "Triple-click on the first sentence of the document" means "point to the first sentence of the document, and then press and release the left mouse button three times."
Quadruple-click	Press and release the left mouse button four times in rapid succession. "Quadruple-click on the first paragraph of the document" means "point to the first paragraph of the document, and then press and release the left mouse button four times."
Choose	Click on a menu command or dialog-box button. "Choose File, Open" means "click on the word *File* (in the menu bar), and then click on the word *Open* (in the File menu)."
Drag	Press and hold the left mouse button while moving the mouse. "Drag the scroll box upward" means "point to the scroll box, press and hold the left mouse button, move the mouse upward, and then release the mouse button."
Scroll	Click on a scroll arrow or within a scroll bar, or drag a scroll box.

Table 1.1   **Mousing Techniques (Continued)**

Select

Click on an object (to select the entire object), or drag over part of a text object (to select part of the text). "Select the file *LETTER.WPD*" means "click on the file name *LETTER.WPD*." "Select the first four letters of the title *Global Travel*" means "drag over the letters *Glob*."

Check

Click on a check box to check (turn on) that option. "Check the Italic option" means "click on the Italic check box to check it."

Uncheck

Click on a check box to uncheck (turn off) that option. "Uncheck the Italic option" means "click on the Italic check box to uncheck it."

STARTING WORDPERFECT

Before you start WordPerfect for Windows, both Microsoft Windows and WordPerfect 6.0 for Windows must be installed on your hard disk. If either of these programs is not installed, please install it now. For help installing Microsoft Windows, see your Windows documentation. For help installing WordPerfect for Windows, see Appendix A of this book.

In addition, if you did not complete the activity in the "Creating Your Work Directory" section of the Introduction, please do so now. Otherwise, you will not be able to perform the tasks in this book.

Note: In this book, we present two types of procedures: bulleted and numbered. A *bulleted procedure*—one whose steps are preceded by bullets (•)—serves as a general reference; you should read its steps without actually performing them. A *numbered procedure*—one whose steps are preceded by numbers (1., 2., and so on)—is a specific hands-on activity; you should perform its steps as instructed.

Here's the general procedure for starting WordPerfect for Windows:

• Turn on your computer.

• If you are already in Windows, skip this step. If you are in a non-DOS operating environment, exit to DOS. At the DOS prompt, type *win* and press *Enter* to start Windows.

- Locate the WordPerfect 6.0 for Windows program icon. Double-click on this icon to start WordPerfect for Windows.

Let's follow this procedure to start WordPerfect for Windows:

1. Turn on your computer. After a brief self-check, your *operating environment* will automatically load. If your operating environment is Windows, skip the rest of this activity (steps 2 through 9) and continue with the next activity. If your operating environment is DOS, continue with step 2 of this activity. If you are in a non-DOS operating environment (for example, GeoWorks), exit from this environment to DOS and continue with step 2. (For help exiting to DOS, see the reference manual for your operating environment.)

2. You may see this prompt:

```
Current date is Sun 11-07-1993
Enter new date (mm-dd-yy):
```

(**Note:** Your current date will be different.) If you do not see a date prompt, skip to step 5.

3. If the current date on your screen is wrong, type the correct date. Use a hyphen (-) to separate the month, day, and year (for example, 12-01-93).

4. Press **Enter**. Remember that after you type a command, you must press the Enter key to send this command to the computer.

5. You may see this prompt:

```
Current time is 0:23:32:56
Enter new time:
```

(Your current time will be different.) If you do not see a time prompt, skip to step 8.

6. If the current time on your screen is wrong, type the correct time. Use the 24-hour format *hh:mm* (for example, 10:30 for 10:30 a.m., and 22:30 for 10:30 p.m.).

7. Press **Enter** to set your computer's internal clock.

8. Your DOS prompt then appears:

```
C:\>
```

(Your prompt may differ somewhat from this example.)

9. Type **win** and press **Enter** to start Windows. After a few moments of furious hard-disk activity (indicated by the blinking of your hard-disk drive pilot light), Windows appears on your screen.

10. When Windows is loaded, look for an on-screen object entitled WPWin 6.0. If this object is an icon (a small box about 0.5-inch square), continue with step 11. If this object is a window (a larger, framed box with icons inside of it commonly referred to as a Program Group), continue with step 12.

11. Use your mouse to move the on-screen pointer to the **WPWin 6.0** icon. Double-click (press the left mouse button two times in rapid succession) on the icon to turn it into a window (see Figure 1.1).

Figure 1.1   **The WordPerfect for Windows program icon**

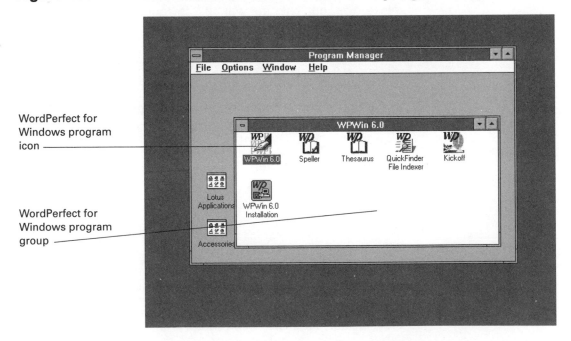

WordPerfect for Windows program icon

WordPerfect for Windows program group

12. Move the mouse pointer to the **WPWin6.0** program icon (see Figure 1.1) and double-click (press the left mouse button two times in rapid succession) on the icon. The WordPerfect

program loads into memory, and a blank document window appears on-screen. Document windows are discussed in the next section.

WordPerfect is a user-customizable program. Users can specify, for example, whether they want WordPerfect to display certain on-screen icons or hide them. To ensure that your WordPerfect screens and the screens in this book's figures look alike, please do the following:

1. Click on the word **View** (point to View and press the **left mouse** button once) in the *menu bar* (the horizontal bar directly under the title bar) to open the *drop-down View menu* (a list of view-related commands).

2. Observe the options. By default, WordPerfect is set to Page view (there is a check mark next to Page in the View menu). Of the other View options, Power Bar, Button Bar, and Status Bar should have check marks next to them, indicating that they are visible on the screen. If all these options are checked, click on **View** again to close the View menu. If one of these options is not checked, please select it now. (**Note:** The Graphics option should also be checked.)

3. If necessary, repeat steps 1 and 2 until all three options (Power Bar, Button Bar, and Status Bar) display a check mark. Your screen should match that shown in Figure 1.2.

THE WORDPERFECT APPLICATION AND DOCUMENT WINDOWS

WordPerfect for Windows is structured around a set of *interactive windows*—rectangular, on-screen boxes in which information passes between the user (you) and the program (WordPerfect). When you start WordPerfect, two windows appear on the screen, one within the other. The larger of these, called the *application window*, frames the entire screen; you use it to communicate with the WordPerfect program. (Remember, the terms *program* and *application* can be used interchangeably.) The smaller window, called the *document window*, fits seamlessly within the application window; you use it to create and edit your WordPerfect documents.

Table 1.2 defines the screen elements that you need to be familiar with when using WordPerfect. Figure 1.3 shows each element's location. (Your screen may not match that shown in the figure.)

Figure 1.2   **WordPerfect upon start-up**

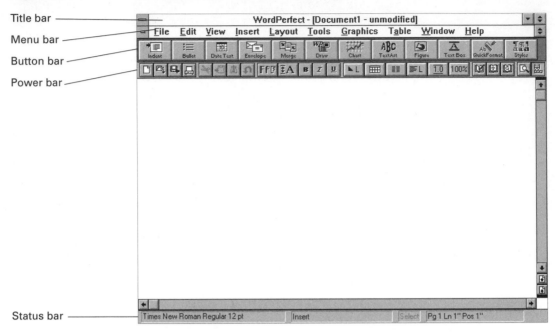

Title bar

Menu bar

Button bar

Power bar

Status bar

Table 1.2   **WordPerfect Screen Elements**

Term	Definition
Application window	The larger of the two start-up windows; it provides an interface between the user and WordPerfect.
Document window	The smaller of the two start-up windows; it holds the currently active WordPerfect document.
Control-menu boxes	Located in the upper-left corner of the screen; they control the size and position of the application window (upper box) and document window (lower box).

Figure 1.3 **The WordPerfect application window**

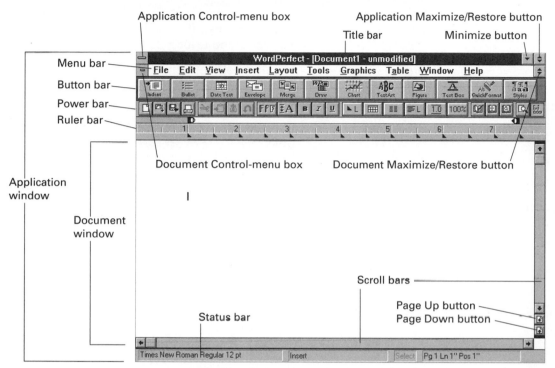

Table 1.2 **WordPerfect Screen Elements (Continued)**

Title bar
: Located at the top of the screen; it displays the name of the application (WordPerfect) and the document (Document1, in this case), and the status of the document (unmodified, in this case).

Maximize/Restore buttons
: Located in the upper-right corner of the screen; they control the size of the application window (upper box) and document window (lower box).

Minimize button
: Located to the left of the application Maximize/Restore button; it reduces the application window to an icon.

Table 1.2   **WordPerfect Screen Elements (Continued)**

Menu bar	Located below the title bar; it lists the Word-Perfect menu options.
Button bar	Located below the menu bar; it provides quick access to WordPerfect commands of your choice.
Power bar	Located below the button bar; it provides quick access to WordPerfect's most frequently used commands and utilities.
Ruler bar	Located below the power bar; it provides on-going page measurement as well as quick access to margins, tabs, and indents. The ruler bar is not displayed by default.
Scroll bars	Located along the right side and bottom of the document window; they are used to display different areas of the active document (each scroll bar contains directional scroll boxes denoted by arrows).
Page Up button	Located directly below the vertical scroll bar; it moves the screen display up one page.
Page Down button	Located below the Page Up button; it moves the screen display down one page.
Status bar	Located along the bottom of the screen; it displays a variety of information relating to the active document.

Let's take a closer look at some of these screen elements. (The remaining elements will be discussed in detail over the next few chapters.)

1. Use the mouse to move the on-screen pointer to the **Control-menu** box of the application window (the upper of the two boxes containing a horizontal bar in the upper-left corner of your screen). Click the mouse (press and release the **left mouse** button once) to open the box; do not double-click, as this would cause you to exit WordPerfect. Note the Control-menu box options: Restore, Move, Size, Minimize, and so on. Click on the **Control-menu box** again to close the box.

2. Use the mouse to move the on-screen pointer to the **Control-menu** box of the document window (the lower of the two boxes in the upper-left corner of the screen) and click the mouse to open the box. Note the similarities in document and application window Control-menu box options.

3. Use the mouse to point to the application window **Maximize/Restore** button (the upper of the two boxes containing an up/down indicator in the upper-right corner of the screen). Click the mouse to restore (shrink) the application window; an inch of space appears at the bottom of the screen. Note that the Maximize/Restore button now contains only an up indicator, indicating that its function is to maximize (rather than re-store) the window. Click on the **Maximize/Restore** button again to remaximize the application window.

4. Repeat step 3, substituting the document Maximize/Restore button (the lower of the two boxes in the upper-right corner of the screen) for the application Maximize/Restore button. Note that when you click on the document **Maximize/Restore** button the first time, the button moves to the upper-right corner of the restored (shrunk) document window; this is the button you click on to maximize the window. Note also that when the document window is restored, it gets its own title bar.

USING THE MENU BAR TO ISSUE COMMANDS

To perform your daily word processing tasks (such as retrieving a document from disk, setting new margins, and so on), you must issue the appropriate WordPerfect commands. You can do this by

* Using the mouse to choose the command from the menu bar

* Using the mouse to choose the command from the button bar, power bar, or ruler bar

* Using the keyboard to enter a command keystroke

For example, to open a new document, you could

* Choose the *New* command from the File option on the menu bar or

* Click on the power bar's *New* button or

* Press *Ctrl+N* from your keyboard (press and hold the Ctrl key, press and hold the N key, and then release both keys).

Please do not perform any of these actions now.

The menu bar is the only method that allows you to issue every available WordPerfect command. The button bar, power bar, and ruler bar provide a subset of the most frequently used commands, as does the keyboard. For this reason, we'll begin our exploration of WordPerfect commands by using the menu-bar approach.

Let's issue some commands by using the menu bar:

1. Move the mouse pointer to the **File** option on the menu bar, and then press and hold down the **left mouse** button. (Do not release this button until indicated in step 4.) The File menu drops down, displaying a set of file-related commands: New, Template, Open, Close, Save, Save As, and so on.

2. Observe the text in the title bar at the top of your screen. WordPerfect displays a brief description (*long prompt*) of the currently selected item—in this case, the File menu.

3. Without releasing the button, drag the mouse pointer down to highlight the **Save As** command. (When you highlight an item in WordPerfect, the item is displayed in reverse video.) The title bar now displays a brief description of the File, Save As command.

4. Release the mouse button to open the Save As dialog box (see Figure 1.4). Dialog boxes prompt you to enter information relating to the selected command (File, Save As, in this case). You will work extensively with dialog boxes during the course of this book.

5. Click the mouse pointer on the **Cancel** button in the upper-right corner of the Save As dialog box to close the box.

6. Click on the **Edit** option of the menu bar. The Edit menu drops down, displaying WordPerfect's editing commands. Note that you can either press and hold the mouse button (as in steps 1 through 4), or press and release (click) the button to display a drop-down menu.

7. Observe that several Edit commands are *dimmed* (Cut, Copy, Paste, and so on). WordPerfect dims menu commands to show that they are unavailable in the current context. For example, the Copy command is dimmed because you have not selected any text to copy. (You'll learn how to select text later in this chapter under "Editing a Document.")

Figure 1.4   **The Save As dialog box**

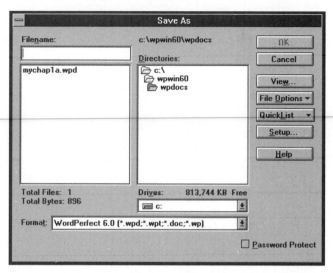

8. Observe also that several commands are followed by ellipses (Find..., Replace..., Go To..., and so on). WordPerfect adds ellipses to menu commands that display dialog boxes. To keep this book easy to read, we chose not to print ellipses when referencing these commands. For example, in step 3 of this listing, we ask you to drag the mouse pointer to the *Save As* command, although *Save As...* is how the command actually appears on your screen.

9. Click on **Edit** again to close the Edit menu.

THE BASICS OF ENTERING TEXT

WordPerfect is a *WYSIWYG* (What You See Is What You Get) word processor; the screen shows you how the text will look when you print your document. Most users prefer WYSIWYG programs because they remove the arcane codes and inaccurate page layouts that plague non-WYSIWYG programs. WordPerfect's WYSIWYG feature encourages you to work in a "visual-intuitive" style in which you treat the word processor as a computerized extension of a typewriter.

In the next several sections, we'll discuss the basics of entering text in a WordPerfect document.

THE TEXT AREA

When you start WordPerfect, a new document window automatically appears, providing you with a blank area for typing called the *text area*. WordPerfect assumes certain settings for margins, page length, line spacing, tab stops, and several other document attributes. Because of these assumptions, called *defaults*, you can begin to type immediately without first having to specify any of the settings yourself.

As you type, characters are inserted in front of a blinking vertical bar called the *insertion point*. To change the location of the insertion point, you simply click the mouse pointer at the desired place in the text.

Let's examine WordPerfect's text area (see Figure 1.5):

1. Observe the insertion point (the blinking vertical bar). Its location determines where the next character you type will be entered into your document. Note that the insertion point of a new document always appears near the upper-left corner (that is, at the beginning) of the document window.

Figure 1.5   **The text area**

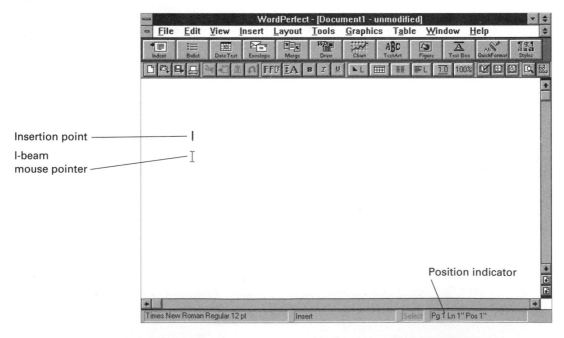

2. Observe the mouse pointer. The pointer changes to an I-beam (see Figure 1.5) when it is within the text area. When moved outside the text area, it becomes an arrow. When the mouse pointer is placed on the border of the button bar, it changes to a hand (indicating that you can move the button bar). Take a moment to verify this.

WORD-WRAP AND THE ENTER KEY

The Enter key on your keyboard is analogous to the Return key on a typewriter. When using a typewriter, you need to hit the Return key whenever you want to end a line. In word processing, when a word does not fit on a line, it automatically flows to the beginning of the next line. This feature is called *word-wrap*. However, you do need to press Enter to

- End a short line (one that does not extend to the right margin)
- End a paragraph
- Create a blank line

Let's type some text in our new document window and practice using the Enter key. (Word-wrap will be demonstrated under "Using the Backspace Key to Delete Text," later in this chapter.)

1. Observe the status bar. *Pg* indicates the current page number. The line number *Ln* and the vertical page position measurement *Pos* reflect the current position of the insertion point. **Note:** *Ln* indicates the distance of the insertion point from the top of the page. *Pos* indicates the distance of the insertion point from the left edge of the page.

2. Type **Cyndi Wood** to enter the characters at the insertion point and observe the status bar. *Pos* shows the new location of the insertion point (about 1.84 inches from the left edge of the paper).

3. Press **Enter** to end the line.

4. Observe the status bar. The line number changes to reflect the new position of the insertion point.

5. Type **3325 Fillmore Avenue** and press **Enter** to end the line.

6. Type **North Hills, NY 11756** and press **Enter**.

7. Press **Enter** to create a blank line.

8. Type **Dear Janet:** and press **Enter** twice to end the line and create one blank line. Your screen should now match Figure 1.6.

Figure 1.6   **Entering text in a document**

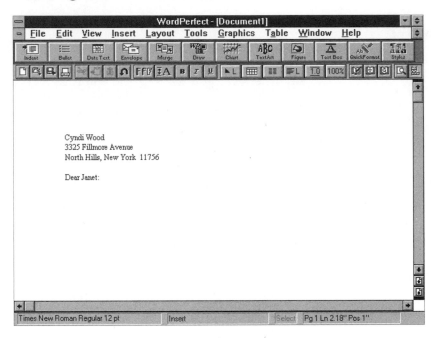

NONPRINTING CHARACTERS

You can choose to have WordPerfect display a number of special
characters on the screen that show the places in the text where
you pressed the spacebar, or the Enter and Tab keys. These *nonprinting characters* (so called because they do not appear on
paper when you print the document) are often useful to see. This
is particularly true when you are working with heavily formatted
documents and need to keep track of your tabs, spaces, blank
lines, and so on.

Here's the general procedure to display WordPerfect's nonprinting characters:

- Click on the *View* menu option to open the View menu.
- Click on *Show ¶* to show nonprinting characters.

Let's display the nonprinting characters of your active document:

1. Examine the screen. Each line of text is short, not reaching the right margin. Note that there are no characters marking the ends of these lines.

2. Click on **View** in the menu bar to open the View menu.

3. Click on **Show ¶** to display the nonprinting characters on your screen.

4. Examine the screen. Each time you pressed Enter, Word-Perfect placed a paragraph mark (¶) in the document. Each time you pressed the spacebar, WordPerfect placed a space mark (·) in the document. These nonprinting characters only appear on the screen when the Show ¶ option is turned on; they will not appear on your printed document. Note that your screen looks busy with the nonprinting characters turned on. We recommend that you work with the Show ¶ option turned off unless you are editing a document and need to see how many spaces or returns there are.

5. Click on **View** on the menu bar to open the View menu.

6. Observe the Show ¶ option. There is a check mark next to the option, indicating that it is on. It will remain on only for this document. If you open a new document and want to see the nonprinting characters, you will have to select the option again.

7. Click on **View** again to close the View menu without making any changes.

USING THE TAB KEY TO ALIGN TEXT

Tabs enable you to align columns of text. These lines are properly aligned:

Line 1 ...

Line 2 ...

These are not:

Line 1 ...

Line 2 ...

Pressing the Tab key moves the insertion point to the next tab stop to the right. *Tab stops* are fixed horizontal positions within a line. By default, WordPerfect's tab stops are set at 0.5-inch increments. Pressing Tab once moves the insertion point 0.5-inch to the right; pressing Tab again moves it another 0.5-inch, for a total of 1 inch (0.5 + 0.5) from the left margin; and so on. (We created the properly aligned example just shown by pressing Tab once at the beginning of each line. We created the improperly aligned example by using the spacebar to indent the second line.

 ## USING THE BACKSPACE KEY TO DELETE TEXT

You can use the Backspace key to delete text one character at a time. Simply press Backspace to delete the single character immediately to the left of the insertion point.

Let's experiment with WordPerfect's Tab, Backspace, and word-wrap features:

1. Choose **View, Ruler Bar** (click on **View**, then click on **Ruler Bar**) to display the ruler bar.

2. Observe the ruler bar. Default tab stops are set every 0.5-inch along the ruler. This means that unless you tell it otherwise, each time you press the Tab key, the insertion point will jump to the next nearest tab stop on the ruler.

3. Press **Tab** to insert a tab at the beginning of the line. This moves the insertion point to the first tab stop, 0.5-inch to the right. Note that WordPerfect displays the tab mark ($\rightarrow$), since the Show ¶ feature is still set to Show from our last exercise. As with the paragraph and space marks, this tab mark will not appear on the printed page.

4. Press **Tab** again to insert another tab. This moves the insertion point to the second tab stop, 1 inch from the left margin.

5. Press **Backspace** twice to remove the tab characters.

6. Type **I have been happy with the service provided by Global Travel.** (including the period). Then press the **spacebar** to insert a space before the next sentence.

7. Type **I would like additional information about your program.** (including the period) and then examine the screen. Notice that the word *about* automatically wraps to the next line, even though you did not press Enter. This is an example of word-wrap. (**Note:** Depending upon the printer you have installed and the font you use, your text may wrap in a different location.

8. Press **Enter** twice to end the paragraph and add one blank line (as shown in the first paragraph in Figure 1.7).

Figure 1.7   **Completed letter in Show mode**

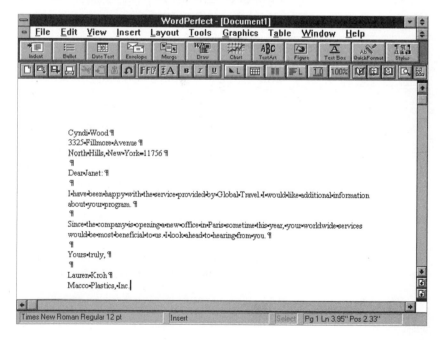

PRACTICE YOUR SKILLS

Complete the entire letter as shown in Figure 1.7.

EDITING A DOCUMENT

As mentioned at the beginning of this chapter, one of the strongest arguments for switching from a typewriter to a word processor is the greatly increased ease of editing your documents. In the time it would take you just to pencil in your desired changes to a typewritten document (without actually retyping it), you could incorporate these changes into a word processed document, print it, and save it on a hard or floppy disk for future revision.

In the next several sections, we'll discuss the rudiments of text editing in WordPerfect.

INSERTING TEXT

By default, WordPerfect runs in *insert mode*; as you type, text to the right of the insertion point is pushed further to the right to make room for your new text.

Here's the general procedure to insert text in a document:

- Place the insertion point (use the mouse to position the I-beam and then click) where you want to add text.

- Type the new text.

Let's practice inserting text in a document:

1. Point to the left of the *p* in *program*, which is located in the second sentence of the paragraph beginning with *I have*. Click the mouse button to place the insertion point directly before the *p* in *program*. (Do not place the insertion point before the space preceding the *p*.) This is where you will insert your new text.

2. Type **corporate travel** and press the **spacebar**. Note that the existing text is pushed to the right of the inserted text.

SELECTING TEXT

It is often easier to work with a block of text rather than with a single character. For example, if you needed to underline a sentence in a paragraph, you would not want to underline each and every character separately (a multistep, tedious task); rather, you would want to underline the entire sentence at once (a single-step, straightforward task). To work with a block of text, you must first select it.

Here's the general procedure to select a block of text:

- Point to the first (or final) character of the text you want to select.

- Press and hold the *left mouse* button.

- Drag across the text to the final (or first) character you want to select.

- Release the mouse button.

Note: As just indicated, you can select text downward (from the first character to the last character) or upward (from the last character to the first character). Both methods are equally effective; use whichever you feel more comfortable with.

 DELETING TEXT

As you know, Backspace deletes the character to the left of the insertion point. To delete the character immediately to the right of the insertion point, press the Del key on the numeric keypad. If you have a PS/2-style Enhanced Keyboard, you may press the Delete key on the auxiliary keypad to the left of the numeric keypad. Pressing either of these keys has the identical effect on the text being deleted.

Note: If you intend to use the numeric keypad Del key to perform your deletions, make sure that Num Lock is off (press the Num Lock key until the indicator light goes out). If Num Lock is on, Del functions as a decimal point key; when you press it, WordPerfect displays a period (.) on the screen instead of performing the deletion.

Here's the general procedure to delete a block of selected text:

- Select the text.

- Press the *Delete* key (or *Del*).

Let's begin by deleting text one character at a time:

   1. Place the insertion point directly to the left of the *A* in *Avenue*, which is located in the heading at the top of the page.

2. Press **Del** (or the **Delete** key) six times to delete the word Avenue. (To keep things simple, we'll only mention Del from here on. Feel free, however, to use the Delete key instead.)

3. Type **Circle**.

4. Place the insertion point to the right of the *y* in *happy*, located in the paragraph beginning with *I have*.

5. Press **Backspace** five times to delete the word happy.

6. Type **very pleased**.

Now let's delete a block (in this case, a single word) of selected text:

1. Point to the left of the *m* in *most* in the first sentence of the paragraph beginning *Since the company*.

2. Press and hold the left mouse button. Then drag over **most** and the *trailing space* (the space that follows the *t* of *most*) to select the text. Do not select the space before most.

3. Release the mouse button. If you don't succeed on the first try, don't panic. Simply release the mouse button and start with step 1 again. Selecting text by dragging takes practice.

4. Press **Del** to delete the selected text.

REPLACING TEXT

You already learned how to insert new text within a document. At times, however, you may want to replace existing text with new text. For example, you may want to replace the standard letter salutation *Dear Sir or Madam* with *To Whom It May Concern*. One way you can do this is by inserting the new text and then deleting the old text. This, however, doubles your work and can grow very tiresome, particularly when you are replacing many blocks of text. Fortunately, WordPerfect provides a more convenient solution.

Here's the general procedure to replace existing text with new text:

- Select the text to be replaced.

- Type the new text.

Let's use this technique to replace some text in our letter:

1. Select the name **Janet** in the salutation *Dear Janet*.

2. Type **Cyndi** to replace *Janet* with *Cyndi*.

PRACTICE YOUR SKILLS

Complete the following corrections, referring to Figures 1.8 and 1.9. **Note:** Replacement text in Figure 1.8 (such as **Circle** or **Cyndi**) is boldface for emphasis only. Do not enter this text in bold. You'll learn about bold formatting in Chapter 4.

1. Delete *the* (in the paragraph *Since the company*). Then type **our**.

2. Delete *ahead* (in the paragraph *Since our company*). Then type **forward**.

3. Delete *Yours truly* in the closing, and then type **Sincerely**.

4. Check your work against Figure 1.9.

Figure 1.8   **Corrections to letter**

Cyndi Wood
3325 Fillmore ~~Avenue~~ **Circle**
North Hills, New York 11756

Dear ~~Janet~~ **Cyndi:**

I have been ~~happy~~ **very pleased** with the service provided by Global Travel. I would like additional information about your **corporate travel** program.

Since ~~the~~ **our** company is opening a new office in Paris sometime this year, your worldwide services would be ~~most~~ beneficial to us. I look ~~ahead~~ **forward** to hearing from you.

~~Yours truly~~ **Sincerely,**

Lauren Kroh
Macco Plastics, Inc.

Figure 1.9   **Final (corrected) letter**

> Cyndi Wood
> 3325 Fillmore Circle
> North Hills, New York 11756
>
> Dear Cyndi:
>
> I have been very pleased with the service provided by Global Travel. I would like additional
> information about your corporate travel program.
>
> Since our company is opening a new office in Paris sometime this year, your worldwide services
> would be beneficial to us. I look forward to hearing from you.
>
> Sincerely,
>
> Lauren Kroh
> Macco Plastics, Inc.

SAVING A DOCUMENT IN A DISK FILE

Before it is saved, a document exists only in computer memory, a temporary storage area. For permanent storage, you must save the document in a disk file (hard or floppy). WordPerfect has two commands that are used to save disk files: File, Save As and File, Save.

THE FILE, SAVE AS COMMAND

You use the File, Save As command to save a disk file for the first time, to save a disk file with a new name, or to save a disk file in a different location (on another disk or in a different directory).

Here is the general procedure to save a disk file using File, Save As:

- Choose *File, Save As* (that is, choose the Save As command from the File menu) to open the Save As dialog box.

- In the Drives and Directories list boxes, select the location (drive and directory) in which you wish to save the disk file, if this location is not already selected.

- In the File Name text box, type the name of the file.

- Click on *OK*.

When you save a disk file, WordPerfect adds the .WPD file-name extension to identify the file as a document file.

Note: In the past, WordPerfect allowed you to choose your own file-name extension. You can still do this. However, keep in mind that your hard disk or floppy disks can hold many other types of files, such as .EXE program files, .NUM spreadsheet files, .DBF database files, and so on. We recommend that you do not add the file extension yourself; let WordPerfect do it automatically.

THE FILE, SAVE COMMAND

You use the File, Save command (rather than File, Save As) to save a disk file with its current name and in its current location. File, Save *updates* a disk file; it replaces the last-saved version of the disk file with the new version of the document on your screen. For example, let's say you used File, Save As to save a business report to your reports directory as REPORT1, and then you re-vised the report by adding an extra closing paragraph. If you then chose File, Save, the new (extra paragraph) report version would replace the last-saved (no extra paragraph) version on the disk. Once you've used File, Save As to name and save a disk file, you should generally use File, Save for all subsequent updates of that disk file. However, if you later want to rename it or save it in a different location, you should use File, Save As.

It's very important to save your active documents as disk files frequently. That way, if something happens to the disk file in memory (for example, a power failure, which erases the contents of computer memory), you will have a recent copy of the document safe on the disk. This precaution will keep retyping to a minimum.

General rules for saving are

- Save at least once every 15 minutes.
- Save before printing.
- Save before spell-checking.

NAMING A DOCUMENT

When you save a disk file for the first time, you must name it. Follow these guidelines when naming disk files:

- A file name can contain from one to eight letters, numbers, or the following special characters: (!@#$%()-{}'~).

- A file name cannot contain spaces.

- A file name should be descriptive so that you can remember the file's contents (for example, JANREPT rather than X117-A).

Let's save the active document as a disk file:

1. Choose **File, Save As** (click on **File** and then click on **Save As**) to open the Save As dialog box.

2. From the Drives list, select the drive that contains the WP-WORK directory, if necessary. This is the work directory you created in the Introduction; it is here that you will store and retrieve all of the disk files you work with in this book. (If you did not yet create the WPWORK directory, please consult the Introduction and create it now.)

3. Double-click on **wpwork** in the Directories list box to select the WPWORK directory. (You might need to double-click on the drive at the top of the directory list and scroll to display the WPWORK directory.)

4. Double-click the mouse pointer in the File Name text box (to select *.* if necessary) and type **mychap1a** to name the document MYCHAP1A (capitalization is not important when you type document names). Your screen should now look like Figure 1.10.

5. Click on **OK** to save the document as a disk file.

6. Observe the title bar. It has changed to display the document's path and name, c:\wpwork\mychap1a.wpd. (As mentioned previously, when you save a disk file, WordPerfect automatically adds the extension .WPD to its name.)

PRINTING A DOCUMENT

When you're ready to print your document, WordPerfect is set up to print one copy of the entire document by default. You can, however, choose to print the current page, multiple pages, multiple

Figure 1.10 **Saving MYCHAP1A to the WPWORK directory**

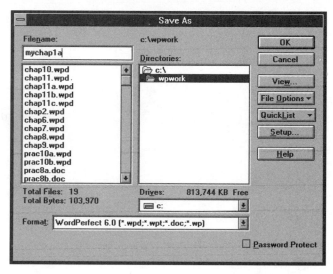

copies, or selected text. You can also print to a disk file rather than to a printer.

Here's the general procedure to print the active document:

- Choose *File, Print*.

- Select any desired options from the Print dialog box.

- Click on *OK* to print the document.

Now let's print MYCHAP1A.WPD:

1. Choose **File, Print** to open the Print dialog box (see Figure 1.11).

2. Click on **Print** to print the document. (Or, if you do not have a printer, click on **Close** to cancel the Print command and return to your document.) Compare your printout with Figure 1.9. Depending on the printer you are using, your printout may vary slightly from the one shown in the figure.

3. If your document failed to print, make sure your printer is on-line, then repeat step 1. If it still won't print, refer to Appendix A for help with selecting your printer.

Figure 1.11   **The Print dialog box**

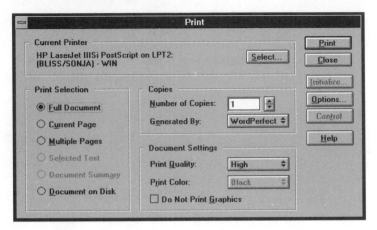

CLOSING A DOCUMENT

When you're finished working with a document—that is, after you've completed, saved, and (if desired) printed it—you should close the document window.

Here's the general procedure to close a document:

- Save the document, if necessary.

- Choose *File, Close* (or double-click on the document *Control-menu* box).

Let's close MYCHAP1A.WPD, since we've saved and printed it:

1. Choose **File, Close** to close the document and remove it from memory.

2. Observe the screen. WordPerfect remains loaded and automatically returns you to a blank, unmodified Document1. The power bar, button bar, and status bar are still visible, but the ruler bar is not displayed.

3. Click on **View** to open the View menu and observe the Show ¶ option. It is off. When you close a document, the Show ¶ option closes with it. Click on **View** again to close the View menu without making any changes.

CREATING A NEW DOCUMENT

After you've closed the active document, you can use Document1 to create your next document, or you can still create another new document.

Here's the general procedure to create a new document (other than Document1):

- Choose *File, New.*

WordPerfect will open a new, blank document window.

Let's create a new document:

1. Choose **File, New** to open a new, blank document window.

2. Type **This is my second document**.

3. Choose **File, Save As** to open the Save As dialog box.

4. Type **mychap1b** to name the document. Note that the desired directory (WPWORK) is still selected; WordPerfect remembered it from the last time you chose it. (If WPWORK is not the active directory, please select it now.)

5. Observe that the OK button has a dark border. This means that OK is the default button. To choose a default button, you simply press Enter. Press **Enter** now as an alternative to clicking on OK.

EXITING WORDPERFECT

Your final step of every WordPerfect session is to exit WordPerfect. Never turn off your computer before doing so, as this could result in the loss of one or more documents.

Here's the general procedure to exit WordPerfect and return to the Windows Program Manager:

- Choose *File, Exit.*

As a safeguard, if you have not saved the latest version of an active document, WordPerfect will prompt you to do so before exiting.

Let's exit WordPerfect:

1. Choose **File, Exit**. The WordPerfect application and document windows disappear, and the Windows Program Manager is displayed.

PRACTICE YOUR SKILLS

You've learned a great deal in this first chapter. The following two activities allow you to apply this knowledge to practical word processing tasks. Please don't think of these activities as tests, but rather as opportunities to hone your WordPerfect skills. It is only through repetition that you'll learn and remember these techniques.

In this activity, you will create and edit the document shown in two stages in Figures 1.12 and 1.13. Then you'll produce the final document shown in Figure 1.14.

1. Start WordPerfect.

2. Enter the text shown in Figure 1.12 (Where the text *(today's date)* appears in Figure 1.12, enter the current date.)

3. Edit the letter as shown in Figure 1.13.

4. Save the document (as a disk file) to your WPWORK directory under the name **myprac1a**.

5. Print the document and compare the results to Figure 1.14.

6. Close the document window.

Figure 1.12   **The first draft of MYPRAC1A.WPD**

(today's date)

Michelle Duncanson
1822 W. 18th Avenue
New York, NY 10021

Dear Michelle:

Thank you so very much for accepting our invitation to the Macco Plastics, Inc. Product Update seminar in June. We hope you will also be able to attend our appreciation dinner immediately before the seminar.

We look ahead to seeing you there!

Sincerely,

B. Lynn Jakat
Seminar Director

Figure 1.13   Editing MYPRAC1A.WPD

(today's date)

Michelle Duncanson
1822 W. 18th ~~Avenue~~ **Street**
New York, NY 10021

Dear Michelle:

Thank you ~~so very much~~ for accepting our invitation to the Macco Plastics, Inc. Product Update
seminar in June. We hope you will also be able to attend our **customer** appreciation dinner
immediately ~~before~~ **following** the seminar.

We look ~~ahead~~ **forward** to seeing you there!

Sincerely,

B. Lynn Jakat
Seminar Director

Figure 1.14   The corrected MYPRAC1A.WPD

(today's date)

Michelle Duncanson
1822 W. 18th Street
New York, NY 10021

Dear Michelle:

Thank you for accepting our invitation to the Macco Plastics, Inc. Product Update seminar in
June. We hope you will also be able to attend our customer appreciation dinner immediately
following the seminar.

We look forward to seeing you there!

Sincerely,

B. Lynn Jakat
Seminar Director

In the next activity, you will create and edit the document shown in two stages in Figures 1.15 and 1.16 to produce the final document shown in Figure 1.17.

1. Open a new document window.

2. Enter the text shown in Figure 1.15.

3. Edit the letter as shown in Figure 1.16.

4. Save the document (as a disk file) to your WPWORK directory under the name **myprac1b**.

5. Print the document and compare the results to Figure 1.17.

6. Close the document window.

7. Exit WordPerfect.

Figure 1.15   **The first draft of MYPRAC1B.WPD**

(today's date)

Deanna Ragonesi
1029 Bodera Drive
Baltimore, MD 21227

Dear Deanna:

This is a confirmation of your reservation for our Product Update seminar in June. Because you are a customer, we want to make every effort to provide you with the support and services you need to make the seminar a successful one.

Enclosed please find a map to the hotel and the conference center. After you sign up at the registration desk, your name will be entered into our national mailing list. This will ensure that you receive product information and dates for future seminars.

Thank you for your interest and welcome to our list of totally satisfied customers.

Sincerely,

B. Lynn Jakat
Seminar Director

Figure 1.16   **Editing MYPRAC1B.WPD**

(today's date)

Deanna Ragonesi
1029 Bodera Drive
Baltimore, MD 21227

Dear Deanna:

This is a confirmation of your reservation for our Product Update seminar in June. Because you are a **valued** customer, we want to make every effort to provide you with the support and services you need to make the seminar a successful one.

Enclosed ~~please~~ **you will** find a map to ~~the~~ **your** hotel and the conference center. After you sign up **at the registration desk**, your name will be entered into our national mailing list. This will ensure that you receive product information and dates for future seminars.

Thank you for your interest and welcome to our **growing** list of ~~totally~~ satisfied customers.

Sincerely,

B. Lynn Jakat
Seminar Director

Figure 1.17   **The corrected MYPRAC1B.WPD**

(today's date)

Deanna Ragonesi
1029 Bodera Drive
Baltimore, MD 21227

Dear Deanna:

This is a confirmation of your reservation for our Product Update seminar in June. Because you are a valued customer, we want to make every effort to provide you with the support and services you need to make the seminar a successful one.

Enclosed you will find a map to your hotel and the conference center. After you sign up at the registration desk, your name will be entered into our national mailing list. This will ensure that you receive product information and dates for future seminars.

Thank you for your interest and welcome to our growing list of satisfied customers.

Sincerely,

B. Lynn Jakat
Seminar Director

SUMMARY

In this chapter, you learned the basics of the document creation-revision-saving-printing cycle, a procedure you'll use frequently in your daily word processing work. You now know how to start and exit WordPerfect; how to enter, insert, delete, and replace text; how to save, name, print, and close a document; and how to create a new document. Congratulations! You're well on your way to mastering WordPerfect for Windows.

Here's a quick reference guide to the WordPerfect features introduced in this chapter:

Desired Result	How to Do It
Start WordPerfect	Start **Windows**, double-click on the **WPWin6.0** icon in the WPWin 6.0 program group
Maximize/Restore a window	Click on the document or application **Maximize/Restore** button
Minimize an application window	Click on the **Minimize** button
Choose a menu command	Click on the menu-bar entry to display the drop-down menu; click on the command; or, press and hold the mouse button on the menu-bar entry; drag down to the command; release the mouse button
End a paragraph or a short line	Press **Enter**
Create a blank line	Press **Enter**
Display/remove nonprinting characters	Choose **View, Show ¶**
Align text columns	Use the **Tab** key
Delete character to the left of the insertion point	Press **Backspace**

Desired Result	How to Do It
Select text	Point to the first (or final) character of the text; press and hold the mouse button; drag across the text to the final (or first) character; release the mouse button
Delete character to the right of the insertion point	Press **Del**
Delete selected text	Select text, press **Del**
Replace selected text	Select text, type the new text
Save a disk file for the first time	Choose **File, Save As**
Rename a document or save a document as a disk file in a new location	Choose **File, Save As**
Save a previously saved disk file with the same name/location	Choose **File, Save**
Print the active document	Choose **File, Print**
Close the active document	Choose **File, Close**; or, double-click on the document **Control-menu** box
Create a new document	Choose **File, New**
Choose a default button	Press **Enter**
Exit WordPerfect	Choose **File, Exit**

In the next chapter, we'll show you how to navigate in WordPerfect. You'll learn how to open a document, display different portions of a document, search for text in a document, control document magnification, and obtain on-line help.

A NOTE ON HOW TO PROCEED

If you wish to stop here, feel free to do so. If you wish to press onward, please proceed directly to the next chapter. Remember to allot enough time to work through an entire chapter in one sitting.

CHAPTER 2: NAVIGATING IN WORDPERFECT

Using File, Open
to Open a
Document

Scrolling through
a Document

Moving through a
Document

Using Edit, Find
to Search for Text

Using Zoom to
Control Document
Magnification

Using Help to
Obtain On-line
Help

Saving the
Modified File

In Chapter 1 you learned how to use the mouse to move around within a one-page document. In this chapter, you'll learn how to use the mouse and the keyboard to navigate through a multipage document. It's essential for you to master these navigational techniques as early as possible in your WordPerfect for Windows career. The more comfortable you feel moving around within a document, the more you'll be able to concentrate on the contents of the document itself.

When you're done working through this chapter, you will know

- How to open a document

- How to use the mouse to scroll through a document

- How to use the keyboard and menus to move through a document

- How to use Edit, Find to search for text

- How to use Zoom to control document magnification

- How to use WordPerfect Help to obtain on-line help

USING FILE, OPEN TO OPEN A DOCUMENT

In Chapter 1 you learned how to create, modify, and save a document as a disk file. Here you'll learn how to open (retrieve) a document that is stored as a disk file. This way, you'll be able to revise previously saved disk files and then reprint and resave them.

Here's the general procedure to open a document:

- Choose *File, Open* to display the Open dialog box.

- Select the desired drive (in the Drives list box) and directory (in the Directories list box), if necessary.

- Click on the desired file (in the Filename list box) and then click on *OK*. Or, simply double-click on the desired file.

When you open a document, a copy of the disk file is placed in a document window on your screen. Because this is a copy of the disk file, and not the disk file itself, you can revise it to your heart's content without changing the original document stored on your disk. (You will, however, change the original document if you save your revised document as a disk file with the same name, and in the same location, as the original. For this reason, if you want to preserve the original document, make sure to give your revised disk file a new name.)

WordPerfect also provides a convenient file-opening shortcut; it keeps track of the last four files that you worked on and places their names as choices at the bottom of the File menu. To open one of these documents, choose File and click on the desired document name.

If you are not running WordPerfect on your computer, please start it now. Close all open documents except for Document1.

Let's begin by opening a document that is stored in your WPWORK directory:

1. Choose **File, Open** to display the Open File dialog box (see Figure 2.1).

Figure 2.1   **The Open File dialog box**

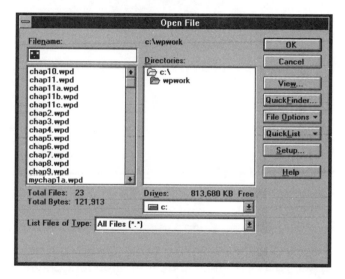

2. If your WPWORK directory is not already selected, select it now (double-click on **wpwork** in the Directories list box). You must tell WordPerfect where to find a document stored as a disk file before you open it.

3. In the File Name list box, click once on **chap2.wpd**. Note that this file name is automatically inserted in the Filename text box. (A *list* box displays a list of options; a *text* box contains text that is either entered automatically or that you can enter when prompted.)

4. Click on **OK** (or press **Enter**) to open the document. A copy of the disk file appears in an active document window; note its title bar, c:\wpwork\chap2.wpd (see Figure 2.2).

Figure 2.2 **CHAP2.WPD, newly opened**

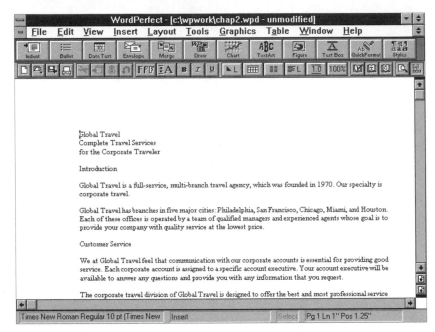

5. Double-click on the document window (not the application window) **Control-menu** box to close CHAP2.WPD. If prompted, do not save changes.

Now let's try the shortcut method for opening this document:

1. Click once on **File** to display the drop-down File menu. Note that CHAP2.WPD appears in the recently accessed files section at the bottom of the menu.

2. Click on **chap2.wpd** to open this document.

SCROLLING THROUGH A DOCUMENT

A WordPerfect document window can only display about half of a standard business-size (8.5-by-11-inch) page at a time. To view the remainder of the page (or to view other pages within the document), you can use the mouse and the vertical and horizontal scroll bars to *scroll* through the document—that is, to display different areas of the document. The vertical scroll bar controls up and down scrolling; the horizontal scroll bar controls side-to-side scrolling.

Scrolling through a document changes the document display, but does not change the position of the insertion point. For example, if the insertion point is at the top of page 2 and you use the vertical scroll bar to scroll down to page 8, the contents of page 8 will be displayed on the screen, but the insertion point will still be at the top of page 2. If you then begin to type, your text is entered at the insertion point on page 2, not on page 8. (You'll learn how to change both the document display and the insertion point position in the next section.)

Table 2.1 lists WordPerfect's vertical and horizontal scrolling options and tells how to perform them. Figure 2.3 identifies the screen elements used for scrolling.

Table 2.1   **Vertical and Horizontal Scrolling Options**

To Scroll	Do This
Up or down one line at a time	Click on the up or down scroll arrow.
To the top, bottom, or middle of a document	Drag the vertical scroll box to the top, bottom, or middle of the scroll bar.
Up or down a screen at a time	Click in the shaded area above or below the vertical scroll box.
Up one page at a time	Click on the Page Up button.
Down one page at a time	Click on the Page Down button.
To the left edge, right edge, or middle of a document	Drag the horizontal scroll box to the left, right, or middle of the scroll bar.
Left or right a screen at a time	Click in the shaded area to the left or right of the horizontal scroll box.

Figure 2.3 **Scrolling terminology**

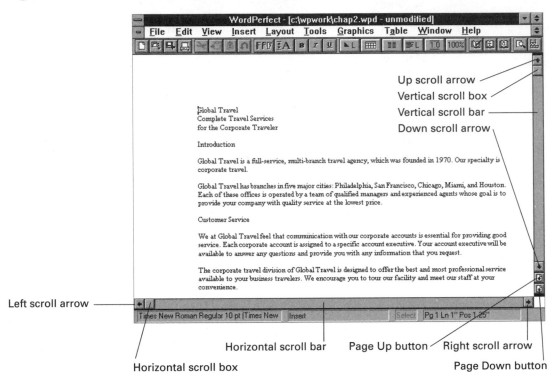

Let's practice using the mouse and scroll bars to scroll through the active document, CHAP2.WPD:

1. Choose **View, Button Bar** to hide the button bar. You will learn more about the button bar in Chapter 8; for now, it isn't necessary to view it.

2. Click on the **down scroll arrow** several times to scroll down through the document one line at a time. Note that the insertion point does not move.

3. Click on the **up scroll arrow** several times to scroll up through the document.

4. Drag the **vertical scroll box** (place the tip of the mouse pointer on the scroll box, press and hold the left mouse button, and slide the mouse pointer down) to the bottom of the scroll bar to scroll to the bottom of the document.

5. Drag the **vertical scroll box** to the middle of the scroll bar to scroll to the middle of the document.

6. Observe the page break—where one page ends and the next begins. (You may have to scroll to see this.) Because CHAP2-.WPD is a two-page document, the page break is located about halfway through the document.

7. Drag the **vertical scroll box** to the top of the scroll bar to scroll to the top of the document. Note that, throughout all of your scrolling, the insertion point has remained at the top of the document.

8. Click in the **vertical scroll bar** below the vertical scroll box to scroll one screen length down through the document.

9. Repeat step 8 as many times as necessary to scroll to the bottom of the document.

10. Click in the **vertical scroll bar** above the vertical scroll box to scroll one screen length up through the document.

11. Repeat step 10 as many times as necessary to scroll up to the top of the document.

12. Click on the **Page Down** button to view page 2.

13. Click on the **Page Up** button to view page 1.

Let's take a moment to observe a common scrolling mistake. Assume you wanted to enter your initials at the end of the active document:

1. Drag the **vertical scroll box** to the bottom of the scroll bar to display the end of the document.

2. Type your initials. The text is inserted at the top of the document (where your insertion point is located), not at the end (where you scrolled to). Note that WordPerfect automatically repositions the document to display the inserted text. To avoid making such a mistake, remember these two things: Text that you type is always inserted at the insertion point, and the insertion point does not move when you use the mouse to scroll through your document.

3. Press **Backspace** to erase your initials.

4. Scroll back down to the end of the document and look at the page indicator in the status bar. It shows the position of the

insertion point (page 1), not the current document display (page 2). Observing the status bar from time to time can help you keep track of the insertion point's position.

MOVING THROUGH A DOCUMENT

When you scroll through a document, you change the document display but not the insertion point. When you *move* through a document, you change both the document display and the insertion point. For this reason, you should scroll when you just want to view different parts of a document, and you should move when you want to view and modify a document.

 USING THE KEYBOARD TO MOVE THROUGH A DOCUMENT

Table 2.2 lists several ways to move through a document by using the keyboard.

Table 2.2   **Keyboard Movement Techniques**

To Move	Press
Up one screen	PgUp (or Page Up on enhanced keyboards)
Down one screen	PgDn (or Page Down)
To the top of the document	Ctrl+Home
To the end of the document	Ctrl+End
To the beginning of a line	Home
To the end of a line	End

Now let's practice using the keyboard to move—rather than to scroll—through a document.

Note: If you intend to use the PgDn and PgUp keys on the numeric keypad, make sure that Num Lock is off.

1. Press **PgDn** (or Page Down) twice to move two screen lengths down through the document. Note that the insertion point has moved along with the document display.

2. Press **PgUp** (or Page Up) twice to move two screen lengths up through the document. Note that the insertion point has moved.

3. Press **Ctrl+End** to move to the end of the document. (**Note:** Press and hold the Ctrl key, press End, then release both keys.)

4. Press **Ctrl+Home** to move to the beginning of the document.

Let's redo our initial-writing task, this time using the correct method:

1. Press **Ctrl+End** to move to the end of the document.

2. Type your initials. They now appear in the desired location, because you used Ctrl+End (not the scroll bar) to move the insertion point along with the document display.

USING EDIT, *GO TO* TO MOVE TO A PAGE

You can use the Edit, Go To command to move to the top of a specified page in the active document. This technique is particularly useful when you are moving through long (multipage) documents.

Here's the general procedure to move to the top of the page:

- Choose *Edit, Go To*.
- Type the page number.
- Click on *OK* (or press *Enter*).

Instead of choosing Edit, Go To from the menu, you can also use the Ctrl+G shortcut key to issue a Go To command. Shortcut keys allow you to issue frequently used commands directly from the keyboard. (For a list of WordPerfect's shortcut keys, see Appendix B.)

Here's the general procedure to use the Ctrl+G shortcut key to move to the top of a page:

- Press *Ctrl+G*. WordPerfect displays the Go To dialog box.
- Type the page number.
- Press *Enter*.

Let's use the Edit, Go To command to move through the document:

1. Choose **Edit, Go To** to open the Go To dialog box (see Figure 2.4; your dialog box may not exactly match the one shown in the figure).

Figure 2.4   **The Go To dialog box**

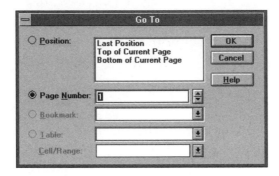

2. In the Page Number text box, type **2** to specify the destination page. Then press **Enter** to move (the document display and the insertion point) to the top of page 2.

3. Choose **Edit, Go To**. Enter **1**—that is, type **1** and then press **Enter**—to move to the top of page 1. (From here on we'll use "enter text" to mean "type text and then press Enter.")

4. Click on **Edit** to display the drop-down Edit menu. Observe the shortcut key for the Go To command. It is Ctrl+G. Click on **Edit** again to close the Edit menu.

5. Press **Ctrl+G** (Go To). The Go To dialog box opens.

6. Enter **2** (type **2** and press **Enter**) to move to the top of page 2.

PRACTICE YOUR SKILLS

1. Use **Edit, Go To** to move to the top of page 1.

2. Use **Ctrl+G** to attempt to move to the top of page 3. Since CHAP2.WPD does not have a page 3, you are moved to the top of the final page (2).

USING EDIT, FIND TO SEARCH FOR TEXT

One of WordPerfect's most powerful features is its ability to quickly locate a specific word or phrase in a document. You can use this feature to move rapidly to any document location. For example, you can move to the sentence containing the phrase "We would like to establish...," even if you have no idea on which page this sentence appears.

Here's the general procedure to use Edit, Find to search for text within a document:

- Place the insertion point where you wish to begin the search. By default, WordPerfect searches from the insertion point downward to the end of the document. To search the entire document, place the insertion point at the top of the document.

- Choose *Edit, Find* to open the Find dialog box.

- In the Find text box, type the search text (the text that you want to find).

- Select any desired search options (covered next).

- Click on *Find Next* (or press *Enter*). WordPerfect highlights the first occurrence of your search text.

- Repeat the previous step as many times as necessary until you have searched through the entire document. Or, cancel your search at any time by clicking on Close. When WordPerfect has reached the end of your document, it displays a message telling you that your search text is "not found."

- Click on *OK* (or press *Enter*) to close this message box.

- Close the Find dialog box.

The Find dialog box provides several menu options which allow you to refine your text searches. By choosing the *Match, Whole Word* option, you can tell Find to locate only whole words that match your search text. By choosing the *Match, Case* option, you can locate only words that exactly match the case (capitalization) of your search text. By selecting options from the Options menu, you can tell WordPerfect how to search your document. For example, if you are searching for text and your insertion point is not at the top of the document, you can tell WordPerfect to continue searching from the beginning of the document once it reaches the end.

Let's experiment with the Edit, Find command:

1. Press **Ctrl+Home** to move the insertion point to the top in preparation for searching the entire document.

2. Choose **Edit, Find** to open the Find Text dialog box (see Figure 2.5).

Figure 2.5   **The Find Text dialog box**

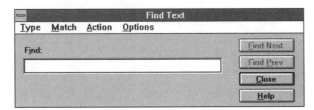

3. In the Find text box, type **vacation**.

4. Click on **Match** to open the Match menu. Note that none of the options are selected. A check mark appears when an option is on.

5. Click on **Match** again to close the menu without selecting any options.

6. Click on **Find Next** (or press **Enter**) four times, pausing each time to examine the found word (when a word is found, it is highlighted in the document). WordPerfect finds the following occurrences of vacation:

   ```
   Vacations
   vacation
   Vacation
   Vacation
   ```

   WordPerfect found the second occurrence just listed—*vacation*—because it exactly matches your search text. It found the last two occurrences (*Vacation*), because by leaving the Match, Case option unselected, you told it to ignore capitalization. It found the first occurrence (*Vacations*) because by leaving the Match, Whole Word option unselected, you also told it to ignore whole-word matching (*vacation* is a partial match of *Vacations*).

7. Click on **Find Next** (or press **Enter**) again. A message box appears, informing you that your search text was "not found." This means WordPerfect has completed its search through the end of the document. Click on **OK** (or press **Enter**) to close this box.

8. Click on **Close** (or press **Esc**) to close the Find Text dialog box.

Now let's refine our search by using the Match, Whole Word and Match, Case options:

1. Move the insertion point to the top of the document (press **Ctrl+Home**).

2. Choose **Edit, Find** to open the Find Text dialog box.

3. Choose **Match, Whole Word**. Whole Word is displayed below the Find text box, indicating that the option is on.

4. Click on **Match** to open the Match menu, and observe that there is a check mark next to Whole Word. Click on **Match** again to close the menu without selecting an option.

5. Click on **Find Next** (or press **Enter**) three times, pausing to examine each found word. Three occurrences are found: *vacation, Vacation,* and *Vacation. Vacations* is not found, because you told WordPerfect to find only whole-word matches of vacation.

6. Click on **Find Next** (or press **Enter**) again; the end-of-document message box appears. Click on **OK** to close this box and then click on **Close** to close the Find Text dialog box.

7. Move the insertion point back up to the top of the document (press **Ctrl+Home**).

8. Choose **Edit, Find** to open the Find Text dialog box.

9. Choose **Match, Case**. (Both Case and Whole Word should now be selected.)

10. Observe the Find Text dialog box. Case Sensitive joins Whole Word below the Find text box. Both options are on.

11. Click on **Find Next** (or press **Enter**) two times. Only one occurrence of your search text is found: *vacation. Vacation* is not found, because you told WordPerfect to find only case-matching occurrences of *vacation*.

12. Click on **OK** to close the end-of-document message box and then click on **Close** to close the Find Text dialog box.

PRACTICE YOUR SKILLS

1. Uncheck the **Whole Word** and **Case** options and then search your entire active document for **news**. (**Hint:** Remember to move the insertion point to the top of the document before beginning the search.) There are three matches.

2. Check **Whole Word** and repeat the search. There is only one match.

3. Uncheck **Whole Word**, check Case, and repeat the search. There are two matches.

4. Uncheck **Case** and close the Find Text dialog box.

USING ZOOM TO CONTROL DOCUMENT MAGNIFICATION

The Zoom feature enables you to control the level of magnification at which a document is displayed on your screen. By default, Zoom is set to 100 percent magnification (where the screen display matches the actual document size), but you can adjust this magnification to anywhere from 50 percent to 200 percent.

A magnification of 50 percent shrinks the on-screen document to half of its actual size, allowing you to view all (or most of) an entire page without scrolling. A magnification of 200 percent enlarges the on-screen document to twice its actual size, allowing you to view text and graphics close up to perform detail work. (WordPerfect allows you to edit a document's text at any Zoom magnification level.)

To specify an exact Zoom magnification (such as 68 percent or 124 percent), you must use the View, Zoom command.

Here's the general procedure to use the View, Zoom command:

- Choose *View, Zoom*.
- Click on the *Other* button.
- Type the desired magnification in the Other box.
- Click on *OK* (or press *Enter*).

For most situations, however, you can use the Zoom buttons in the power bar to quickly zoom in (increase the magnification) to and zoom out (decrease the magnification) of a document. These buttons include the Zoom button (the sixth button from the right; it displays a percentage) and the Page Zoom Full button (the second button from the right; it displays a magnifying glass).

Note: Page Zoom Full toggles between fitting the full page width and length on the screen and 100 percent magnification.

Here's the general procedure to use the Zoom button on the power bar:

- Place the mouse pointer on the *Zoom* button.
- Press and hold the *left mouse* button.
- Select the magnification you want.
- Release the mouse button.

The Zoom buttons can also be used as a navigational tool, allowing you to quickly move the insertion point to the part of the page you wish to edit.

Here's the general procedure to use Page Zoom Full to move the insertion point:

- Click on the *Page Zoom Full* button to view the entire page.
- Place the insertion point where you want to edit text.
- Click on the *Page Zoom Full* button to return to 100 percent magnification.

The document window will automatically reorient to the new position of the insertion point.

Let's try using Zoom as a navigational tool to edit an entry in the tabbed table at the bottom of the first page.

1. Move the insertion point to the top of the document (press **Ctrl+Home**).

2. Observe the Zoom button, the sixth button from the right on the power bar. It reads 100 percent.

3. Click on the **Page Zoom Full** button. WordPerfect displays a miniature view of the page (see Figure 2.6). Observe the Zoom button. It displays the current magnification.

4. Move the mouse pointer to the first line of the tabbed table at the bottom of page 1. Click to position the insertion point.

5. Click on the **Page Zoom Full** button to return to 100 percent magnification.

6. Delete **/Motel** (you might need to scroll to find it) in the first line of the tabbed table.

Figure 2.6   **Page 1 of CHAP2.WPD in Page Zoom Full view**

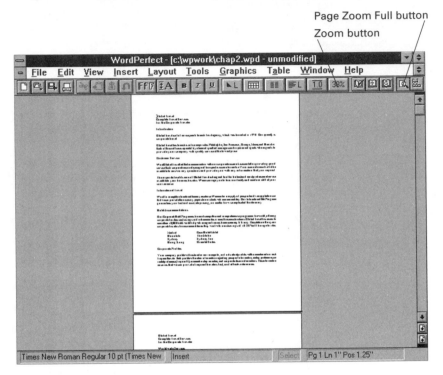

USING HELP TO OBTAIN ON-LINE HELP

WordPerfect Help is an extensive on-line help system that provides you with "how-to" information on every aspect of the WordPerfect program. The beauty of WordPerfect Help is its accessibility. No matter what you are doing in WordPerfect (choosing a command from the menu, editing a document, filling in a dialog box, and so on), Help is only a keystroke—or mouse click—away.

USING THE HELP INDEX TO OBTAIN HELP

The WordPerfect Help index provides an overview (similar to a table of contents) of the topics for which Help information is available.

Here's the general procedure to use the Help index:

- Choose *Help, Contents* to open the Help index.

- To get help for a specific topic, click on any underlined word or phrase in the index.

- To jump to a new Help window, click on any solid-underlined word or phrase.

- To pop up a definition of a word or phrase without moving from the current screen, point to a dotted-underlined word or phrase, then click the *left mouse* button.

- To close the WordPerfect Help window, double-click on the window's *Control-menu* box.

Let's practice using WordPerfect Help:

1. Choose **Help, Contents** to display the WordPerfect Help index (see Figure 2.7).

Figure 2.7   **The WordPerfect Help index**

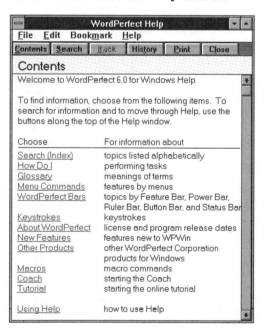

2. Move the mouse pointer to the entry **Using Help** (at the bottom of the contents list). The mouse pointer changes to a hand. Click to view the step-by-step instructions (see Figure 2.8).

Figure 2.8　　　**Using Help**

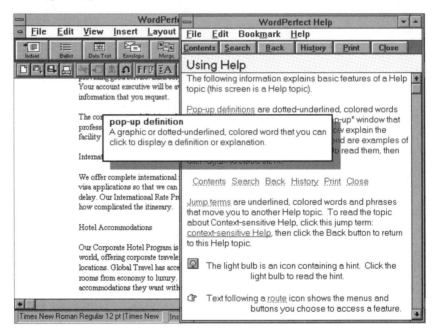

3. Read the Help text. The text explains some of the features of WordPerfect Help.

4. Click on **pop-up definitions** to display a pop-up dialog box defining pop-up definitions (see Figure 2.8). You can click on any dotted-underlined word or phrase and WordPerfect Help will display a pop-up definition of it.

5. Click anywhere to hide the pop-up definition box.

6. Click on the dotted-underlined **Jump terms** to display its pop-up definition. You can click on jump words (solid-underlined words or phrases) to jump to related Help topics. Let's try it.

7. Click to hide the Jump terms pop-up definition box.

8. Click on **context-sensitive Help** to jump to the Context-Sensitive Help window.

9. Read the Help text to learn how to get context-sensitive help in a WordPerfect dialog box, menu, or window. We will use context-sensitive help later in this chapter.

10. Click on **Using Help** (at the bottom of the window) to return to the Using Help window.

11. Click on **Search** to display the pop-up definition for Search.

You can search for specific Help topics by typing in keywords. Let's try it:

12. Click on the **Search** button (at the top of the dialog box) to open the Search dialog box.

13. Type **find** to display the section of the WordPerfect Help index beginning with the word *find* (see Figure 2.9).

Figure 2.9   **The Search dialog box**

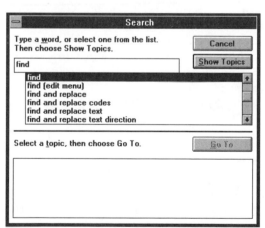

14. Click on **Show Topics** to display a list of WordPerfect Help topics related to *find* (see Figure 2.10).

15. Click on **Find Text** to select the topic (see Figure 2.10).

16. Click on **Go To** to move to the Find Text Help window.

Figure 2.10   **The Search dialog box displaying topics related to *find***

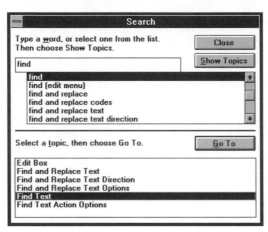

17. Read the Help text. The Help text explains how to use the Edit, Find command to find specific text in a document.

18. Close the WordPerfect Help window by double-clicking on its **Control-menu** box, in the upper-left corner of the Help title bar. (Do not double-click on the application or document window Control-menu boxes, as this would close the WordPerfect program or the active document.)

USING THE F1 KEY TO OBTAIN CONTEXT-SENSITIVE HELP

In addition to the Help index and the Search dialog box, WordPerfect Help offers you context-sensitive help—information related to your current working context. For example, if a dialog box is open and you ask for context-sensitive help, Help displays information about that particular dialog box. Context-sensitive help quickly provides information about specific dialog boxes, menu commands, or areas of the screen.

There are two ways to obtain context-sensitive help:

• Press *F1*; WordPerfect displays the Help window related to your current working context.

OR

• Press *Shift+F1*; the mouse pointer changes to an arrow with a question mark attached.

- Make any menu choice or click on the desired part of the application window and WordPerfect opens a related Help window.

Note: In addition to the methods listed above, most WordPerfect dialog boxes display a Help button which you can use to open the Help topic for the dialog box.

Let's use the F1 (Help) key to obtain context-sensitive help:

1. Choose **Edit, Go To** to open the Go To dialog box.

2. Press **F1** (Help) and click on **OK**, if necessary, to open the Help window for the Go To command (see Figure 2.11). This is an example of context-sensitive help, in which WordPerfect provides help relative to your current working context.

Figure 2.11   **Help window for the Go To command**

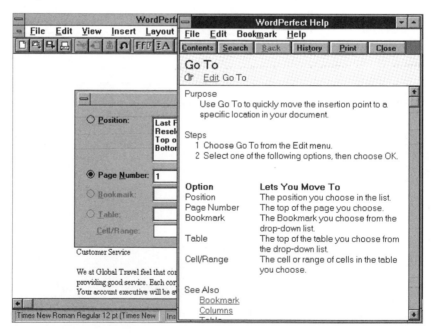

3. Close the Help window (double-click on its **Control-menu** box).

4. Click on **Cancel** to close the Go To dialog box.

Now let's use the Shift+F1 method to obtain context-sensitive help:

1. Press **Shift+F1** to activate WordPerfect's context-sensitive help. Note that the mouse pointer now has a question mark attached to it (see Figure 2.12).

Figure 2.12   **Context-sensitive help pointer**

Context-sensitive help pointer

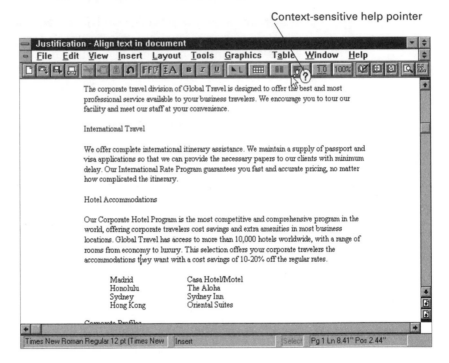

2. Choose **File, Print** to open the Help window on the Print command.

3. Close the Help window (double-click on its **Control-menu** box).

4. Close the Print dialog box (click on **Close**).

5. Press **Shift+F1** to reactivate context-sensitive help.

6. Click the mouse pointer on the **New** button on the power bar (the first button from the left) to open the WordPerfect Help window for new documents.

7. Close the Help window.

SAVING THE MODIFIED FILE

Let's end this work session by using File, Save As to rename the active document and save it (as a disk file) to your WPWORK directory. By using the File, Save As command, you preserve the original version of the document (CHAP2.WPD) along with your revised version. If you instead were to use the File, Save command to save the active document, you would preserve the revision (as CHAP2.WPD), but delete the original.

1. Choose **File, Save As** to open the Save As dialog box.

2. In the File Name text box, type **mychap2** to rename the document.

3. If your **wpwork** directory is not already selected, select it now.

4. Click on **OK** (or press **Enter**) to save your modified CHAP2-.WPD document under the name MYCHAP2.WPD.

5. Double-click on the document window (not the application window) **Control-menu** box to close the document.

SUMMARY

In this chapter, you learned the basics of navigating in WordPerfect. You now know how to open a document, scroll and move through a document, search for text, control document magnification, and obtain on-line help.

Here's a quick reference guide to the WordPerfect features introduced in this chapter:

Desired Result	How to Do It
Open a document	Choose **File, Open**; select the drive and directory; click on the disk file; and then click on **OK** (or double-click on the file)
Open a recently used document	Choose **File**; click on the document name at the bottom of the File menu

Desired Result	How to Do It
Scroll up or down one line	Click on the **up** or **down scroll arrow**
Scroll to the top, bottom, or middle of a document	Drag the **vertical scroll box** to the top, bottom, or middle of the scroll bar
Scroll up or down a screen	Click in the **vertical scroll bar** above or below the vertical scroll box
Scroll down one page	Click on the **Page Down** button
Scroll up one page	Click on the **Page Up** button
Scroll left or right a column	Click on the **left** or **right scroll arrow**
Scroll to the left edge, right edge, or middle of a document	Drag the **horizontal scroll box** to the left, right, or middle of the scroll bar
Scroll to the left or right a screen at a time	Click in the **horizontal scroll bar** to the left or right of the horizontal scroll box
Move up one screen	Press the **PgUp** key
Move down one screen	Press the **PgDn** key
Move to the top of the document	Press **Ctrl+Home**
Move to the end of the document	Press **Ctrl+End**
Move to the beginning of a line	Press **Home**
Move to the end of a line	Press **End**
Move to the top of a page	Choose **Edit, Go To** or press **Ctrl+G**; type the page number; click on **OK** or press **Enter**

Desired Result	How to Do It
Search for text	Place the insertion point where you want to begin searching; choose **Edit, Find**; type the search text; select any desired search options; click on **Find Next** (or press **Enter**)
Specify an exact Zoom magnification	Choose **View, Zoom**; click on the **Other** button; press **Tab**; type the desired magnification in the Other box; click on **OK** (or press **Enter**)
Use the Zoom button to control magnification	Place the mouse pointer on the **Zoom** button; press and hold the **left mouse** button; select the desired magnification; release the mouse button
Use the Page Zoom Full button as a navigational tool	Click on the **Page Zoom Full** button; position the insertion point; click on the **Page Zoom Full** button
Open Help contents	Choose **Help, Contents**
Get help from the Contents window	Click on any underlined word or phrase
Jump to a new Help window	Click on any solid-underlined word or phrase
Pop up a definition of a word or phrase	Point to a dotted-underlined word or phrase; click the **left mouse** button
Search for help	Choose **Help, Contents**; click on the **Search** button; type the keyword you want to search for help on; click on **Show Topics**; select a topic from the Topics list; click on **Go To** to go to the Help window for that topic

Desired Result	How to Do It
Obtain context-sensitive help	Press **F1**; or, press **Shift+F1** and make any menu choice or click on the desired part of the application window
Close the WordPerfect Help window	Double-click on the window's **Control-menu** box

In the next chapter, you'll learn how to edit text. Editing includes replacing found text, moving text, and copying text. You'll also be introduced to a handy way to undo an editing action.

IF YOU'RE STOPPING HERE

If you need to break off here, please exit WordPerfect. If you want to proceed directly to the next chapter, please do so now.

CHAPTER 3:
EDITING TEXT

Techniques for
Selecting Text

Using Edit,
Replace to
Replace Found
Text

Moving and
Copying Text

Fixing Mistakes

In Chapter 1, you learned the basics of editing—how to insert, select, replace, and delete text. In this chapter we'll introduce you to some of WordPerfect for Windows's more advanced editing techniques. You'll learn sophisticated ways to select text and then move and copy this text to other locations in your document. You'll find out how to use the Edit, Replace command (Edit, Find's more powerful cousin) to find text and replace it with new text of your choice. Finally, we'll show you how to use the Undo and Undelete commands to rescue yourself from a potentially catastrophic word processing mistake.

When you're done working through this chapter, you will know

- How to use the mouse, the keyboard, and menus to select text
- How to use the Edit, Replace command to replace found text
- How to move and copy text
- How to use the Undo command to reverse your last operation
- How to use Undelete to retrieve your last three deletions

TECHNIQUES FOR SELECTING TEXT

Before you can move or copy text, you must select it. You can do this by using the mouse, the keyboard, or menus. Table 3.1 lists WordPerfect's text-selection techniques.

Table 3.1   **Text-Selection Techniques**

Selection Technique	How to Do It
Dragging	Point at one end of the text you want to select. Press and hold the left mouse button. Move (drag) the mouse pointer to the other end of the text. Release the mouse button. All the text between the two ends is selected.
Using the Shift key	Place the insertion point at one end of the text. Press and hold Shift, and then click the left mouse button at the other end of the text you want to select (do not drag). Release Shift. All the text between the two ends is selected.
Selecting a word	Point anywhere inside the word and double-click the left mouse button. The trailing space is automatically selected along with the word.

| Table 3.1 | Text-Selection Techniques (Continued) |

Selection Technique	How to Do It
Selecting a sentence	Point anywhere inside the sentence and triple-click the left mouse button. Or, point in the *selection bar* area (the blank vertical bar on the left side of the document window) next to the sentence and click the left mouse button. End punctuation and trailing spaces are automatically selected along with the sentence.
Selecting multiple lines	Point in the selection bar next to the first or last line of the text you want to select. Press and hold the left mouse button, and then drag down or up. Release the mouse button. All the lines you "dragged" are selected.
Selecting a paragraph	Point anywhere inside the paragraph and quadruple-click the left mouse button. Or, point in the selection bar area next to the paragraph, click the *right* mouse button, and select Paragraph. The ending paragraph mark is selected along with the paragraph.
Selecting an entire document	Choose Edit, Select, All.
Extending an existing selection	While holding Shift, click beyond the existing selection. The selection extends to that point.
Deselecting an existing selection	Make another selection, or click the left mouse button in the text area anywhere outside the existing selection.

If you are not running WordPerfect on your computer, please start it now. Close all open documents except for Document1. Let's begin this chapter's activities by opening a new document file and then using the mouse-dragging method to select text:

1. Click on the **Open** button (second from the left in the power bar; it shows a file folder being opened) to display the Open File dialog box. Clicking on the Open button is equivalent to choosing the File, Open command from the menu.

2. If your **WPWORK** directory is not already selected, select it now.

3. In the Filename list box, double-click on **chap3.wpd** to open the document file. Double-clicking on a list-box item is often equivalent to clicking once on the item and then clicking on OK (or pressing Enter).

4. Point to the left of the *C* in *Corporate* in the third line of the document.

5. Drag to the right to select **Corporate** and the trailing space.

6. Release the mouse button. Your screen should resemble Figure 3.1.

Now let's use the whole-word selection technique:

1. Point to the word **five** in the first paragraph of the document.

2. Double-click the mouse button to select the entire word **five**. Note that selecting *five* deselects *Corporate*.

3. Examine the selected text. The trailing space after *five* is also selected.

Now let's use the sentence and paragraph selection techniques:

1. Move the mouse pointer into the selection bar—the blank vertical bar between the left edge of the document window and the left edge of the document text (see Figure 3.2). Note that the pointer changes from an I-beam into an arrow.

2. Point in the selection bar next to the line beginning with *Global Travel is a full-service*. Click the mouse button to select the first sentence.

3. Point in the selection bar next to *Global Travel has branches in*. Double-click the mouse button to select the entire paragraph.

Figure 3.1   **Dragging the mouse to select text**

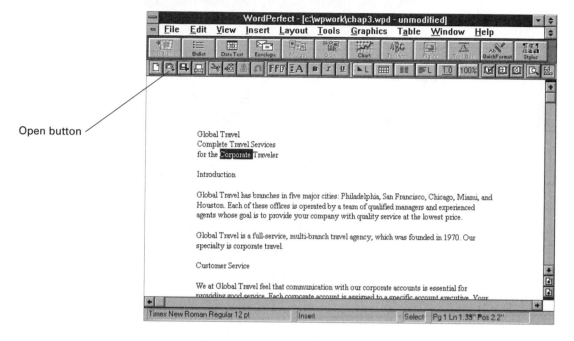

Open button

Figure 3.2   **The selection bar**

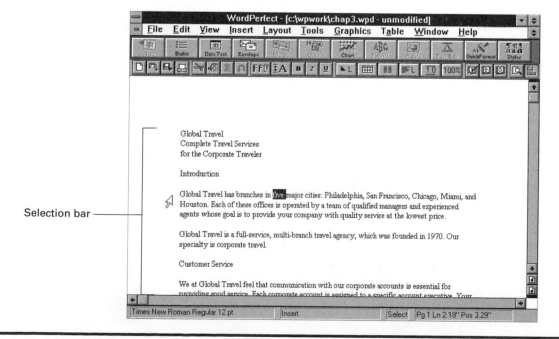

Selection bar

4. Point in the selection bar next to *Introduction*. Press and hold the mouse button, and then drag down to the last line of the second paragraph (before *Customer Service*) to select multiple lines of text.

Let's use the Shift key to select a block of text and then extend this selection:

1. Place the insertion point before the *C* in *Corporate* in the third line of the document.

2. Press and hold **Shift**, and then click the mouse pointer in the space after *five* to select all the text from *Corporate* to *five*. Release Shift (see Figure 3.3).

Figure 3.3   **Selecting text with the mouse and the Shift key**

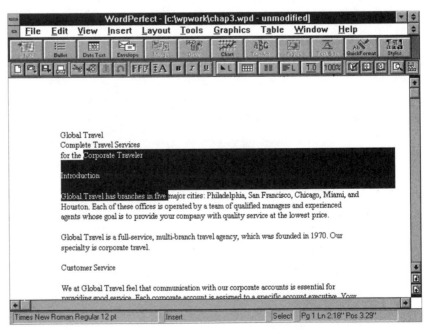

3. Point to the right of the *s* in *offices* in the next line down. Press and hold **Shift**, and then click the mouse button to extend the selection through to the end of *offices*. Release Shift.

Finally, let's use the menu to select the entire document:

1. Choose **Edit, Select, All** (click on **Edit**, click on **Select**, and then click on **All**) to select the entire document.

2. Click anywhere within the text area to deselect the text.

PRACTICE YOUR SKILLS

1. Select the first sentence of the paragraph beginning with *Global Travel has branches in five major cities*, using the mouse-dragging technique.

2. Deselect the sentence.

3. Select the same sentence as in step 1, this time using the selection bar to select the entire sentence without dragging. (For help, refer to Table 3.1, earlier in this chapter.)

4. Use the double-clicking technique to select each of the following words in the first paragraph: **Global, Philadelphia, offices, qualified, price**. Note that double-clicking selects the trailing space or punctuation after a word.

5. Select the first line of the document. Extend the selection to include the first four lines.

USING EDIT, REPLACE TO REPLACE FOUND TEXT

In Chapter 2, you learned how to use Edit, Find to search for text in a document. Here you'll learn how to use the Edit, Replace command to search for text and replace it with new text of your choice.

Edit, Replace is one of WordPerfect's most powerful commands. Let's say you typed a 100-page document that made frequent reference to a man named *Pablo Sitauskus* and then you found out that the correct spelling was *Sitauskis*. Normally you'd have to find each occurrence of *Sitauskus* and retype it—an ugly task considering the length of the document. Using Edit, Replace, however, you could issue a single command that would automatically (and rapidly) replace every occurrence of *Sitauskus* with *Sitauskis*.

Here's the general procedure to use Edit, Replace to replace found text in a document:

- Place the insertion point where you wish to begin the search/replace operation (Edit, Replace only permits you to search from the insertion point downward). To search an entire document, place the insertion point at the top of the document.

- Choose *Edit, Replace* to open the Find and Replace Text dialog box.

- In the Find text box, type the *search text* (the text you wish to find).

- If necessary, select your desired Match options.

- In the Replace With text box, type the *replace text* (the text you wish to replace the search text).

- Click on *Find* (or press *Enter*); WordPerfect highlights the first occurrence of your search text.

- Click on either *Replace* (to replace the found text and search for the next occurrence), *Find* (to leave the found text unchanged and search for the next occurrence), or *Replace All* (to replace all occurrences of the search text throughout the rest of the document).

- Repeat the previous step as needed until you have searched through the entire document, or cancel your search at any time by clicking on *Close.*

- Close the Find and Replace Text dialog box.

Let's use the procedures just described to find and replace some text in the active document:

1. Press **Ctrl+Home** to move the insertion point to the top of your document in preparation for searching an entire document.

2. Choose **Edit, Replace** to open the Find and Replace Text dialog box (see Figure 3.4).

Figure 3.4   **The Find and Replace Text dialog box**

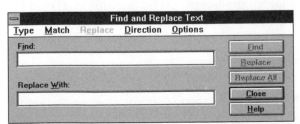

3. In the Find text box, type **20**. This is the text we will search for and replace.

4. Press **Tab** to select the Replace With text box and then type **50**. This is the text that will replace the search text (20).

5. Click on **Find** to find the first occurrence of *20*.

6. Click on **Replace** to replace *20* with *50* and search for the next occurrence of *20*.

7. Click on **Find** to leave *20-30%* unchanged and search for the next occurrence of *20*.

8. Click on **Replace** to replace *20* with *50* and search for the next occurrence of *20*. Because there are no more occurrences of *20*, the Not Found message box appears.

9. Click on **OK** to close the message box.

10. Click on **Close** to close the Find and Replace Text dialog box.

You'll have a chance to use the Replace All command in the "Practice Your Skills" section at the end of this chapter.

MOVING AND COPYING TEXT

Another of WordPerfect's powerful editing features is its ability to move and copy text within a document. You can, for example, quickly and easily move a table of numbers from the top of the fifth page of a business report to the bottom of the 11th page, or copy a four-line address to several locations within the body of a letter.

THE CLIPBOARD

Windows provides a temporary storage area called the *Clipboard* for when you move or copy text. When selected text is *cut* (removed) or *copied*, it is placed on the Clipboard. *Pasting* inserts a copy of the Clipboard contents before the insertion point. You'll notice that the Copy button, which is the sixth button from the left on the power bar, resembles a clipboard. Entries remain on the Clipboard, either until you cut or copy another entry to it or until you exit from Windows.

MOVING TEXT

Here's the general procedure to move text within a document:

- Select the text to be moved.

- Choose *Edit, Cut* (or click on the *Cut* button—fourth from the left in the power bar; it shows a pair of scissors) to cut the selected text from the document and place it on the Clipboard. See the previous section for a discussion of the Clipboard.

- Place the insertion point where you want to move this text.

- Choose *Edit, Paste* (or click on the *Paste* button—it shows a jar of paste) to paste the cut text before the insertion point.

Let's practice moving text from one location to another within a document:

1. Drag in the selection bar to select the paragraph beginning with *Global Travel is a full-service* and the trailing blank line. (**Note:** If you have difficulty selecting the trailing blank line, select it *first* and then drag up to select the *Global Travel* paragraph.)

2. Choose **Edit, Cut** to remove the selected text from the document and place it on the Windows Clipboard.

3. Place the insertion point before the *G* in *Global Travel has branches*.

4. Choose **Edit, Paste** to paste a copy of the Clipboard contents before the insertion point (see Figure 3.5).

 COPYING TEXT

Here's the general procedure to copy text within a document:

- Select the text to be copied.

- Choose *Edit, Copy* (or click on the *Copy* button—fifth from the left in the power bar) to copy the selected text to the Clipboard.

- Place the insertion point where you want to copy this text.

- Choose *Edit, Paste* (or click on the *Paste* button) to paste the Clipboard text before the insertion point.

Figure 3.5   **Page 1 of CHAP3.WPD, after pasting**

Cut button   Paste button

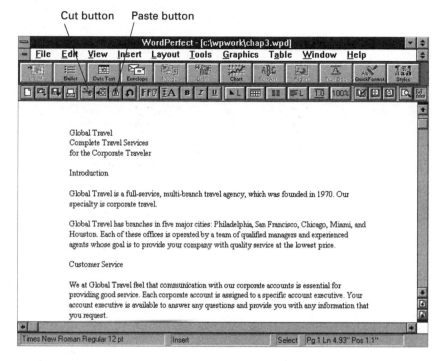

Now let's practice copying text within a document:

1. Select the first four lines of the document (the three-line page heading and the trailing blank line).

2. Choose **Edit, Copy** to place a copy of the selected text on the Clipboard. Note that the selected text is not removed from the document, as it is when you choose Edit, Move.

3. Use **Ctrl+G** (Go To) to place the insertion point at the top of page 2. (**Note:** If you don't see the insertion point, click at the top of page 2 to place the insertion point there.)

4. Choose **Edit, Paste** to paste a copy of the Clipboard contents before the insertion point (see Figure 3.6).

As demonstrated earlier, you can also use the power bar to paste text from the Clipboard. Let's try this:

1. Place the insertion point at the top of page 3.

Figure 3.6 **Page 2 of CHAP3.WPD, after pasting**

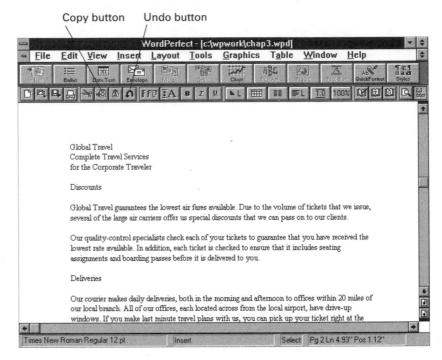

2. Click on the **Paste** button (the one showing a paste jar). Because a copy of the text is still on the Clipboard, you do not need to copy the text again before pasting.

3. Use **File, Save As** to save the document as **mychap3**.

FIXING MISTAKES

WordPerfect provides you with two commands that can save you a lot of work if you accidentally issue a command or delete something that you later decide you want.

USING UNDO TO REVERSE YOUR LAST OPERATION

WordPerfect provides an Undo command that allows you to reverse (undo) the last operation that you performed. Because Undo can reverse only your *last* operation, you must use it immediately after performing the operation.

Here's the general procedure to reverse your last operation:

- Choose *Edit, Undo*, or click on the *Undo* button (the eighth button from the left in the power bar—it shows a U-turn arrow).

Let's use the power bar Undo button to reverse a potentially catastrophic text-replacement mistake:

1. Select the entire document. (Choose **Edit, Select, All**.)

2. Type your first initial. Surprise! All that's left in the document window is a single letter.

3. Click on the **Undo** button (the one showing an arrow that looks like a U-turn sign) to restore the original text. All is well.

4. Deselect to avoid deleting the entire document again.

USING UNDELETE TO RECOVER DELETED INFORMATION

When you delete text, it is not immediately lost. The Edit, Undo command allows you to undelete text immediately after you delete it, and the *Edit, Undelete* command goes two steps further. It enables you to retrieve your last three deletions. When you choose Edit, Undelete, the Undelete dialog box opens. It displays five options, and the most recent deletion that was made appears highlighted in your document at the insertion point (see Figure 3.7). You can use the Previous and Next buttons to cycle through the three deletions that are stored in memory. Click on *Previous* to display the previous deletion. Click on *Next* to display the most recent deletion. Click on *Restore* to place the appropriate text at the insertion point. Click on *Cancel* to close the Undelete dialog box. Click on *Help* to get help for the Undelete command.

Let's practice deleting and undeleting text:

1. Point to the left of the *G* in *Global Travel*, at the top of page 1, and then drag down to select through the second line of the heading.

2. Release the mouse button.

3. Press **Del** to delete the selected text.

4. Select **corporate**, in the last line of the paragraph below *Introduction*.

5. Press **Del** to delete the selected text.

Figure 3.7   **The Undelete dialog box**

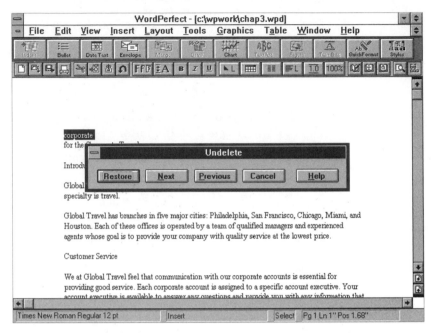

6. Place the insertion point at the top of the document (press **Ctrl+Home**).

7. Choose **Edit, Undelete**. The Undelete dialog box opens. The most recent deletion, *corporate*, is selected at the location of the insertion point (see Figure 3.7). You don't want to restore *corporate* at the current position of the insertion point. Instead, restore the previous deletion, which was the letter heading.

8. Click on **Previous** to view the previous deletion.

9. Now click on **Restore** to restore the text at the location of the insertion point.

10. Choose **File, Save** to update the document—that is, to save it with the same name and in the same location.

11. Close the document window.

PRACTICE YOUR SKILLS

In Chapters 2 and 3, you've learned how to navigate within a document, and how to select, replace, move, and copy text. The following two Practice Your Skills activities give you the opportunity to apply these techniques to realistic word processing situations. After each activity step, a chapter reference is provided (in parentheses) to inform you where the relevant technique for that step was introduced.

Follow these steps to produce the final document shown in Figures 3.8 and 3.9 from the original document PRAC3.WPD:

1. Open **prac3.wpd** (Chapter 2). (You'll have to scroll through your WPWORK directory.)

2. Replace all occurrences of *Mayco* with **Macco** (Chapter 3). (**Hint:** Select *Replace All* in the Replace dialog box.)

3. Move the second paragraph on page 1 (beginning with *Congratulations to all*), and its trailing blank line, before the first paragraph on page 1 (beginning with *As we expected*) (Chapter 3).

4. Copy the three-line heading and the trailing blank line on the top of page 1 to the top of page 2 (Chapter 3).

5. Save the document as **myprac3a** (Chapter 2).

6. Print the document and compare it to Figures 3.8 and 3.9 (Chapter 1).

7. Close the document (Chapter 1).

Follow these steps to produce the final document shown in Figures 3.10 and 3.11 from the original document PRAC3B.WPD:

1. Open **prac3b.wpd** (Chapter 2).

2. Replace all case-matching occurrences of *Territory* with **Region** (Chapter 3).

3. Move the heading *3. Computer Study* and the subsequent paragraph before the heading *2. Regional Updates* (Chapter 3). (**Hint:** Include the blank line following the paragraphs.)

4. Change *3. Computer Study* to **2. Computer Study** (Chapter 1).

5. Change *2. Regional Updates* to **3. Regional Updates** (Chapter 1).

Figure 3.8   **Page 1 of the completed document MYPRAC3A.WPD**

Macco Plastics Inc.
Quarterly Sales Report
First Quarter

1. Introduction

Congratulations to all of you! An initial review of the sales figures for the nation reveals a surge in sales in all of Macco's sales areas. major new clients have been added and many new products are on the way.

As we expected when we entered the field, computer-related products, such as keyboard housings and protective carrying cases, are accounting for a major portion of this upswing.

2. Regional Updates

Midwestern Territory

After several years of falling sales due to the slump in the auto industry, Shannon Heilman and her folks have something to celebrate. The recent boom in auto manufacturing has led to renewed demand of Macco products in Detroit.

Northeastern Territory

Elizabeth Graham and her group are doing a great job in Nashua. They have secured major contracts for a wide range of new and existing products. Much of this business is coming from Computer Equipment Corporation, a major client of Macco's.

Southern Territory

Scott Helland and his group have done a fine job of maintaining relations with Becker's Product Development Division in Boca Raton. They have been working closely with Becker to decrease manufacturing costs.

3. Computer Study

A companywide study will begin in March, under the direction of Susan Milanowski and Sandra Rodriquez in data processing, to determine how to most effectively implement automation in our firm. We will be making a large commitment to productivity gains via computerization sometime late this year.

Figure 3.9   **Page 2 of the completed document MYPRAC3A.WPD**

Macco Plastics Inc.
Quarterly Sales Report
First Quarter

4. Quarterly Meeting

The quarterly meeting will take place in Memphis this time. You will find the agenda attached to this report.

5. Conclusion

If the recovery continues at the current pace, this year should be a banner year for all of us at Macco. We want to thank all of you for the outstanding jobs you have done and, most important, for standing by Macco in hard times. Keep up the good work!

Adho Magee
Regional Coordinator
Macco Plastics, Inc.

Figure 3.10   **Page 1 of the completed document MYPRAC3B.WPD**

Macco Plastics Inc.
Quarterly Sales Report
First Quarter
(today's date)

1. Introduction

Congratulations to all of you! An initial review of the sales figures for the nation reveals a surge in sales in all of Macco's sales regions. Major new clients have been added and many new products are on the way.

As we expected when we entered the field, computer-related products, such as keyboard housings and protective carrying cases, are accounting for a major portion of this upswing.

2. Computer Study

A companywide study will begin in March, under the direction of Susan Milanowski and Sandra Rodriquez in data processing, to determine how to most effectively implement automation in our firm. We will be making a large commitment to productivity gains via computerization sometime late this year.

3. Regional Updates

Midwestern Region

After several years of falling sales due to the slump in the auto industry, Shannon Heilman and her folks have something to celebrate. The recent boom in auto manufacturing has led to renewed demand of Macco products in Detroit.

Northeastern Region

Elizabeth Graham and her group are doing a great job in Nashua. They have secured major contracts for a wide range of new and existing products. Much of this business is coming from Computer Equipment Corporation, a major client of Macco's.

Southern Region

Scott Helland and his group have done a fine job of maintaining relations with Becker's Product Development Division in Boca Raton. They have been working closely with Becker to decrease manufacturing costs.

Figure 3.11   **Page 2 of the completed document MYPRAC3B.WPD**

Macco Plastics Inc.
Quarterly Sales Report
First Quarter
(today's date)

4. Quarterly Meeting

The quarterly meeting will take place in Memphis this time. You will find the agenda attached to
this report.

5. Conclusion

If the recovery continues at the current pace, this year should be a banner year for all of us at
Macco. We want to thank all of you for the outstanding jobs you have done and, most important,
for standing by Macco in hard times. Keep up the good work!

Adho Magee
Regional Coordinator
Macco Plastics, Inc.

6. Add the current date as a fourth line to the three-line heading on the top of page 1 (Chapter 1).

7. Copy the entire date line into the heading on the top of page 2 (Chapter 3).

8. Save the document as **myprac3b** (Chapter 2).

9. Print the document and compare it to Figures 3.10 and 3.11 (Chapter 1).

10. Close the document (Chapter 1).

SUMMARY

In this chapter, you learned how to use the mouse, keyboard, and menus to select text; how to use the Edit, Replace command to replace found text; how to move and copy text; how to use the Undo command to reverse your last operation; and how to use the Undelete command to restore deleted information.

Here's a quick reference guide to the WordPerfect features introduced in this chapter:

Desired Result	How to Do It
Select text by dragging	Point at one end of the text to be selected; press and hold the **left mouse** button; drag the mouse pointer to the other end of the text; release the mouse button
Select text by using the Shift key	Place the insertion point at one end of the text; press and hold **Shift**; click at the other end of the text; release Shift
Select a word	Point anywhere inside the word and double-click the **left mouse** button
Select a sentence	Point anywhere inside the sentence and triple-click the **left mouse** button; or, place the mouse pointer in the selection bar next to the sentence; click the **left mouse** button
Select a paragraph	Point anywhere inside the paragraph and quadruple-click the **left mouse** button

Desired Result	How to Do It
Select multiple lines	Point in the selection bar next to the first or last line of text to be selected; press and hold the **left mouse** button; drag down or up; release the mouse button
Select an entire document	Choose **Edit, Select, All**
Extend an existing selection	While holding **Shift**, click beyond the existing selection
Deselect an existing selection	Make another selection. Or, click the **left mouse** button in the text area anywhere outside the existing selection
Replace found text in a document	Place the insertion point where you wish to begin; choose **Edit, Replace**; type the search text in the Find text box; type the replace text in the Replace With text box; select your desired search options; click on **Find** (or press **Enter**) to find the first occurrence; then click on **Replace, Find Next**, or **Replace All**; repeat the above steps until you have searched through the entire document (or cancel your search at any time by clicking on **Close**); close the Replace dialog box
Move text within a document	Select the text to be moved; choose **Edit, Cut** (or click on the power bar **Cut** button); place the insertion point where you want to move this text; choose **Edit, Paste** (or click on the power bar **Paste** button)
Copy text within a document	Select the text to be copied; choose **Edit, Copy** (or click on the power bar **Copy** button); place the insertion point where you want to copy this text; choose **Edit, Paste** (or click on the power bar **Paste** button)
Undo your last operation	Choose **Edit, Undo** (or click on the power bar **Undo** button)

Desired Result	How to Do It
Undelete deleted text	Place the insertion point where you want to undelete the text; choose **Edit, Undelete**; select the deletion you want to undo; click on **Restore** to restore the deleted text

In the next chapter, you'll learn the basics of character formatting—how to apply and remove character styles (such as bold and italic) and how to change fonts (typestyles) and point sizes for your text.

IF YOU'RE STOPPING HERE

If you need to break off here, please exit from WordPerfect. If you want to proceed directly to the next chapter, please do so now.

CHAPTER 4: CHARACTER FORMATTING

Applying Text
Attributes

Learning about
the Reveal Codes
Area

Applying Fonts
and Point Sizes

The overall effectiveness of a document is directly related to the way it looks. A brilliantly written business report, for example, can be severely undermined by an inappropriate typestyle, print too small to read comfortably, a dizzying barrage of italics or underlining, tables whose columns don't line up, an overbusy page layout, and so on. These next three chapters are devoted to formatting—controlling the way your documents look. We'll proceed logically: This chapter covers WordPerfect for Windows's smallest formatting units, characters; Chapter 5 covers its intermediate units, paragraphs; and Chapter 6 covers its largest units, pages.

When you're done working through this chapter, you will know

- How to apply and remove text attributes
- How to change fonts and point sizes

APPLYING TEXT ATTRIBUTES

You can enhance the appearance of your documents and emphasize selected text through the application of text attributes (bold, italic, underline, and so on). In this book, for example, we chose to bold certain headings (such as **Desired Result** and **How to Do It**, which appear in each chapter). WordPerfect provides two methods for applying text attributes: the Font dialog box and the text attribute buttons in the power bar.

USING THE FONT DIALOG BOX TO APPLY TEXT ATTRIBUTES

There are three ways to access the Font dialog box:

- Choose *Layout, Font* or
- Place the mouse pointer anywhere on the text area and press the *right mouse* button to open the Text quick menu and select *Font* or
- Press *F9* (the shortcut key).

Here's the general procedure to use the Font dialog box to apply text attributes:

- Select the desired text.
- Choose *Layout, Font* to open the Font dialog box.
- Select your desired text attribute options.
- Click on *OK* (or press *Enter*) to apply your chosen attributes.

Here's the general procedure to use the Font dialog box to remove text attributes:

- Select the desired text.
- Choose *Layout, Font*.
- Deselect the text attribute options you wish to remove.
- Click on *OK* (or press *Enter*).

If you are not running WordPerfect on your computer, please start it now. Close all open documents except for the start-up document—Document1. Let's begin by opening CHAP4.WPD and modifying its text attributes:

1. Click on the **Open** button (the power bar button showing an open file folder) to display the Open dialog box.

2. If your **WPWORK** directory is not already selected, select it now.

3. In the File Name list box, double-click on **chap4.wpd** to open the document.

4. Select **Introduction** (be sure to select the entire word), near the top of the document.

5. Choose **Layout, Font** to open the Font dialog box. (See Figure 4.1. Your Font dialog box may not exactly match that shown in the figure.)

6. In the Appearance box, check (click on) the **Bold** option. Note that the Resulting Font box shows you how your attribute choice (Bold) will look.

Figure 4.1   **The Font dialog box**

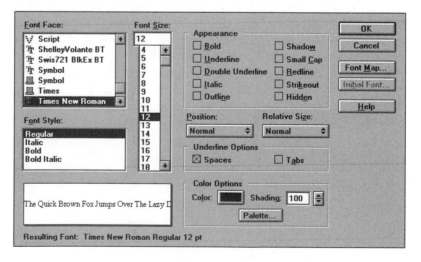

7. Click on **OK** (or press **Enter**) to bold your selected text and return to the document.

8. Deselect **Introduction** to verify that it is bolded. You can see text attributes better when the text is deselected.

9. Select **Customer Service**, the next heading on page 1.

10. Choose **Layout, Font** to open the Font dialog box. Check **Bold** and then click on **OK** (or press **Enter**) to bold *Customer Service*.

Now let's see how to remove the text attribute that you just applied and then restore it:

1. If **Customer Service** is not selected, select it now.

2. Choose **Layout, Font**.

3. Uncheck **Bold** and then click on **OK** (or press **Enter**) to unbold *Customer Service*.

4. Choose **Edit, Undo** to reverse step 3—that is, to rebold *Customer Service*.

ACCESSING THE FONT DIALOG BOX THROUGH THE TEXT QUICK MENU

The Font dialog box makes formatting text very easy, but it is a pain in the neck to choose Layout, Font every time you want to format something. Fortunately, there is an easier way. You can use WordPerfect's *Text quick menu* to access the Font dialog box without ever touching the menu.

The Text quick menu appears in the typing area. It eliminates moving the mouse pointer up to the menu and searching for some of the most commonly used text commands. You can use the Text quick menu to Cut, Copy, Paste, and Undelete text as well as perform some other commands (for example, spell check) that are covered later in this book.

Here's the general procedure to access WordPerfect's Text quick menu:

• Place the mouse pointer anywhere on the text area.

• Click the *right mouse* button.

To close a quick menu without selecting anything, simply press Esc.

Note: WordPerfect has several quick menus. If you click the right mouse button and a menu other than the Text shortcut menu appears, don't panic. Move your mouse pointer back into the text area (place it right on the text) and click the right mouse button again.

Let's use the quick menu to access the Font dialog box and apply text attributes (italic and underline) to your document's first line:

1. Select **Global Travel**, the first line.

2. Place the mouse pointer anywhere on the text area and click the **right mouse** button. The quick menu shown in Figure 4.2 is displayed. You perform any of the commands on the quick menu by simply pressing the right mouse button to display the quick menu and selecting the command (clicking on the command with the left mouse button). And, to make life even easier, WordPerfect has different quick menus depending upon where your mouse pointer is and what text is selected. You might want to experiment with the right mouse button to determine what the different quick menus are.

Figure 4.2   **WordPerfect's Selected Text quick menu**

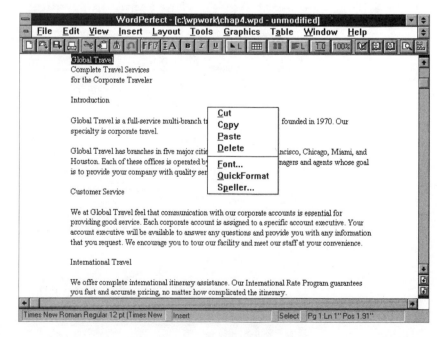

3. Choose **Font** (point to **Font** and click the **left mouse** button) to open the Font dialog box. Wasn't that fantastic!

4. In the Appearance box, check **Italic**. Observe the Resulting Font box text; the text is italicized.

5. Check **Underline** (in the Appearance box) to apply a single underline. Observe the Resulting Font box; the text is italicized and underlined.

6. Click on **OK** (or press **Enter**) to italicize and underline your selected text, *Global Travel*. Deselect the text to see the multiple styles more clearly.

7. Select **Global Travel** again.

8. Place the mouse pointer anywhere in the text area, click the **right mouse** button (to display the quick menu) and select **Font** (to open the Font dialog box).

9. Uncheck **Italic** and then click on **OK** to remove the italic text attribute. Deselect *Global Travel* to verify that the italics (but not the underline) have been removed, as shown in Figure 4.3.

Figure 4.3 **Global Travel, after removing italics**

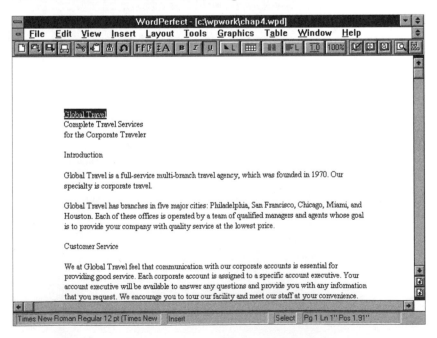

USING THE POWER BAR TO APPLY TEXT ATTRIBUTES

The power bar provides quick access to a few of the most commonly used text attribute options, including bold, italic, and underline.

Here's the general procedure to use the power bar to apply text attributes:

- Select the desired text.

- Click on the desired power bar text attribute button.

Here's the general procedure for using the power bar to remove text attributes:

- Select the desired text.

- Click on the power bar button of the text attribute you wish to remove.

Note: Occasionally when you use the power bar to remove text attributes, you might need to click on the text attribute button twice.

Let's practice using the power bar to apply text attributes:

1. Move to the top of the document.

2. Choose **View, Show ¶** to display the nonprinting characters.

3. Select the paragraph beginning with *Global Travel has branches in five* (double-click in the selection bar).

4. Click on the **Bold** button (the button with a boldface *B*, in the middle of the power bar) to bold the entire paragraph.

5. Observe the Bold button on the power bar. Note that the button now appears to be "pushed in."

6. Deselect the paragraph and place the mouse pointer before the paragraph mark at the end of the paragraph. Observe the Bold button; it doesn't appear to be pushed in. When you place the insertion point before the paragraph mark, WordPerfect doesn't see the character formatting you just applied to the rest of the paragraph. This is because paragraph marks don't carry character formatting applied within the paragraph.

7. Select the paragraph again and choose **Layout, Font**. Note that the Bold check box is grayed. Because the end of the paragraph is selected, WordPerfect is a little confused. It is telling you that Bold formatting is applied somewhere in the

selected text, but not to the entire selection (that is, to the end of the paragraph).

8. Uncheck **Bold** and then click on **OK**.

9. Click on the **Bold** button to rebold the selected text.

10. Click on the **Italic** button (the button with an italicized *I* to the right of the Bold button) to italicize the text.

11. Click on the **Underline** button (the button with an underlined *U* to the right of the Italic button) to single-underline the text (see Figure 4.4).

Figure 4.4　　**Text, after applying bold, italic, and underline text attributes**

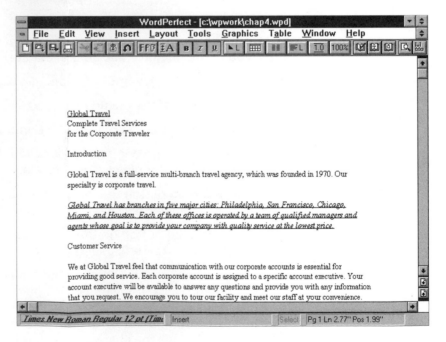

12. Click on the **Underline** button again to remove the underline from the selected text.

13. Choose **View, Show ¶** to turn off the display of nonprinting characters.

PRACTICE YOUR SKILLS

1. Remove the italic and bold character formats from the paragraph *Global Travel has branches*.

2. Select the entire document and then italicize it.

3. Use the **Undo** command to reverse step 2.

4. Remove the underline from the first line (*Global Travel*), and then bold and italicize it.

5. Bold and italicize the first line of the heading on page 2 (*Global Travel*).

USING QUICK FORMAT TO COPY TEXT ATTRIBUTES

Once you have applied one or more text attributes to your selected text, you can easily use *Quick Format* to copy (repeat) these attributes to newly selected text. Quick Format allows you to copy character or paragraph formats from a character or paragraph and apply them to any other character or paragraph in your document. (You will learn how to use Quick Format to copy paragraph formats in the next chapter.)

Here's the general procedure to copy text attributes using Quick Format:

*   Choose *View, Show ¶*.

*   Select the text that is formatted (do not select the paragraph marker at the end of the line).

*   Choose *Layout, Quick Format*.

*   Select the new text.

Note: If you wish to use the technique just described to repeat text attributes, you must select text only. If you select a paragraph mark, then WordPerfect will repeat paragraph formats instead of character formats.

Let's use Quick Format to repeat text attributes:

1. Scroll to the bottom of the document. (Drag the **vertical scroll box** to the bottom of the scroll bar.)

2. Select **Flight Insurance**.

3. Open the **Font** dialog box (choose **Layout, Font** or click the **right mouse** button and choose **Font**).

4. Check **Italic** and **Underline** in the Appearance box; then click on **OK** to italicize and underline the selected text.

5. Deselect **Flight Insurance**.

6. Choose **View, Show ¶** to display nonprinting characters. When you copy character formatting, you need to make sure you don't select the paragraph mark at the end of the line. It is easiest to do this if you can see the paragraph mark. If you include the paragraph mark in your selection, WordPerfect will copy the paragraph format instead of the character formats.

7. Select **Flight Insurance** (do not select the paragraph mark at the end of the line).

8. Choose **Layout, Quick Format** to turn on the Quick Format option. Your mouse pointer turns into an I-beam with a paint roller, indicating that WordPerfect is ready to roll your character formats onto new text.

9. Select **Telex** to copy the character formats from *Flight Insurance* to *Telex*. Note that Telex is italicized and underlined.

10. Choose **Layout, Quick Format** to turn off the Quick Format option. If you don't turn off the option, WordPerfect will continue to copy character formatting each time you select text.

11. Use **Ctrl+G** (Go To) to move to the top of page 2.

12. Select **Complete Travel Services**. Click on the **Bold** button, and then click on the **Italic** button to bold and italicize the selected text. Deselect the text.

13. Select **Complete**. Because you are copying character formatting, you really only need to select some of the formatted text. You can select as little as one character to copy.

14. Click on the **right mouse** button to display the shortcut menu. Choose **Quick Format** to turn on the Quick Format option.

15. Click on **Layout** to display the Layout menu. Note that the Quick Format option has a check mark next to it, even though you used the shortcut menu to turn on the option.

16. Click on **Layout** again to close the Layout menu without selecting anything.

17. Click on the **Page Up** button on the scroll bar to move to the top of the document.

18. Select **Complete Travel Services** to copy the character formatting.

19. Click the **right mouse** button and choose **Quick Format** to turn off the Quick Format option.

20. Choose **View, Show ¶** to turn off the nonprinting characters.

21. Deselect the text, if necessary, and use **File, Save As** to save the disk file as **mychap4**. (**Note:** If you try to save a document with text selected, a dialog box appears asking you if you want to save the selected text. If this happens to you, just click on Entire File, then click on OK.)

PRACTICE YOUR SKILLS

1. Bold the heading *International Travel*.

2. Use **Quick Format** to bold the following headings:

Corporate Profiles

Worldwide Services

Discounts

Deliveries

Auto Rentals

Hotel Accommodations

Newsletter

3. Remove the italics and underlining from *Flight Insurance* and *Telex*.

4. Use the **Font** dialog box to bold and italicize *for the Corporate Traveler* at the top of page 1.

5. Use **Quick Format** to copy these multiple styles to *for the Corporate Traveler* at the top of page 2.

6. Compare your document to the printouts depicted in Figures 4.5 and 4.6.

7. Update the disk file (use **File, Save**).

Figure 4.5   **Page 1 of MYCHAP4.WPD**

Global Travel
Complete Travel Services
for the Corporate Traveler

Introduction

Global Travel is a full-service multi-branch travel agency, which was founded in 1970. Our specialty is corporate travel.

Global Travel has branches in five major cities: Philadelphia, San Francisco, Chicago, Miami, and Houston. Each of these offices is operated by a team of qualified managers and agents whose goal is to provide your company with quality service at the lowest price.

Customer Service

We at Global Travel feel that communication with our corporate accounts is essential for providing good service. Each corporate account is assigned to a specific account executive. Your account executive will be available to answer any questions and provide you with any information that you request. We encourage you to tour our facility and meet our staff at your convenience.

International Travel

We offer complete international itinerary assistance. Our International Rate Program guarantees you fast and accurate pricing, no matter how complicated the itinerary.

Corporate Profiles

Your company profile is stored in our computer. In addition, individual profiles are maintained on each of your frequent travelers. Each profile contains passport information, seating and car rental preference, frequent-flyer membership number, and corporate discount numbers. This information ensures that we can provide frequent travelers fast, cost-effective service.

Worldwide Services

Global Travel's Reservation Center handles all of your weekend and after-hour reservations and changes. The reservation center can be reached toll-free, 24 hours a day. The worldwide service emergency numbers will be clearly marked on your travel itineraries.

Discounts

Global Travel guarantees the lowest air fares available. Due to the number of tickets that we issue, several large air carriers offer us special discounts that we can pass on to our clients. Our quality-control specialists check each of your tickets to guarantee that you have received the lowest rate available. In addition, each ticket is checked to ensure that it includes seating assignments and boarding passes before it is delievered to you.

Figure 4.6   **Page 2 of MYCHAP4.WPD**

Global Travel
Complete Travel Services
for the Corporate Traveler

Deliveries

Our courier makes daily deliveries twice a day to offices within 20 miles of our local branch. Each one of our offices is located across from the local airport and has a drive-up window. If you make last minute travel plans with us, you can pick up your ticket at the drive-up window on your way to the airport.

Auto Rentals

We guarantee the lowest prices on all car rentals. We will match the type of car with the information provided in the profile for each of your frequent travelers. Each car that is rented through Global Travel carries an extra $50,000 worth of liability insurance.

Hotel Accommodations

Our Corporate Hotel Program is the most competitive and comprehensive program in the world. We offer cost savings and extra amenities in most business locations. Global Travel has access to more than 10,000 hotels worldwide, with a range of rooms from economy to luxury. Your corporate travelers get the accommodations they want with a savings of 20-30% off regular rates.

Newsletter

All clients receive our montly newsletter covering a variety of travel topics.

Additional Services

Global Travel also provides the following services for our corporate customers:

Personal Vacations

Our corporate clients are invited to discuss their vacation and personal travel plans with an agent from Global Travel's Vacation division.

Flight Insurance

We supply all clients with $250,000 worth of flight insurance.

Telex

Telex service is available for international hotel confirmations.

LEARNING ABOUT THE REVEAL CODES AREA

Until now, you've been making a number of changes to documents. For example, you've enhanced text by underlining it, or by making it bold or italic; you've even used multiple character formats. While you've been making these enhancements, WordPerfect for Windows has been implementing them behind the scenes by inserting special *codes*. These codes tell your printer how to handle your changes. To print a word in bold, for example, WordPerfect inserts codes telling the printer to print bold characters in that location.

To keep the typing area free of clutter, WordPerfect does not display these codes as you type. The program does, however, make it possible for you to move between the typing area and the *Reveal Codes* area and edit codes in either place.

Here's the general procedure to view the Reveal Codes area:

• Choose *View, Reveal Codes*.

Note: The codes are displayed at the bottom of the typing area. Ordinarily, you need not be concerned with the Reveal Codes area when you are typing. But, when you need to go back and undo formatting—underlining, for example—you must delete the code that tells the printer what and how to format.

INTERPRETING PAIRED CODES

When you apply a character format (or text attribute), paired codes (two codes) are created. For example, when you select text and use the Font dialog box to boldface it, WordPerfect inserts a [Bold] code immediately before and after the selected text. All of the text between the paired codes will appear bold when it is printed or displayed on the screen.

Whenever you press Enter, WordPerfect places a hard return code [HRt] in the document, which indicates a manual line break. An [SRt] soft return code is placed at the end of a line when text wraps. When you move the insertion point through a document, the codes area moves with the insertion point, so that it displays the same text that is displayed in the typing area.

Note: If you scroll through the document, the Reveal Codes area does not move. It stays with the insertion point.

Let's view the Reveal Codes area and examine some paired codes:

1. Place the insertion point to the left of the *I* in the *Introduction* heading, near the top of page 1.

2. Choose **View, Reveal Codes** to display the codes area at the bottom of the screen (see Figure 4.7).

3. Examine the Reveal Codes area in the lower half of the document window. The codes area displays all the keys that you press, including any formatting attributes that you have added to the document.

Figure 4.7   **The Reveal Codes area**

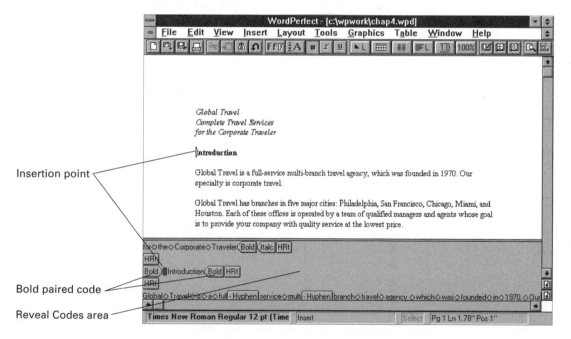

4. Observe the Bold paired codes. These codes enclose any text that you make bold.

5. Place the insertion point in the paragraph *Global Travel has branches* and observe the [HRt] and [SRt] codes. The [HRt] code is displayed whenever you press the Enter key. The [SRt] code appears whenever WordPerfect uses word-wrap

to place text on a new line. (Notice that [HRt] and [SRt] are not paired.)

6. Observe the insertion point in the typing area; the insertion point appears as a blinking vertical bar.

7. Observe the insertion point in the codes area. Here, it is displayed as a thick bar (located in the paragraph *Global Travel has branches*).

8. Choose **View, Reveal Codes** to hide the codes area.

WORKING WITH CODES

WordPerfect inserts codes as you type. However, as was mentioned earlier, to keep the typing area uncluttered, they are not visible except through the Reveal Codes area. Let's apply some text enhancements while in Reveal Codes in order to watch the program insert them:

1. Choose **View, Reveal Codes** to display the codes area.

2. Press the **down arrow** key several times to move the insertion point down several lines. (If you use the numeric keypad, make sure Num Lock is off.) As you move the insertion point through the document, the codes area "mirrors" the typing area.

3. Go to page 2 (Use **Ctrl+G**).

4. Select **Additional Services**, near the bottom of page 2.

5. Observe the [Select] code in the codes area, to the left of *Additional*. This code is inserted whenever you select text; when you deselect text, the code is removed.

6. Click on the **Bold** button (on the power bar).

7. Observe the Bold codes. The paired codes [Bold] appear before and after the selected text.

8. Click on the **Underline** button (on the power bar).

9. Observe the Underline codes. The Underline paired codes [Und] are inserted before and after the selected text.

10. Click on the **Italic** button (on the power bar).

11. Observe the Italic codes. The Italic paired codes [Italc] are inserted, along with the underline and bold codes, before and after the selected text.

DELETING CODES

When you use the power bar or Font dialog box to remove text attributes from selected text, the codes at the beginning and at the end of the selected text are removed. You can also remove text attributes directly from the codes area.

Here's the general procedure to remove a code from the codes area:

- Place the mouse pointer on the code.
- Press and hold the *left mouse* button.
- Drag the code up and out of the Reveal Codes area.

OR

- Place the insertion point immediately to the right or left of the code.
- Press *Backspace* or *Del*, respectively.

Note: We do not recommend using this second method due to its greater potential for error.

With the Reveal Codes area displayed, let's use two methods to remove character formats. We'll use the power bar and we'll also delete codes by dragging them out of the Reveal Codes area.

1. In the typing area, verify that *Additional Services* is still selected.
2. Click on the **Underline** button on the power bar to remove the Underline character format.
3. Observe the codes area; both of the Underline codes are removed.
4. In the codes area, place the mouse pointer on the Italic code (**[Italc]**).
5. Press and hold the **left mouse** button.
6. Drag the **[Italc]** code completely out of the codes area (into the typing area).
7. Release the mouse button.
8. Observe the codes area; both of the Italic codes are removed.
9. Choose **View, Reveal Codes** to hide the codes area.

APPLYING FONTS AND POINT SIZES

Earlier in this chapter, you learned how to change the attributes of selected text by adding or removing character formats. You can also change the shape and size of your selected text by changing the text's font and point size. The *font* determines the shape (type-style) of the text; the *point size* determines the size of the font (one point equals $1/72$ of an inch). The sentence you are reading, for example, is printed in 10-point Universe font. You can use the Font dialog box or the power bar to apply fonts and point sizes.

Note: The specific fonts and point sizes that WordPerfect provides are dependent upon your currently selected printer. PostScript-type laser printers, for example, offer a large variety of fonts and point sizes, whereas low-end dot-matrix printers offer a much more limited selection.

 ## USING THE FONT DIALOG BOX TO APPLY FONTS AND POINT SIZES

Here's the general procedure to use the Font dialog box to apply fonts and point sizes:

- Select the desired text.

- Open the Font dialog box (choose *Layout, Font* or click the *right mouse* button and choose *Font*).

- Select your desired font and/or point size.

- Click on *OK* (or press *Enter*).

Let's select some text and use the Font dialog box to change its font and point size:

1. Move to the top of the document (press **Ctrl+Home**).

2. Select the lines **Complete Travel Services** and **for the Corporate Traveler** in the heading at the top of page 1.

3. Choose **Layout, Font**.

4. Click on the **down arrow** next to the Font Face list box to scroll through your available fonts. Note that the font names are listed in alphabetical order. Observe the current font (Times New Roman) and the representative text in the Resulting Font box.

5. Select **Helvetica**. You may need to scroll up through the list to find Helvetica. Observe the change in the Resulting Font box text. (If you do not have Helvetica, choose another font.)

6. Click on the **down arrow** next to the Font Size list box to view the available point sizes for Helvetica.

7. Select **14**. Observe the change in the Resulting Font box text.

8. Click on **OK** to apply your chosen font and point size to the selected text. Deselect and compare your screen to Figure 4.8.

Figure 4.8   **Lines 2 and 3 of the heading, after changing the font and point size**

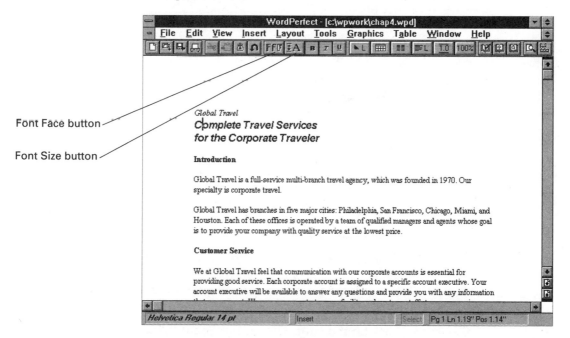

In a previous activity, you used Quick Format to copy text attributes. Now let's use Quick Format to copy the font and point size:

1. Select **Complete** in the heading *Complete Travel Services* (remember, when you are copying character formats, you only need to select a piece of the formatted text).

2. Choose **Layout, Quick Format** to turn on the Quick Format option.

3. Click on the **Page Down** button on the scroll bar to display the top of page 2 without moving the insertion point.

4. Select **Complete Travel Services** and **for the Corporate Traveler**, lines 2 and 3 in the page heading. Quick Format copies the font and point size from *Complete* at the top of page 1. The text is now Helvetica, 14 point. **(Note:** Earlier in this chapter, you also added bold and italic attributes to this text.)

5. Click on the **Save** button (the third from the left in the power bar, it shows a floppy disk) to update the document.

6. Choose **Layout, Quick Format** to turn off the Quick Format option.

USING THE POWER BAR TO APPLY FONTS AND POINT SIZES

Here's the general procedure to use the power bar to apply fonts and point sizes:

- Select the desired text.

- Click on the *Font Face* or *Font Size* button (respectively, the ninth and tenth buttons from the left in the power bar).

- Select your desired font or point size.

Let's use the power bar to change the font and the point sizes:

1. Select **Global Travel**, the first line on page 2.

2. Click on the **Font Face** button (located on the power bar, it displays three *F*'s in varying fonts) to open the Font list box. Note that the box currently displays Times New Roman. Select **Helvetica** (you might need to scroll up to view Helvetica).

3. Click on the **Font Size** button (located on the power bar, it displays an *A* with sizing arrows) to open the Font Size list box. Note that the box currently displays 12. Select **24** (you may need to scroll).

PRACTICE YOUR SKILLS

1. Move to the top of page 1.

2. Change the font and point size of the first line, *Global Travel*, to **Helvetica** and **24**.

3. Deselect and compare your screen to Figure 4.9.

4. Save the disk file and close the document.

Figure 4.9   **The completed heading**

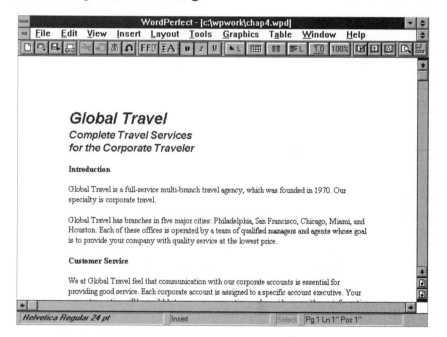

 CHANGING THE FONT FOR THE ENTIRE DOCUMENT

In addition to changing the font and size for selected text, you can change the font and size for the entire document.

Here's the general procedure to change the font and size for the entire document:

• Place the insertion point at the top of the document.

- Open the Font dialog box (choose *Layout, Font* or click the *right mouse* button and choose *Font*).
- In the Font list box, select the desired font.
- In the Size list box, select the desired point size.
- Click on *OK* (or press *Enter*).

Let's change the font and point size for a new document:

1. Close MYCHAP4.WPD, if necessary. (Save changes if prompted to do so.)

2. Choose **File, chap4.wpd** to reopen CHAP4.WPD.

3. Verify that the insertion point is located at the top of the document. (If it isn't, press **Ctrl+Home.**)

4. Open the **Font** dialog box.

5. Choose **Helvetica** from the Font list box and **14** from the Size list box.

6. Click on **OK** (or press **Enter**) to change the font and size for the entire document to Helvetica, 14 point.

7. Observe the document. The font and size have changed.

8. Close CHAP4.WPD without saving changes.

SUMMARY

In this chapter, you learned the basics of character formatting. You now know how to apply and remove text attributes, how to edit and delete codes, and how to change fonts and point sizes.

Here's a quick reference guide to the WordPerfect features introduced in this chapter:

Desired Result	How to Do It
Use the Font dialog box to apply text attributes	Select the desired text; choose **Layout, Font**; select your desired text attribute options; click on **OK** (or press **Enter**)

Desired Result	How to Do It
Use the Font dialog box to remove text attributes	Follow the procedure just described to deselect the style options you wish to remove
Use the power bar to apply text attributes	Select the desired text; click on the desired power bar text attribute button
Access WordPerfect's Text shortcut menu	Place the mouse pointer anywhere on the text area; click the **right mouse** button
Use the power bar to remove text attributes	Select the desired text; click on the power bar button of the text attribute you wish to remove
Copy character formatting	Choose **View, Show ¶**; select the text whose format you wish to repeat; choose **Layout, Quick Format**; select the text you wish to format; repeat as necessary until all text is formatted; choose **Layout, Quick Format** to turn off the Quick Formatting; choose **View, Show ¶**
Reveal codes	Choose **View, Reveal Codes**
Hide the Reveal Codes area	Choose **View, Reveal Codes**
Delete codes	Display the Reveal Codes area; place the mouse pointer on the code you want to delete; press and hold the **left mouse** button; drag the code out of the Reveal Codes area (into the text area)
Use the Font dialog box to apply fonts and point sizes	Select the desired text; choose **Layout, Font**; select your desired font and/or point size; click on **OK** (or press **Enter**)

Desired Result	**How to Do It**
Use the power bar to apply fonts and point sizes	Select the desired text; click on the **Font Face** or **Font Size** button; select your desired font or point size
Change the font and size for the entire document	Place the insertion point at the top of the document; open the Font dialog box (choose **Layout, Font,** or click the **right mouse** button and choose **Font**); in the Font list box, select the desired font; in the Size list box, select the desired point size; click on **OK** (or press **Enter**)

In the next chapter, you will learn the basics of paragraph formatting. You'll find out how to work with tab stops and paragraph indents, how to align paragraphs, and how to set line spacing.

IF YOU'RE STOPPING HERE

If you need to break off here, please exit WordPerfect. If you want to proceed directly to the next chapter, please do so now.

CHAPTER 5: LINE FORMATTING

Working with Tabs

Setting Indents and Line Breaks

Setting Paragraph Justification

Setting Line Spacing

When you finish typing and editing, you should ask yourself how you can make your document look so attractive and interesting that people will want to read it. In WordPerfect for Windows, you can enhance the appearance of your document in many ways. This chapter discusses enhancements known as *line formatting* (also called *paragraph formatting*); the next chapter looks at *page formatting*.

When you're done working through this chapter, you will know

- How to clear, set, and remove tabs for selected text
- How to clear, set, add, delete, move, and reset tabs for the entire document
- How to indent paragraphs
- How to align paragraphs
- How to change line spacing

WORKING WITH TABS

As you learned in Chapter 1, you use tabs to align text at preset tab stops across the page. This type of alignment is particularly important in tables, where several categories of information must line up in precise columns. In the first part of this chapter, you'll learn how to clear default tab stops, and how to set, change, and clear custom tab stops.

 ## SELECTING PARAGRAPHS FOR PARAGRAPH FORMATTING

Before you set custom tab stops, you must first select the paragraph(s) you want to work with. As you learned in the last chapter, when you select a paragraph for character formatting (text attributes, font, point size, and so on), you must select the entire paragraph. However, when you select a paragraph for paragraph formatting (tab stops, indents, line spacing, and so on), you do not have to select the entire paragraph.

To select a single paragraph for paragraph formatting:

- Place the insertion point anywhere in the paragraph. You do not have to select (highlight) any characters.

To select multiple paragraphs for paragraph formatting:

- Select (highlight) a portion of each paragraph. It is not necessary to select every character in every paragraph.

The techniques just described are paragraph selection shortcuts. If you feel more comfortable selecting entire paragraphs for paragraph formatting, please do so.

TAB TYPES

In WordPerfect for Windows, tab stops are set by default every half inch from the left edge of the paper. Table 5.1 shows WordPerfect's available tab types. These tabs can be useful in aligning text in tables, creating charts and reports, and displaying numeric data.

Table 5.1   **Tab Types**

Tab Type	Alignment
Left	First letter of word
Right	Last letter of word
Center	Center of word or phrase
Decimal	Column of numbers aligned at common character, usually a decimal point (.)
...Left	First letter of word, preceded by a series of dots, or leaders
...Center	Text centered under tab stop, preceded by a series of dots, or leaders
...Right	Last letter of word, preceded by a series of dots, or leaders
...Decimal	Column of numbers aligned at alignment character, preceded by series of dots, or leaders

Note: It's important to understand the distinction between alignment and justification. By *alignment*, we mean the use of tabs to indent paragraphs, align columns of text in a table, and so on. *Justification*—which you'll learn about later in this chapter—refers to the appearance of the text at the left and right margins.

EXAMINING THE RULER

In WordPerfect, you can use the ruler to set various paragraph formats, including tab settings, indents, and margins. You can also use the menu to change these features.

Here's the general procedure to display the ruler:

• Choose *View, Ruler Bar*.

The ruler is displayed at the top of the document window. To view the current settings of a paragraph, place the insertion point in the paragraph and examine the ruler. The ruler displays the current tab settings and margins.

The ruler components are shown in Figure 5.1. If you close the document or open a new document, the ruler will no longer be displayed.

Figure 5.1   **Ruler components**

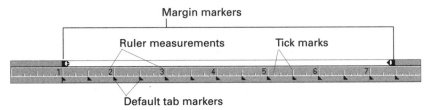

Note: The further you progress in this book, the more succinct our activity instructions tend to be. For example, instead of saying "Click on the Open button, select the WPWORK directory, and then double-click on CHAP5.WPD to open it," we now simply say "Open CHAP5.WPD from your WPWORK directory." If you are unsure of how to perform a certain WordPerfect task, use the index, the end-of-chapter quick reference guides, or WordPerfect Help to jog your memory.

If you aren't running WordPerfect for Windows, please start it now. All documents should be closed except for the default Document1.

Let's display and examine the ruler:

1. Open **chap5.wpd** from your WPWORK directory.

2. Choose **View, Ruler Bar** to display the ruler (see Figure 5.2).

3. Observe the ruler measurements. Generally, the ruler measurement is in inches.

Figure 5.2   **CHAP5.WPD with ruler displayed**

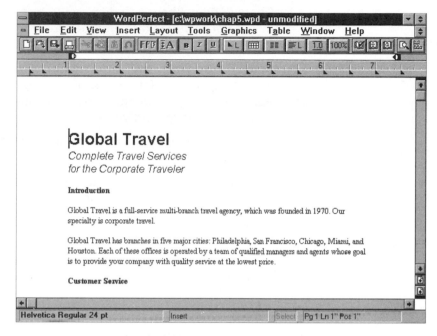

4. Observe the left and right margin markers—the two small, black brackets and triangles that point toward each other, located at the top of the ruler, directly below the power bar.

5. Observe the tab markers—the small black triangles directly below the ruler measurements. The default tab settings are left-aligned tabs set at 0.5-inch increments.

6. Choose **View, Ruler Bar** to hide the ruler.

PRACTICE YOUR SKILLS

Display the ruler again.

ADDING A ROW TO A TABBED TABLE

We're going to complete a *tabbed table* (a table that uses tabs to separate text into columns). We'll add a new row to the table by typing a line of information that we'll later align in columns.

Let's begin our exploration of tabs by adding text to a tabbed table:

1. Choose **View, Show ¶** to display the nonprinting characters. It is easier to add text to a tabbed table if you can see where the tabs, spaces, and returns are.

2. Scroll down and examine the tabbed table following the heading *Discounts* (at the bottom of page 1). Note that the *Paris* discount percentage (20%) is misaligned. We will fix this in the next few activities.

3. Place the insertion point in the first blank line after the tabbed table.

4. Press **Tab** to move the insertion point to the first default tab stop (0.5 inch to the right), and then type **Hong Kong**.

5. Press **Tab** to move to the next available tab stop, and then type **25%**.

6. Press **Enter** to create a new blank line. Compare your screen to Figure 5.3.

Figure 5.3   **Adding text to the Discounts tabbed table**

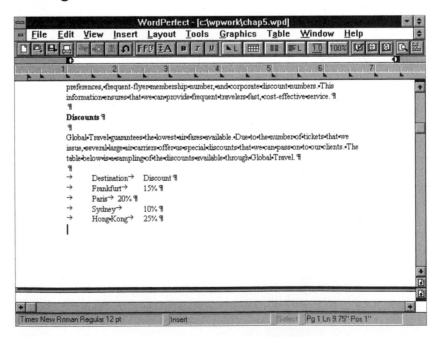

7. Choose **View, Show ¶** to turn off the nonprinting characters. (While nonprinting characters are helpful when you are editing your document, they do make your screen more difficult to read. So, we recommend that you show nonprinting characters only when you need to edit.)

CLEARING DEFAULT TABS FOR SELECTED TEXT

If you want to set your own tabs, you must first clear the default tabs. Furthermore, if you select text that you want to manipulate, only the tabs for that text will be affected; tab settings for the rest of the document will remain intact.

Here's the general procedure to clear all tabs for selected text:

- Select the desired paragraph.

- Press and hold *Shift*.

- Drag to select the tab markers on the ruler.

- Point to the shaded tab area.

- Drag the tabs off the ruler (down into the typing area).

Let's select text and then clear the tabs:

1. Point to the left of the *D* in *Destination*, and drag down to select the rest of the text in the table (through *Hong Kong*).

2. Press and hold **Shift**.

3. On the ruler, point to the left of the tab marker at the 1-inch mark. Press and hold the **left mouse** button; drag to the right to select all of the **tab stops**; then release the mouse button and Shift. The tab area appears highlighted. Compare your screen to Figure 5.4.

4. Point to the shaded area between any two tab markers. Drag the selected tab markers down off the ruler; then release the mouse button. All of the tabs for the selected lines of text have been cleared from the ruler (see Figure 5.5). You'll notice that the tab area is no longer highlighted.

5. Click anywhere in the tabbed table to deselect, and then observe the text. Because there are no tab stops on the part of the ruler above the text, the text appears to be bunched together at the left margin.

Figure 5.4   **Selected text and tab markers**

Selected tab stops

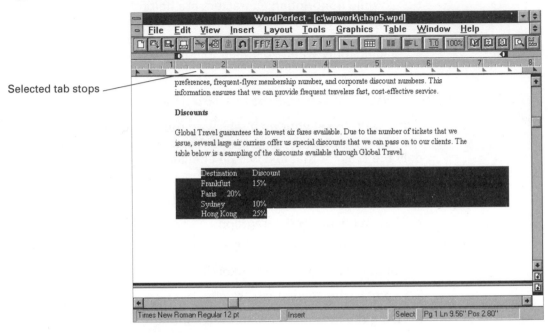

Figure 5.5   **Cleared tabs**

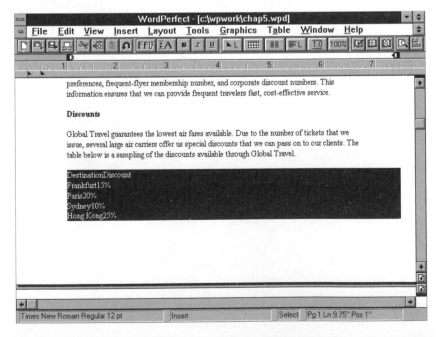

SETTING CUSTOM TABS FOR SELECTED TEXT

Now that all the default tab stops have been removed, the next step is to create new tab stops for the table.

Here's the general procedure to set tab stops:

- Select the text for which you want to set tabs.

- Select the desired tab type by clicking on the *Tab Set* button on the power bar and selecting the appropriate option: Left-aligned, Center-aligned, Right-aligned, Decimal, Left-aligned dot leader, Center-aligned dot leader, Right-aligned dot leader, or Decimal dot leader.

- Point at the desired tab-stop position in the ruler (directly under the tick marks) and click the *left mouse* button.

When you point to a tab stop on the ruler, and then press and hold the mouse button, a broken vertical line called the *ruler guide* appears in the window. At the same time, the position indicator in the status bar displays the distance from the left edge of the page. You can use the ruler guide and/or the position indicator to place your tab exactly where you would like it.

Now let's set some new left-aligned tab stops to fix the savings-percentage misalignments. First we need to select the entire table (all five lines). Let's use our multiple paragraph selection shortcut to do this:

1. Select all the text from *Discount* (in the first line) up to and including *Hong Kong* (in the last line). (**Note:** Do not select the entire Hong Kong line.) Even though the first and last lines of the table are only partially highlighted, they are fully selected. Any paragraph formatting changes you now make will apply equally to all five lines.

2. Observe the ruler. Note that above the text there are no tab stops on the ruler.

3. Observe the Tab Set button (located near the middle of the power bar; currently, it displays a triangle with an L). The *L* on the Tab Set button indicates that if you set a tab stop now, WordPerfect will left-align it. As indicated earlier in this section, the power bar Tab Set button determines the alignment of the next tab stop that you set; a left-aligned tab stop

is the default. We want to set a left-aligned tab, so we don't need to change the Tab Set button.

4. Point directly beneath the 2-inch tick mark in the ruler. Click the **left mouse** button to set a left-aligned tab stop at 2 inches.

5. Observe the text. The first column in the tabbed table is now 1 inch from the left margin (and 2 inches from the left edge of the paper).

PRACTICE YOUR SKILLS

1. Set a second left-aligned tab stop at 3.5 inches. The second column in the table is now properly aligned.

2. Compare your screen to Figure 5.6.

Figure 5.6 **Setting tab stops for the Discounts tabbed table**

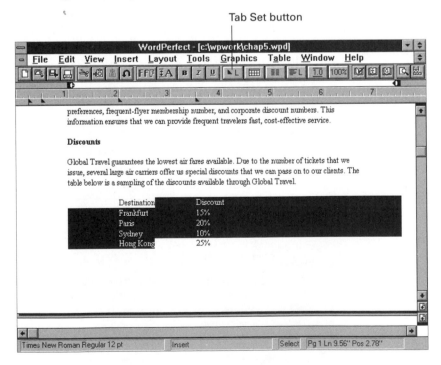

SETTING DIFFERENT TYPES OF TABS

As mentioned in the previous section, WordPerfect provides eight types of tab stops: left-aligned, center-aligned, right-aligned, decimal, left-aligned dot leader, center-aligned dot leader, right-aligned dot leader, and decimal dot leader.

Note: We don't cover dot leader tabs in this book. For information about setting and using them, see WordPerfect Help or your WordPerfect for Windows manual.

Let's use the ruler and the Tab Set button to experiment with some of these tab stops:

1. Scroll down to the tabbed table following the *Hotel Accommodations* section, near the top of page 2.

2. Use the multiple paragraph selection shortcut to select the body (lower four lines) of the tabbed table. (**Hint:** Place the I-beam anywhere in the first line and drag down to select a portion of each line.)

3. Clear the default tab stops (press and hold **Shift**, drag to select the **tab stops**, then drag them off the ruler).

4. Place the mouse pointer on the **Tab Set** button and press and hold the **left mouse** button to display the tab options (see Figure 5.7).

5. Drag down to select **Right** to right-align the next tab stop you set. (The Tab Set button displays a triangle pointing to the left because the text flows to the left of a right-aligned tab stop.)

6. Set a right-aligned tab stop at 4.5 inches.

7. From the Tab Set button, select the **Decimal** tab option to decimal-align the next tab stop you set. (This time, the Tab Set button displays a decimal point in the center of the triangle.) Decimal tabs are used to align numbers containing decimals.

8. Set a decimal tab stop at 6 inches.

Figure 5.7   **Tab Set button options**

Tab Set options ——

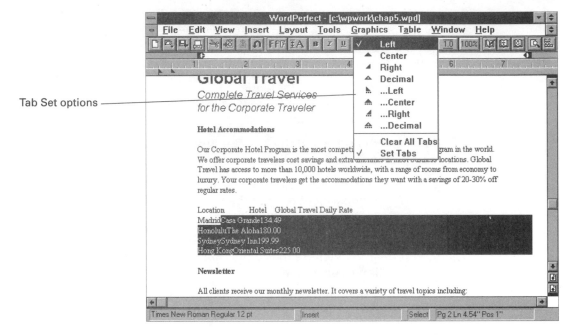

PRACTICE YOUR SKILLS

1. Prepare to set tab stops for the heading (top line) of the tabbed table. (**Hint:** Select the entire line of text.)

2. Set a centered tab stop at 3.5 inches.

3. Set a right-aligned tab stop at 6 inches.

4. Deselect the text and note that the heading and body columns are misaligned (see Figure 5.8). We will fix this in the next activity.

CHANGING THE POSITIONS OF CUSTOM TAB STOPS

WordPerfect allows you to quickly and easily change the positions of your custom tab stops.

Here's the general procedure to change the position of tab stops:

• Select the desired paragraph(s).

• In the ruler, drag the custom tab stop to a new position.

Figure 5.8   **The Hotel Accommodations table, misaligned**

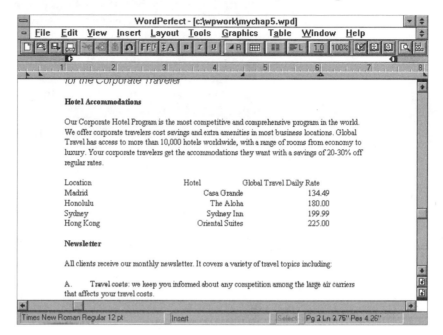

CLEARING CUSTOM TAB STOPS

WordPerfect also allows you to quickly clear (delete) your custom tab stops. Here's the general procedure to clear a custom tab stop:

- Select the desired paragraph(s).

- Drag the custom tab stop down into the text area.

Now let's fix the Hotel Accommodations table's misalignment by changing and clearing tabs:

1. Select the **body** (four lines) of the tabbed table (do not select the last paragraph marker).

2. Drag the decimal tab stop at 6 inches to *5.75 inches* to adjust the position of the table's numbers. WordPerfect displays the position of the tab stop in the Page Indicator area of the status bar as you drag the tab stop to its new location.

3. Place a centered tab stop at 3.5 inches. Note that this causes a severe misalignment. Why? Because there is now an

undesired tab stop in the ruler (the right-aligned tab stop at 4.5 inches), which prevents the final column of text (*Global Travel Daily Rate*) from moving to its intended decimal tab-stop location at 5.75 inches.

4. Drag the undesired right-aligned tab stop at 4.5 inches down off the ruler into the text area, then release the mouse button to clear this tab stop. Note that the misalignment problem has been fixed.

5. Deselect and save the disk file as **mychap5** (use **File, Save As**).

6. Compare your screen to Figure 5.9.

Figure 5.9   **The Hotel Accommodations table, properly aligned**

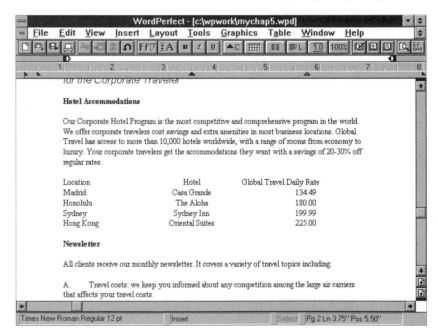

SETTING TABS FOR THE ENTIRE DOCUMENT

If you know that you are going to use a particular tab stop setting throughout your document, you can quickly and easily change the tab stops for the entire document before you begin typing.

Here's the general procedure to change tab stops for the entire document:

- Place the insertion point at the top of the document.

- Delete the default tab stops (press *Shift*, select the tab stops, and drag them off the ruler).

- Set the appropriate tab stops.

Note: You need to set new tabs for the entire document *before* you start typing.

USING THE TAB SET DIALOG BOX TO MANAGE YOUR *CUSTOM* TAB STOPS

We've shown you how to use the power bar and ruler to manage your custom tab stops. This is generally the preferred method of tab management because it is quick, easy, and provides immediate visual feedback. You can, however, perform all of the tab-management tasks already presented in this chapter (clearing, setting, and changing tab stops) by using the Tab Set dialog box (see Figure 5.10).

Figure 5.10   **The Tab Set dialog box**

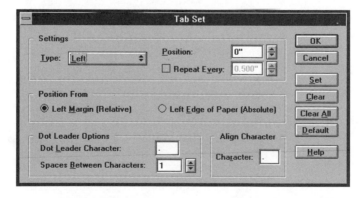

The advantage of using the Tab Set dialog box is that you can specify exact tab-stop positions that you couldn't choose by using the mouse and ruler (for example, 3.12 inches or 6.78 inches). The disadvantages are that you must type in your tab-stop positions and that you see how your tab-stop settings affect the selected paragraph(s) only when you exit the Tab Set dialog box.

Here's the general procedure to use the Tab Set dialog box for managing custom tab stops:

- Select the desired paragraph(s).

- Choose *Layout, Line, Tab Set* to open the Tab Set dialog box.

- Click on *Clear All* to clear the default tab stops for the selected paragraph(s).

- In the Settings box, select the type and position of the tab you want to set or clear.

- In the Position From box, select the appropriate option.

- Click on *Set* (to set the tab) or *Clear* (to clear it).

- Click on *OK* (or press *Enter*).

Note: We recommend that you use the power bar and ruler for managing your custom tab stops, except in those rare instances when you need to set an exact tab-stop position that you cannot choose with the mouse and the ruler.

SETTING INDENTS AND LINE BREAKS

Margins define the upper, lower, left, and right page boundaries of an entire document (see "Setting Margins" in Chapter 6 for details on this WordPerfect feature). *Indents* define the left and right boundaries of selected paragraphs within a document.

By default, a paragraph's left and right indents are set equal to the document's left and right margins. However, you can modify a paragraph's left and/or right indents without changing the document's margins. Figure 5.11 illustrates the relationship between margins and indents. (**Note:** Your screen will not match Figure 5.11 exactly.)

INDENT TYPES

Table 5.2 defines the three types of indents and Figure 5.12 shows them.

Figure 5.11   **Margins and indents**

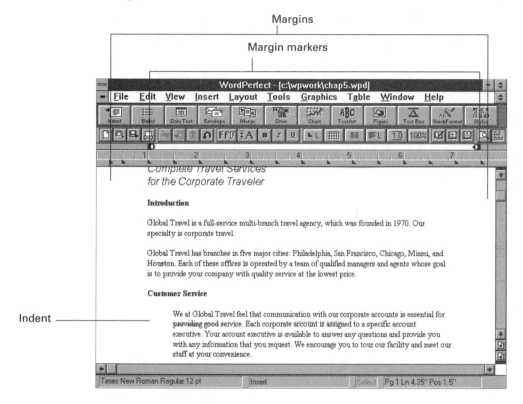

Table 5.2   **Types of Indents**

Indent Type	Description
Hanging indent	The left boundary for every line of a paragraph except the first line is indented. Thus, the first line of the paragraph seems to "hang" over the others.
Left indent	The left boundary of every line in a paragraph is indented (pushed in) from the left margin.
Double indent	The left and right boundaries of every line in a paragraph are indented (pushed in) from their respective margins.

Figure 5.12   Types of indents, illustrated

Hanging indents

Left indents

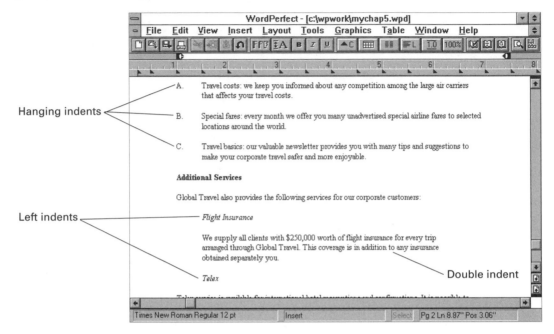

Double indent

The tab settings for a paragraph determine how far the paragraph will be indented from the margin. For example, if the first tab of a left-indented paragraph is one inch from the left margin, the paragraph will be indented one inch from the left margin. To change the amount of indentation, change the tab settings.

Note: When you indent a paragraph, only the text between the insertion point and the end of the paragraph will be affected. Furthermore, you can indent only one paragraph at a time.

CREATING LEFT INDENTS

Here's the general procedure to create a left indent:

- Place the insertion point where you want the indent to begin (within the paragraph that you want to indent).

- Choose *Layout, Paragraph, Indent*.

- If you wish to indent the paragraph to the next tab stop, choose *Layout, Paragraph, Indent* again.

Let's left-indent a couple of paragraphs in our document:

1. Scroll to place the *Additional Services* heading, near the bottom of page 2, at the top of the window.

2. Place the insertion point to the left of the *T* in *Telex service* (the paragraph below the *Telex* heading).

3. Choose **Layout, Paragraph, Indent**. The paragraph is indented from the left margin to the first tab stop, at the 1.5-inch mark on the ruler.

4. Place the insertion point to the left of the *W* in *We supply* (the paragraph below the *Flight Insurance* heading).

5. Choose **Layout, Paragraph, Indent**. The paragraph is indented from the left margin to the first tab, at the 1.5-inch mark.

6. Choose **Layout, Paragraph, Indent** again. The paragraph is indented further, from the first tab stop to the second tab stop, at the 2-inch mark. Compare your screen to Figure 5.13.

Figure 5.13   **Paragraph left-indented twice**

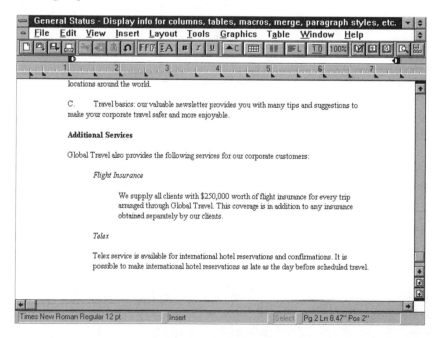

REMOVING INDENTS

The most accurate way to remove an indent is to delete it in the reveal codes area. To tell the printer to print an indented paragraph, WordPerfect inserts an Indent code.

Here's the general procedure to remove an indent:

- Place the insertion point in the paragraph containing the indent you wish to remove.

- Choose *View, Reveal Codes*.

- Place the mouse pointer on the Indent code you wish to remove and drag it out of the Reveal Codes area.

- Choose *View, Reveal Codes* to hide the Reveal Codes area.

Let's remove one of the indents from the *We supply* paragraph:

1. Verify that the insertion point is to the left of the *W* in *We supply* (the paragraph below the *Flight Insurance* heading).

2. Show the codes area (choose **View, Reveal Codes**).

3. Observe the Indent codes ([Hd Left Ind]). There are two codes before the *W* in *We*.

4. Place the mouse pointer on one of the **[Hd Left Ind]** codes (before *We supply*).

5. Drag the code out of the Reveal Codes area. (Drag it into the text area to delete it instead of just moving it to a new location.)

6. Select the remaining indent code in the *We supply* paragraph and delete it.

7. Hide the codes. Notice that the paragraph is once again aligned with the left margin.

PRACTICE YOUR SKILLS

1. Delete the **Indent** code from the Telex service paragraph (below the Telex heading). (**Hint:** You must show the codes area before you can delete the Indent code.)

2. Hide the codes.

CREATING DOUBLE INDENTS

Here's the general procedure to create a double indent:

- Place the insertion point where you want the left indent to begin.

- Choose *Layout, Paragraph, Double Indent*.

Let's create a double-indent for a few paragraphs:

1. Place the insertion point to the left of the *W* in the paragraph beginning with *We supply* (below the *Flight Insurance* heading).

2. Choose **Layout, Paragraph, Double Indent**. The paragraph is now indented from the left and right margins to the first tab stop (see Figure 5.14).

3. Choose **Layout, Paragraph, Double Indent** again. The paragraph is indented further from the left and right margins.

Figure 5.14   **Double-indented paragraph**

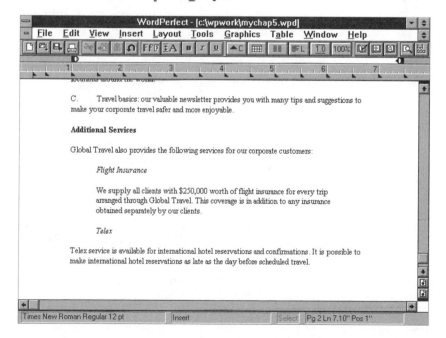

Now, let's look at the code for a double-indented paragraph:

1. Verify that the insertion point is located in the paragraph beginning *We supply*.

2. Show the codes area (choose **View, Reveal Codes**).

3. Observe the two [Hd Left/Right Ind] codes before the *W* in *We*.

4. Delete one of the [Hd Left/Right Ind] codes (drag it out of the codes area).

5. Hide the codes (choose **View, Reveal Codes**).

PRACTICE YOUR SKILLS

1. Create a double-indent for the following paragraph:

   • Telex service (below the *Telex* heading)

2. Save the file.

 ## CREATING HANGING INDENTS

As you know, a hanging indent occurs when the first line of a paragraph is not indented, and every other line of the paragraph is.

Here's the general procedure to create a hanging indent:

• Place the insertion point where you want the hanging indent to begin.

• Choose *Layout, Paragraph, Hanging Indent*.

Note: To create a hanging indent for a lettered, numbered, or bulleted paragraph, you must place a tab between the first character and the paragraph text that follows it.

Let's create a hanging indent:

1. Scroll up to place the *Newsletter* subheading, near the middle of page 2, at the top of the window.

2. Place the insertion point to the left of the *A.* in the paragraph that begins *A. Travel costs*.

3. Choose **Layout, Paragraph, Hanging Indent**. The second line of the paragraph is indented from the left margin to the first

tab setting (at the 1.5-inch mark). It does not wrap below the heading letter.

4. Observe your hanging indent. The second line is indented 0.5 inch, while the first line remains at the left margin—that is, unindented.

PRACTICE YOUR SKILLS

1. Create a hanging indent for the paragraph that begins *B. Special fares*.

2. Create a hanging indent for the paragraph the begins *C. Travel basics*.

3. Save the file.

4. Compare your screen to Figure 5.15.

Figure 5.15   **Completed hanging indents**

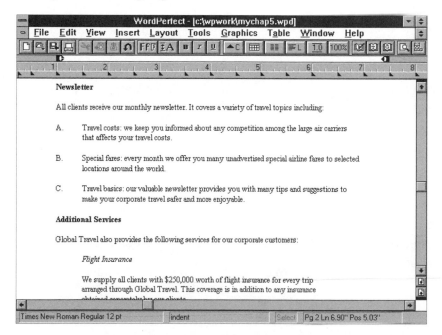

SETTING PARAGRAPH JUSTIFICATION

Paragraph *justification* determines how text is positioned between the left and right indents. WordPerfect for Windows provides five types of paragraph justification, each defined in Table 5.3. Figure 5.16 illustrates how paragraph justification appears on your computer screen.

Table 5.3 **The Five Paragraph Justification Types**

Type	Alignment
Left	Lines of text are flush left (aligned evenly along the left indent) and ragged right (uneven along the right indent); left aligned is the default paragraph-alignment setting.
Centered	Lines of text are centered between the indents; both the left and right sides of a centered paragraph are ragged.
Right	Lines of text are flush right and ragged left, the opposite of left aligned.
Full	Lines of text are both flush left and flush right; in a Full justified paragraph, WordPerfect adjusts the spacing between words so that they stretch from the left indent to the right indent.
All	Short lines of text are both flush left and flush right; in an All justified paragraph, WordPerfect adjusts the spacing between letters so that the text stretches from the left indent to the right indent.

JUSTIFYING SELECTED PARAGRAPHS

Here's the general procedure to set paragraph justification for selected paragraphs:

- Select the desired paragraph(s).
- Point to the *Justification* button on the power bar.
- Press and hold the *left mouse* button.

Figure 5.16   Paragraph justification types

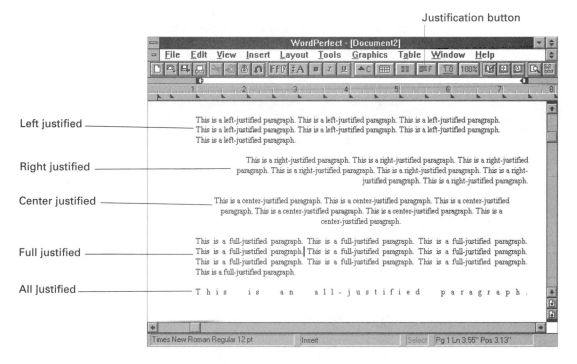

- Select the appropriate alignment.
- Release the mouse button.

Here's the general procedure to use the menu to justify selected text:

- Select the paragraph.
- Choose *Layout, Justification.*
- Select the type of justification that you wish to apply.

Note: When you justify the entire document, WordPerfect inserts an *open code*, a single code that turns on the feature but does not have a corresponding code to turn it off. Therefore, the change will affect the entire document (or remainder of the document), unless another justification code is encountered further down in the document.

Let's center some selected text:

1. Select the first three lines of the document, the heading at the top of page 1. (Press **Ctrl+Home** to move to the top of page 1.)

2. Observe the Justification button (located on the power bar; it displays an *L* and a miniature paragraph). WordPerfect's default justification is Left (that is, lines of text are justified along the left margin).

3. Point to the **Justification** button.

4. Press and hold the **left mouse** button.

5. Drag to select **Center**; then release the mouse button. The selected heading is now centered.

6. Deselect the heading and compare your screen to Figure 5.17.

Figure 5.17 **Centered heading**

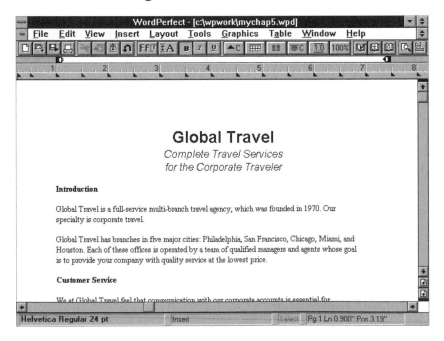

PRACTICE YOUR SKILLS

1. Center all three lines of the heading on the top of page 2.

2. Deselect the heading and update the disk file (use **File, Save**).

SETTING LINE SPACING

Line spacing is the vertical distance between lines of text. Word-Perfect provides four line-spacing options:

- 1.0 sets the line spacing to one single line: Single always maintains a minimum of 12-point (1/6-inch) spacing.

- 1.5 sets the line spacing to a line-and-a-half.

- 2.0 sets the line spacing to two lines.

- Other allows you to specify exact line spacing that will not adjust according to font size.

You can set line spacing for multiple paragraphs or for an entire document. Line spacing affects the text from where you insert the setting to the end of the document, unless you change the line-spacing further down in the document.

Here's the general procedure to set line spacing:

- Place the insertion point where you want the desired line spacing to begin.

- Point to the *Line Spacing* button on the power bar.

- Press and hold the *left mouse* button.

- Drag to select the appropriate line spacing.

- Release the mouse button.

Let's use the above procedure to change the line spacing of MYCHAP5.WPD:

1. Move to the top of the document.

2. Point to the **Spacing** button (located on the power bar next to the Justification button; it displays a 1.0).

3. Press and hold the **left mouse** button, drag to select **1.5**, and then release the mouse button. The line spacing for all of the text from the insertion point to the end of the document is now increased to 1.5.

SETTING LINE SPACING FOR SELECTED PARAGRAPHS

Here's the general procedure to set line spacing for selected text:

- Select the text.
- Point to the *Spacing* button.
- Press and hold the *left mouse* button.
- Drag to select the appropriate line spacing.
- Release the mouse button.

Let's change the line spacing for a table in our document:

1. Scroll to place *Discounts*, near the top of page 2, at the top of the window.
2. Point to the left of the *D* in *Destination*, at the top of the table.
3. Drag to select the text in the table.
4. Point to the **Line Spacing** button on the power bar.
5. Press and hold the **left mouse** button, drag to select **1.0**, and then release the mouse button. The line spacing for the selected text is set for 1.0.

PRACTICE YOUR SKILLS

1. Change the line spacing to 1.0 for the table below the *Hotel Accommodations* section, on page 3.
2. Deselect the text.
3. Save the file, and compare your screen to Figure 5.18.
4. Close the file.

PRACTICE YOUR SKILLS

In Chapters 4 and 5, you learned the basics of character and paragraph formatting. The following two Practice Your Skills activities give you the opportunity to apply these formatting techniques to realistic word processing situations.

Figure 5.18   **Contents of single-spaced table**

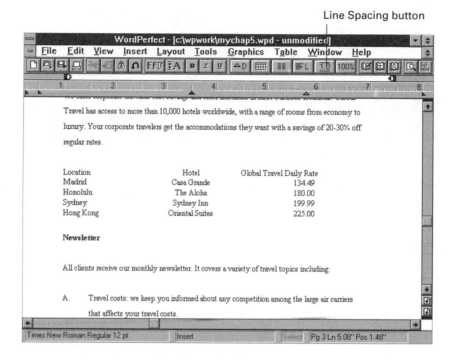

Follow these steps to produce the final document shown in Figures 5.19 and 5.20 from the original document PRAC5A.WPD:

1. Open **prac5a.wpd** (Chapter 2).

2. Bold the following headings (Chapter 4):

    I. Introduction

    II. Computer Study

    III. Regional Updates

    IV. Quarterly Meeting

    V. Conclusion

3. Using the **Font** dialog box, change the font and point size of the three-line heading on the top of page 2 to 14-point Helvetica (Chapter 4).

Figure 5.19   **Page 1 of MYPRAC5A.WPD**

Macco Plastics Inc.
Quarterly Sales Report
First Quarter

I. Introduction

Congratulations to all of you! An initial review of the sales figures for the nation reveals a surge in sales in all of Macco's sales regions. Major new clients have been added and many new products are on the way.

As we expected when we entered the field, computer-related products, such as keyboard housings and protective carrying cases, are accounting for a major portion of this upswing.

II. Computer Study

A companywide study will begin in March, under the direction of Cathy Donaldson and Bill Schuster in data processing, to determine how to most effectively implement automation in our firm. We will be making a large commitment to productivity gains via computerization sometime late this year.

III. Regional Updates

Midwestern Region

After several years of falling sales due to the slump in the auto industry, Blair Williams and his folks have something to celebrate. The recent boom in auto manufacturing has led to renewed demand of Macco Products in Detroit.

Northeastern Region

John Martinson and his group are doing a great job in Nashua. They have secured major contracts for a wide range of new and existing products. Much of this business is coming from Computer Equipment Corporation, a major client of Macco's.

Southern Region

Mark Daley and his group have done a fine job of maintaining relations with Becker's Product Development Division in Boca Raton. They have been working closely with Becker to decrease manufacturing costs.

Figure 5.20   **Page 2 of MYPRAC5A.WPD**

Macco Plastics Inc.
Quarterly Sales Report
First Quarter

IV. Quarterly Meeting

The quarterly meeting will take place in Memphis this time. You will find the agenda attached to this report.

V. Conclusion

The following items will be discussed at the next managers' meeting:

A.   Marketing and sales strategies for the introduction of the new System 400 and System 500 product lines.

B.   Current available positions resulting from the early retirement program and normal attrition of personnel.

C.   Development of the new expense form to facilitate the prompt payment of - travel reimbursements - other out-of-pocket expenses and - commissions.

If the recovery continues at the current pace, this year should be a banner year for all of us at Macco. We want to thank all of you for the outstanding jobs you have done and, most important, for standing by Macco in hard times. Keep up the good work!

John Smith
Regional Coordinator
Macco Plastics Inc.

4. Copy the formatting in step 3 for the three-line heading on the top of page 1 (Chapter 4).

5. Scroll to the bottom of page 1 (Chapter 2).

6. Create a double indent in the paragraph beginning with *After several years* (this chapter).

7. Repeat the indents in step 6 for the paragraphs beginning with *John Martinson* and *Mark Daley* (this chapter).

8. Center the three-line heading on the top of pages 1 and 2 (this chapter).

9. Save the disk file as **myprac5a** (Chapter 2).

10. Print the document and compare it to Figures 5.19 and 5.20 (Chapter 1).

11. Close the document (Chapter 1).

Follow these steps to produce the final document shown in Figures 5.21 and 5.22.

1. Open **prac5b.wpd** (Chapter 2).

2. Using the Font dialog box, italicize the first line on page 1, *Macco Plastics, Inc.*, and change the point size to 24-point (Chapter 4).

3. Copy the formatting in step 2 to the first line on page 2 (Chapter 4).

4. Single-underline the following subheadings (near the bottom of page 1) (Chapter 4):

   Midwestern Region

   Northeastern Region

   Southern Region

5. Create a hanging indent for the paragraph beginning with *A. Marketing and sales* (this chapter).

6. Repeat the hanging indent for the paragraphs beginning with *B. Current available positions* and *C. Development of the* (this chapter).

7. Save the disk file as **myprac5b** (Chapter 1).

Figure 5.21   **Page 1 of the completed document MYPRAC5B.WPD**

Macco Plastics Inc.

Quarterly Sales Report
First Quarter

I. Introduction

Congratulations to all of you! An initial review of the sales figures for the nation reveals a surge in sales in all of Macco's sales regions. Major new clients have been added and many new products are on the way.

As we expected when we entered the field, computer-related products, such as keyboard housings and protective carrying cases, are accounting for a major portion of this upswing.

II. Computer Study

A companywide study will begin in March, under the direction of Cathy Donaldson and Bill Schuster in data processing, to determine how to most effectively implement automation in our firm. We will be making a large commitment to productivity gains via computerization sometime late this year.

III. Regional Updates

Midwestern Region

After several years of falling sales due to the slump in the auto industry, Blair Williams and his folks have something to celebrate. The recent boom in auto manufacturing has led to renewed demand of Macco Products in Detroit.

Northeastern Region

John Martinson and his group are doing a great job in Nashua. They have secured major contracts for a wide range of new and existing products. Much of this business is coming from Computer Equipment Corporation, a major client of Macco's.

Southern Region

Mark Daley and his group have done a fine job of maintaining relations with Becker's Product Development Division in Boca Raton. They have been working closely with Becker to decrease manufacturing costs.

Figure 5.22   **Page 2 of the completed document MYPRAC5B.WPD**

Macco Plastics Inc.
Quarterly Sales Report
First Quarter

IV. Quarterly Meeting

The quarterly meeting will take place in Memphis this time. You will find the agenda attached to this report.

V. Conclusion

The following items will be discussed at the next managers' meeting:

A.   Marketing and sales strategies for the introduction of the new System 400 and System 500 product lines.

B.   Current available positions resulting from the early retirement program and normal attrition of personnel.

C.   Development of the new expense form to facilitate the prompt payment of - travel reimbursements - other out-of-pocket expenses and - commissions.

If the recovery continues at the current pace, this year should be a banner year for all of us at Macco. We want to thank all of you for the outstanding jobs you have done and, most important, for standing by Macco in hard times. Keep up the good work!

John Smith
Regional Coordinator
Macco Plastics Inc.

8. Print the document and compare it to Figures 5.21 and 5.22 (Chapter 1).

9. Close the document (Chapter 1).

SUMMARY

In this chapter, you learned the basics of paragraph formatting. You now know how to set, change, and clear tab stops; how to set and repeat paragraph indents; how to create new lines within a paragraph; how to align paragraphs; and how to set line spacing.

Here's a quick reference guide to the WordPerfect features introduced in this chapter:

Desired Result	How to Do It
Display the ruler	Choose **View, Ruler Bar**
Select multiple paragraphs for paragraph formatting	Select (highlight) at least a portion of each paragraph
Clear all tabs for selected text	Select the desired paragraph; press and hold **Shift**; drag to select the tab markers on the ruler; point to the shaded tab area; drag the tabs off the ruler (down into the typing area)
Set custom tab stops	Select the text for which you want to set tabs; select the desired tab type by pressing on the **Tab Set** button on the power bar and selecting the appropriate option: Left, Center, Right, Decimal, ...Left, ...Center, ...Right, and ...Decimal; point at the desired tab-stop position in the ruler (directly under the tick marks); and click the **left mouse** button
Change the position of tab stops	Select the desired paragraph(s); in the ruler, drag the custom tab stop to a new position

Desired Result	How to Do It
Clear a custom tab stop	Select the desired paragraph(s); drag the custom tab stop down into the text area
Use the Tab Set dialog box for managing tab stops	Select the desired paragraph(s); choose **Layout, Line, Tab Set** to open the Tab Set dialog box; enter your desired settings to change or clear tab stops; click on **OK** (or press **Enter**)
Create a left indent	Place the insertion point where you want the indent to begin (within the paragraph that you want to indent); choose **Layout, Paragraph, Indent**; if you wish to indent the paragraph to the next tab stop, choose **Layout, Paragraph, Indent** again
Remove an indent	Place the insertion point in the paragraph containing the indent you wish to remove; choose **View, Reveal Codes**; place the mouse pointer on the Indent code you wish to remove; drag it out of the Reveal Codes area; choose **View, Reveal Codes** to hide the Reveal Codes area
Create a double indent	Place the insertion point where you want the left indent to begin; choose **Layout, Paragraph, Double Indent**
Create a hanging indent	Place the insertion point where you want the hanging indent to begin; choose **Layout, Paragraph, Hanging Indent**

In the next chapter, you'll learn the basics of page formatting. You'll find out how to use headers and footers and how to set margins and page breaks. You'll also learn how to work in Draft view and how to control document printing.

IF YOU'RE STOPPING HERE

If you need to break off here, please exit WordPerfect. If you want to proceed directly to the next chapter, please do so now.

CHAPTER 6:
PAGE FORMATTING

Exploring
WordPerfect's
Views

Pagination

Creating Headers
and Footers

Changing Margins

Centering Text
Vertically

Controlling the
Printing of Your
Documents

In Chapters 4 and 5, you learned how to format your documents at the character and paragraph levels. In this chapter, we'll introduce WordPerfect for Windows's final level of formatting—*page formatting*. You face some new challenges as your documents get longer. Many powerful formatting features are controlled at the page level, including headers and footers, margins, and page breaks. You can center several lines of text vertically on a page, number the pages of your document, and view the entire document on your screen before you print it.

When you're done working through this chapter, you will know

- How to preview the document before you print it
- How to work in Draft view
- How to insert and delete hard page breaks
- How to create headers and footers
- How to use the ruler to change margins
- How to align text vertically on a page

EXPLORING WORDPERFECT'S VIEWS

WordPerfect for Windows provides you with three views to work in: Page view, Draft view, and Two Page view. In Chapters 1–5, you have worked solely in Page view. In this chapter, we will explore the other WordPerfect views.

PAGE VIEW

As you learned earlier, Page view is a full WYSIWYG (What You See Is What You Get) environment. Your text is formatted in the document window as it will look when it is printed. For example, headers and footers are displayed at the top and bottom of each page as they will print. (You will learn more about headers and footers later in this chapter.)

Each time you start a new page in Page view, WordPerfect creates the entire page. You can scroll to the bottom of the page even if there is no text on the page.

Here's the general procedure to move to Page view from any other view:

- Choose *View, Page*.

DRAFT VIEW

Draft view imitates the WYSIWYG environment of Page view; however, certain features such as headers and footers and some special formatting aren't displayed. In addition, when you work in Draft view, WordPerfect doesn't automatically create an entire page each time you start a new page. Because there is not as much information for WordPerfect to process and display, you can generally work faster in Draft view.

Note: We recommend that you create and format text in Draft view, and then add the finishing touches to it in Page view.

Here's the general procedure to move to Draft view from any other view:

● Choose *View, Draft*.

TWO PAGE VIEW

Two Page view provides a miniature view of how your document will look when it is printed. You can use Two Page view to examine and adjust the layout of a document before you actually print it. When you work in Two Page view, two consecutive pages of your document are displayed side-by-side in the same window.

Note: While you can edit text in Two Page view, we recommend that you use it only to view and modify page layout because the text is so small and difficult to read.

Here's the general procedure to use the Two Page view option:

● Place the insertion point on the first page you want to view.

● Choose *View, Two Page*.

● Edit your document as necessary.

● Choose *View, Page* to return to Page view.

If you aren't running WordPerfect for Windows, please start it now. All documents should be closed except for the default, Document1.

Let's open VIEWS.WPD and take a look at WordPerfect's views:

1. Open **views.wpd** from your WPWORK directory. By default, WordPerfect opens files in Page view (see Figure 6.1). There is a header visible at the top of the page (you will learn more about headers later in this chapter). If you scroll down to the bottom of the page, the footer is also visible.

2. Choose **View, Draft** to switch to Draft view (see Figure 6.2).

3. Observe the screen. Although the header and footer are still there, you can't see them on your screen. If you print the document, the header and footer will print. You can work

Figure 6.1   **VIEWS.WPD in Page view**

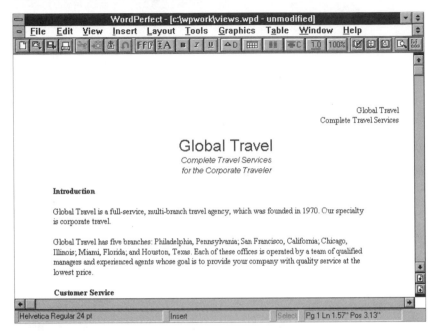

Figure 6.2   **VIEWS.WPD in Draft view**

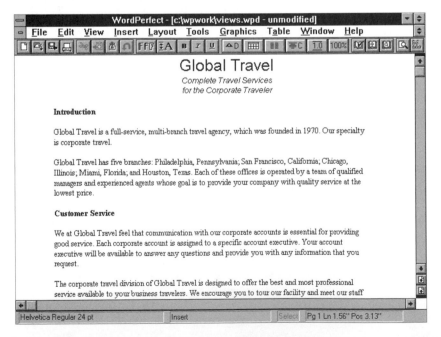

faster in Draft view because WordPerfect doesn't have to process and display as much information.

4. Choose **View, Two Page** to switch to Two Page view (see Figure 6.3). Two Page view provides a miniature display of two pages of your document as they will print, including headers and footers.

Figure 6.3   **VIEWS.WPD in Two Page view**

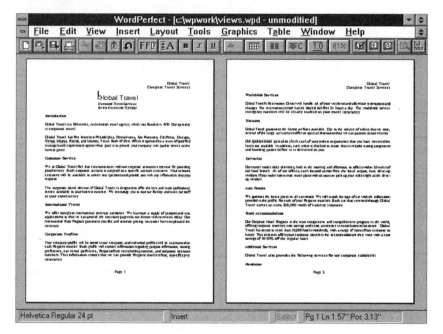

5. Press **PgDn** twice to view pages 2 and 3 of the document. The insertion point moves to page 3 (as shown in the Position indicator on the status bar).

6. Place the insertion point at the top of the document (press **Ctrl+Home**).

7. Close VIEWS.WPD without saving changes.

PAGINATION

Pagination means dividing text into pages, separated by discrete page breaks, and usually numbered sequentially. In WordPerfect for Windows, there are two kinds of page breaks: automatic and manual.

AUTOMATIC (SOFT) PAGE BREAKS

When you type enough lines of text to fill a page, WordPerfect automatically inserts a page break. An *automatic* page break is inserted by the program itself and is also known as a *soft page break*. In Draft view, the soft page break shows up in the document window as a solid horizontal line that extends from the left edge of the window to the right edge.

When WordPerfect inserts an automatic page break, it inserts an [SPg] code in the Reveal Codes area. This code tells the printer to break the page there.

Note: You can't see any difference between an automatic page break and a manual page break in Page view or Two Page view.

Let's open CHAP6.WPD and take a look at some automatic page breaks:

1. Open **chap6.wpd** from your WPWORK directory.

2. View the document in Two Page view (choose **View, Two Page**). The document is four pages long, with the third and fourth pages containing only a few lines. (The actual number of lines will vary, depending on the printer you have selected.)

3. Press **PgDn** twice to view the next two pages (3 and 4) of the document.

4. Switch to Draft view (choose **View, Draft**) to view the page breaks (see Figure 6.4). The automatic page break appears as a *single* solid line, and the manual page break between pages 3 and 4 as a *double* solid line.

5. Scroll up to place *Worldwide Services* (at the bottom of page 1) at the top of your screen.

6. Place the insertion point to the left of the *W* in *Worldwide*. Notice that an automatic page break separates the body paragraph. (**Note:** If you have a different printer installed, your page might not break at the same place.)

Figure 6.4 **Automatic and manual page breaks**

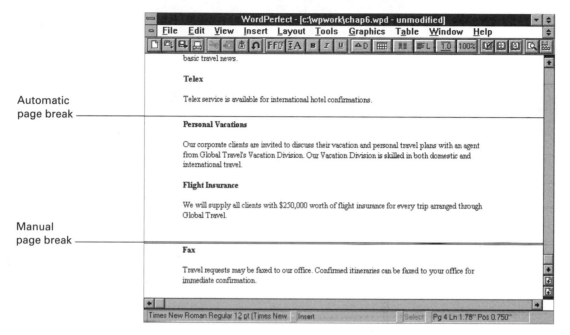

Automatic page break ──

Manual page break ──

MANUAL (HARD) PAGE BREAKS

By inserting automatic page breaks, WordPerfect saves you the trouble of deciding where to break each page. However, sometimes you may want to specify where a page should begin or end. For example, it's common practice to begin each section of a document (particularly if the section begins with a heading) on a new page, even if the program would not automatically break the page there. This is particularly true if the section begins with a heading.

A manual, or *hard,* page break is used to break a page where *you* wish; it is a way of overriding the program. A manual page break necessarily occurs before the page would break automatically; you cannot force WordPerfect for Windows to exceed a specific number of text lines per page.

In Draft view, a manual page break appears as a double horizontal line extending from the left edge of the window to the right edge. Figure 6.4 shows a manual page break in Draft view. In the Reveal Codes area, a manual page break is indicated by the code [HPg], for "hard page."

Deleting a Manual Page Break

There are two ways to delete a manual page break:

- Place the insertion point directly above the page break and press *Del.*

OR

- Delete the manual page break code ([HPg]) from the Reveal Codes area.

Let's delete the manual page break before *Fax:*

1. Place the insertion point above the *F* in *Fax* (at the top of page 4).

2. Press **Del** to delete the manual page break.

Inserting a Manual Page Break

Here's the general procedure to insert a manual page break:

- Place the insertion point to the left of the first character that you want on the new page.

- Choose *Insert, Page Break* (or press *Ctrl+Enter*).

Let's insert some hard page breaks in our document:

1. Place the insertion point to the left of the *I* in *Introduction*, near the top of page 1.

2. Choose **Insert, Page Break** to insert a hard page break. A double line appears on the screen, indicating that a hard page break has been inserted.

3. Scroll to place *Worldwide Services* at the top of the window.

4. Observe the soft page break, indicated by the single horizontal line. Notice that the page break causes the paragraph under the *Discounts* heading to be split between pages 2 and 3.

5. Place the insertion point to the left of the *W* in *Worldwide*.

6. Choose **Insert, Page Break** to insert a hard page break. Because page 2 now contains less text, the soft page break has been removed.

Note: To be certain of the exact positions of hard and soft page breaks, you might want to view them in the Reveal Codes area (see Chapter 4).

PRACTICE YOUR SKILLS

Place a hard page break before *Additional Services,* near the bottom of page 3. Compare your screen to Figure 6.5.

Figure 6.5 **Inserted hard page break**

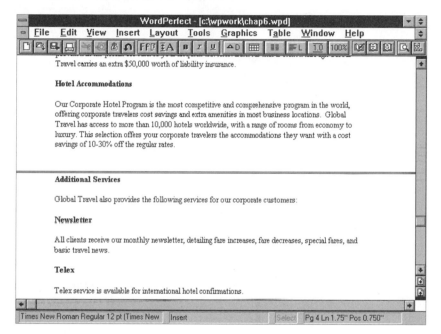

CREATING HEADERS AND FOOTERS

A *header* is text that is automatically printed at the top of every page in a document, and a *footer* is text that is automatically printed at the bottom of every page. Headers and footers are used extensively in word processing to do such things as number each page in a document, place a current date on each page, print the document title and/or author name on each page, and so on.

You can create up to two different headers and two different footers per document. You would use a second header and footer if you were planning to print a two-sided, bound document, and wanted different (alternating) headers and footers on left and right pages.

In Draft view, headers and footers are created in their own "mini-document area" (a blank screen with a Header/Footer feature bar), and each can be as long as one page. Of course, a header or footer longer than a few lines begins to limit the space for regular text.

Most WordPerfect for Windows's enhancement features work within headers and footers. For example, you can create a header or footer with text that is centered, aligned flush right, boldface, or underlined.

CREATING A HEADER

Here's the general procedure to create a header:

- Place the insertion point in the first paragraph on the first page on which you want the header to print.

- Choose *Layout, Header/Footer.*

- Select *Header A* or *B* (it doesn't matter whether you use A for the first or second header).

- Click on *Create.*

- Type the text for the header.

- Select the text and use the *Justification* button to align it.

- Click on *Placement* to select the appropriate placement for the header (whether you want it to appear on every page, odd pages, or even pages).

- Click on *OK.*

- Click on *Close.*

Once created, the header is not displayed in the typing area in Draft view; however, you can view it in Two Page or Page view. The header (or footer) information is contained in a single code; for example

```
[Header A:Every page, [Open Style][Just][Just]Global Travel[HRt]Complete...
```

You can remove a header by deleting its code in the Reveal Codes area.

Let's create a header for our document:

1. Place the insertion point at the top of page 2 (above *Introduction*) so that the header will first print on the second page of the document. As a general rule, it is not necessary to place a header or footer on page 1.

2. Choose **Layout, Header/Footer** to open the Headers/Footers dialog box, shown in Figure 6.6.

3. Verify that *Header A* is selected in the Select box.

4. Click on **Create** to open the Header A window (see Figure 6.7).

Figure 6.6   **Headers/Footers dialog box**

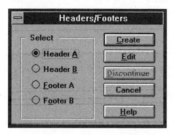

Figure 6.7   **Header A window**

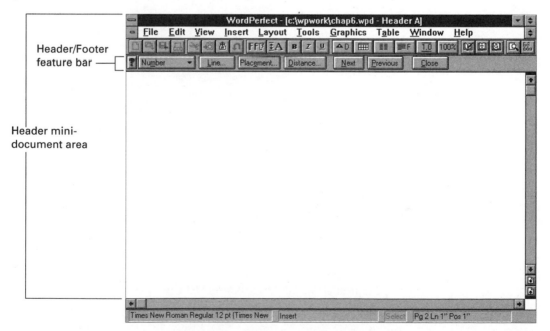

5. Observe the Header/Footer feature bar. It provides easy access to several of the features most often used in creating headers and footers.

6. In the Header A window, type **Global Travel**, and press **Enter** to end the line and move to the next line.

7. Type **Complete Travel Services**.

8. Select all of the header text.

9. Use the **Justification** button to right-justify the text.

10. Click on **Placement** to open the Placement dialog box, shown in Figure 6.8.

Figure 6.8　　　**Placement dialog box with right-justified header**

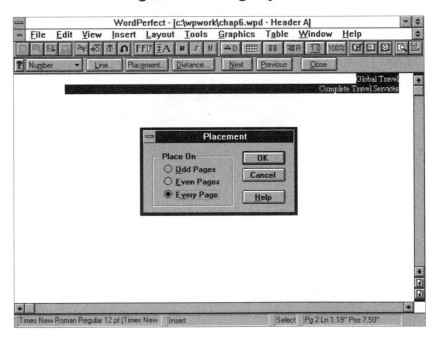

11. Verify that *Every Page* is selected in the Place On box. This will place the header on every page, from the page on which the insertion point is located to the end of the document.

12. Click on **OK** to close the Placement dialog box.

13. Click on **Close** to close the Header window and return to Draft view. Don't panic if you can't see the header you just created. Remember, you can only see the header and footer in the Page and Two Page views.

14. Switch to Two Page view (choose **View, Two Page**), and press **PgDn** to move through the document and observe the header. It appears at the top of every page except the first page.

15. Return to Draft view (choose **View, Draft**).

16. Place the insertion point at the top of page 2, if necessary. (**Note:** *Introduction* is the first line on page 2.)

AUTOMATIC PAGE-NUMBERING

You can insert an automatic page-numbering code in a header or footer. The code tells the program to automatically place a page number at the code's position when the document is printed.

Here's the general procedure to insert a page number in a header or footer:

- In the Header or Footer window, place the insertion point where you want the page number to appear.

- Click on the *Number* button on the Header/Footer feature bar.

- Click on *Page Number*.

The automatic page number is displayed on your screen and appears as a *Pg Num Disp: Lev:1;1* code in the Reveal Codes area. This code tells WordPerfect where to place the page number in each header or footer.

CREATING A FOOTER

Here's the general procedure to create a footer:

- Place the insertion point on the first page that you want the footer to print.

- Choose *Layout, Header/Footer*.

- Select *Footer A or B* (it doesn't matter whether you use A for the first or second footer).

- Click on *Create*.

- Type the text for the footer.

- Use the *Justification* button to align the text.
- Click on *Placement* to select the appropriate placement for the footer (whether you want it to appear on every page, odd pages, or even pages).
- Click on *OK.*
- Click on *Close.*

You can remove a footer by deleting its code in the Reveal Codes area.

Let's create a footer that uses automatic page numbering:

1. Verify that the insertion point is at the top of page 2 to begin the footer on the second page of the document.

2. Choose **Layout, Header/Footer** to open the Header/Footer dialog box.

3. Click on **Footer A** to select it.

4. Click on **Create** to create the footer.

5. In the Footer A window, type **Page** to include the word *Page* in the footer. Then press the **spacebar** to insert a space after the word.

6. Click on the **Number** button in the Header/Footer feature bar to open the Number drop-down list. You can choose to place an automatic page number, secondary number, chapter number, or volume number in your footer.

7. Click on **Page Number** to place the page number in the footer.

8. Place the insertion point immediately to the left of the page number.

9. Display the Reveal Codes area and observe the footer code. The *Pg Num Disp: Lev:1;2* tells WordPerfect to place the page number of each page in the footer, beginning with page 2. (**Note:** If your code displays only *Page Num Disp*, then press the left or right arrow key until the insertion point is located directly in front of the page number code.)

10. Hide the Reveal Codes area.

11. Select all of the footer text.

12. Use the **Justification** button to center the footer (see Figure 6.9).

Figure 6.9   **Centered footer**

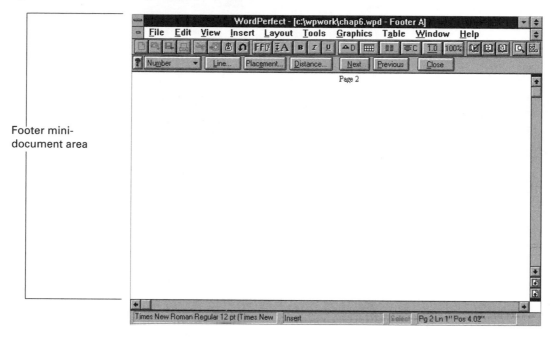

Footer mini-
document area

13. Click on **Placement** to open the Placement dialog box.

14. Verify that *Every Page* is selected. This will print the footer on every page from the insertion point to the end of the document.

15. Click on **OK** to close the Placement dialog box.

16. Deselect the text if necessary, and compare your screen to Figure 6.9.

17. Click on **Close** to close the Footer A window.

PRACTICE YOUR SKILLS

1. Switch to Two Page view and examine the footers you created in the last activity.

2. Compare your screen to Figure 6.10.

3. Return to Draft view.

4. Save the file as **mychap6**.

Figure 6.10   **The header and footer in Two Page view**

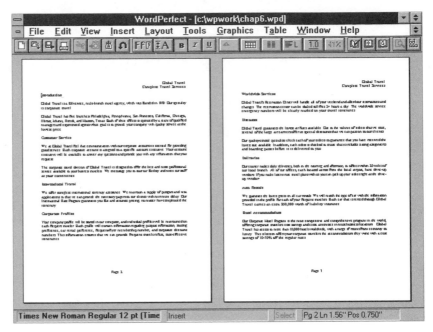

CHANGING MARGINS

Margins define the length of the line on which text appears on your screen and in print. The left and right margins are measured in inches from the left and right edges of the paper, respectively. If you are using 8.5-by-11-inch paper and the left and right margins are 1 inch each, 6.5 inches remain for text on each line.

You can change the margins for selected paragraphs or for the entire document. If you do not select text, the entire paragraph in which the insertion point is located and all of the text from the insertion point to the end of the document will be affected, unless WordPerfect encounters a different margin setting further down in the document.

New left and right margins are set from the cursor position forward (down) in your document. If you wish to change margin settings for the entire document, be sure to first place the insertion point at the top of the document. In WordPerfect for Windows, the top, bottom, left, and right margins each have default settings of 1 inch. The margin markers on the ruler show the left and right margin settings. You can change the margin settings by using the Margins dialog box or by moving the margin markers on the ruler with the mouse pointer.

The general procedure to set left and right margins for the entire document on the ruler is to place the insertion point at the top of the document, show the ruler (choose *View, Ruler Bar*), and then drag the margin markers to a different setting.

Let's change the left and right margins of MYCHAP6.WPD:

1. Show the ruler (choose **View, Ruler Bar**).

2. Move to the top-left margin of the document, before the *G* in *Global Travel* (press **Ctrl+Home**).

3. Observe the left and right margin markers located at the top of the ruler (see Figure 6.11). The left margin is set at the 0.75-inch mark, the right margin at the 7.5-inch mark.

Figure 6.11 **MYCHAP6.WPD with margin markers and position displayed**

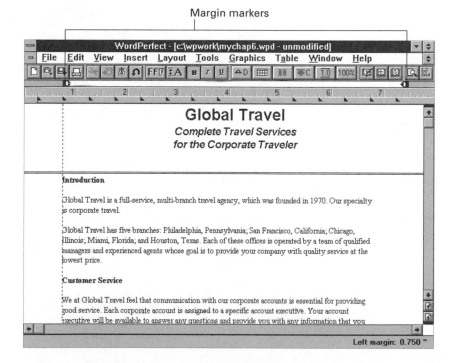

4. Point to the **left margin** marker (make sure you point to the bracket part of the margin marker—see Figure 6.11 if you are unsure which part of the margin marker to point to). Press and hold the **left mouse** button and observe the lower-right corner of the status bar. It displays the position of the left margin (currently at 0.75 inch). As you move the margin marker, its new position is displayed in the status bar.

5. Drag the marker to the 1-inch mark (use the status bar and the ruler guide to help you place the margin marker).

6. Release the mouse button. The left boundary of the text is now aligned with the new left margin setting, from the insertion point to the end of the document.

7. Verify that the insertion point is at the top of the document.

8. Drag the right margin marker to the 7-inch mark and compare your screen to Figure 6.12.

Figure 6.12   **Setting new left and right margins**

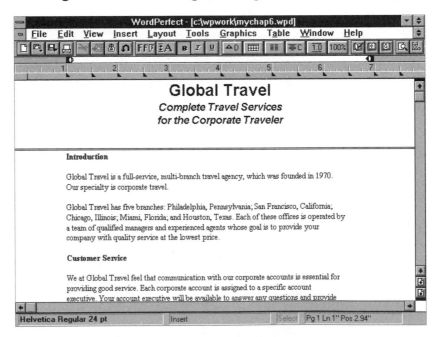

USING THE MARGINS DIALOG BOX TO SET MARGINS

While you can use the ruler to set right and left margins for your document, the only way that you can set the top and bottom margins is through the Margins dialog box.

Here's the general procedure to use the Margins dialog box:

- Choose *Layout, Margins*.
- Enter the appropriate measurements in the Left, Right, Top, and Bottom text boxes.
- Click on *OK* (or press *Enter*).

Let's use the Margins dialog box to change the margins for the document:

1. Verify that the insertion point is at the top of the document (press **Ctrl+Home**).

2. Choose **Layout, Margins** to open the Margins dialog box (see Figure 6.13).

Figure 6.13   **The Margins dialog box**

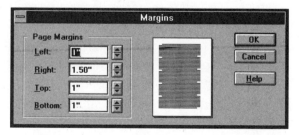

3. Type **1.5** to change the left margin to 1.5 inches.

4. Press **Tab** twice to skip the Right text box and move to the Top text box.

5. Type **.75** to change the top margin to 0.75 inch.

6. Press **Tab** to move to the Bottom text box; then type **.75** to change the bottom margin to 0.75 inch.

7. Click on **OK**.

PRACTICE YOUR SKILLS

1. Change the top and bottom margins to 1 inch. (**Hint:** Use the Margins dialog box.)

2. Save the file.

CENTERING TEXT VERTICALLY

Title pages, charts, tables, and brief letters are examples of short pages that may require special treatment. In such cases, you might want to center the text vertically, between the top and bottom margins.

Here's the general procedure to center text vertically on a page:

- Place the insertion point on the desired page.

- Choose *Layout, Page, Center.*

- Choose *Current Page* to turn centering on for the current page; choose *Current And Subsequent Pages* to center the current page and all pages that follow; or, choose *Turn Centering Off* to remove the centering from a page that was previously centered.

- Click on *OK.* All text on the desired page will be centered vertically.

Note: When you center a page vertically, WordPerfect inserts a [Cntr Cur Pg] code in the codes area. Deleting this code will return the text to its previous position on the page.

Let's create a title page, which will consist of a heading centered vertically on the page, for our document:

1. Place the insertion point on page 1, which contains the three-line heading.

2. Click on the **Page Zoom Full** button (the second button from the right on the power bar) to see page 1 in Full Page view. The text appears near the top of the page.

3. Click on the **Page Zoom Full** button again to return to 100 percent magnification in Draft view.

4. Verify that the insertion point is on page 1.

5. Choose **Layout, Page, Center** to open the Center Page(s) dialog box (see Figure 6.14).

Figure 6.14   **The Center Page(s) dialog box**

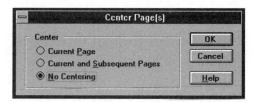

6. Click on **Current Page** to center only the heading page. You can use the Center Page(s) dialog box to center every page of the document (by selecting *Current and Subsequent Pages*), or to remove centering (by selecting *No Centering*).

7. Click on **OK** to close the dialog box and center the heading vertically on the page.

8. Show the Reveal Codes area. The [Cntr Cur Pg] code is inserted at the top of the codes area, before the heading text.

9. Hide the codes.

10. Switch to Two Page view to preview pages 1 and 2. The text on page 1 is now centered between the top and bottom margins (see Figure 6.15).

11. Page down to observe the rest of the document. Only the first page is centered vertically between the margins.

12. Return to Draft view.

13. Save the document.

CONTROLLING THE PRINTING OF YOUR DOCUMENTS

Several times in this book, you've used the File, Print command to print your active document. Let's revisit this very powerful command and learn how to use some of its more advanced features. In addition to printing a single copy of your entire document, File Print allows you to select a printer and to print the current page, multiple pages, multiple copies, or selected text.

Figure 6.15   **Heading centered vertically**

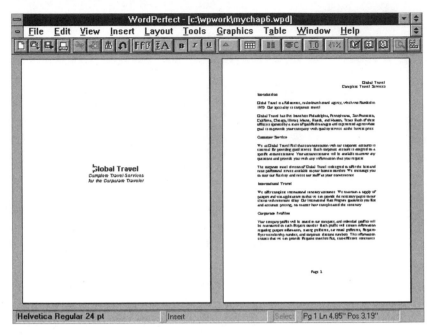

Here's the general procedure to use the Print dialog box to control how your documents print:

- If you wish to print selected text, select that text.

- Choose *File, Print* to open the Print dialog box.

- Choose the desired Print options (see Table 6.1).

- Click on *OK* (or press *Enter*).

PRINT DIALOG BOX OPTIONS

The Print dialog box provides the options shown in Table 6.1. Figure 6.16 shows the Print dialog box.

Let's practice using the print options in the Print dialog box. (If you do not have a printer, please skip this activity.)

1. Move the insertion point to the top of the document.

2. Choose **File, Print** to open the Print dialog box (see Figure 6.16).

Table 6.1   **Print Dialog Box Options**

Option	Description
Current Printer	In this area, you specify the printer you want to use. You can either print to the default printer (shown on the left side of the Current Printer box), or you can click on Select to choose another printer.
Print Selection	In this area, you specify the portion of the document that you wish to print. Choose *Full Document* to print the entire document. Choose *Current Page* to print the page where the insertion point is located. Choose *Multiple Pages* to print a range of pages. If you selected text in your document before issuing the File, Print command, choose *Selected Text*. Choose *Document Summary* to print a summary of the document if you created one with the File, Document Summary command. Choose *Document on Disk* if you want to print a document stored on disk without opening it in the document window.
Copies	In this text box, you enter the number of copies that you wish to print. The default is one copy.
Generated By	If you want to print multiple copies, you can select Printer in this list box. Then, instead of having to send your document to the printer for each copy, WordPerfect only has to send the document once, and the printer sends the document for each copy thereafter.
Document Settings	In this area of the dialog box, you specify the quality of the print job. You can choose *High*, *Medium*, or *Draft*. You can also specify the print color and tell WordPerfect not to print any graphics in your document.

Figure 6.16   **The Print dialog box**

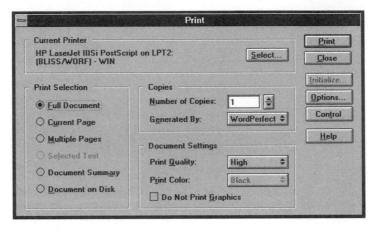

3. In the Print Selection area of the box, choose the **Current Page** option (click on the circle to the left of the option). Click on **Print** to print only the current page (the page on which the insertion point is located), which in this case is page 1. After a page has been sent to the printer, the Print dialog box is automatically closed.

4. Choose **File, Print** to reopen the Print dialog box.

5. In the Print Selection area of the box, select the **Current Page** option.

6. Double-click in the **Number of Copies** text box to select the current value (1); type **2** to tell WordPerfect to print two copies of the current page. Click on **Print** to print these copies.

7. Select all text from the heading *Customer Service* down to the empty paragraph before *International Travel*.

8. Choose **File, Print** to reopen the Print dialog box. In the Print Selection box, note that *Selected Text* is an available option. Whenever you select text in the active document, the Selected Text option becomes available in the Print dialog box.

9. Change the Number of Copies text box back to **1**, if necessary.

10. Choose **Selected Text**, if necessary, and then click on **Print** to print only your selected text.

11. Press **Ctrl+Home** to deselect and move to the top of the document.

USING THE PRINT BUTTON TO ACCESS THE PRINT DIALOG BOX

In addition to choosing File, Print, WordPerfect provides a Print button on the power bar that you can use to open the Print dialog box. To do this, click on the Print button (it displays a miniature printer).

Let's end this chapter's activities by using the Print button to access the Print dialog box and print your entire document. (If you do not have a printer, please skip this activity.)

1. Click on the **Print** button (the one showing a printer) to open the Print dialog box.

2. Click on **Print** to print the entire document.

3. Save the disk file and close the document.

SUMMARY

In this chapter, you learned the basics of page formatting. You now know how to switch between WordPerfect's views, how to insert and delete manual page breaks, how to create headers and footers, how to paginate your document, how to center text vertically, how to change the margins, and how to control the printing of your documents.

Congratulations on completing your foundation of WordPerfect for Windows formatting techniques! You now know how to format your documents at the character, paragraph, and page levels. These skills will allow you to create highly professional-looking documents.

Here is a quick reference guide to the WordPerfect for Windows features introduced in this chapter:

Desired Result	How to Do It
Change to Draft View	Choose **View, Draft**
Change to Two Page View	Choose **View, Two Page**
Change to Page View	Choose **View, Page**

Desired Result	How to Do It
Insert manual page breaks	Place the insertion point to the left of the first character that you want on the new page; choose **Insert, Page Break** (or press **Ctrl+Enter**)
Delete manual page breaks	Place the insertion point directly above the page break; press **Del**
Create a header	Place the insertion point in the first paragraph on the first page on which you want the header to print. Choose **Layout, Header/Footer**, select **Header A** or **B**; click on **Create**. Type the text for the header; select the text and choose the appropriate justification; click on **Placement** and select the appropriate placement; click on **OK**; click on **Close**
Insert a page number in the header or footer	In the Header or Footer window, place the insertion point where you want the page number to appear; click on the **Number** button; click on **Page Number**
Create a footer	Place the insertion point on the first page that you want the footer to print; choose **Layout, Header/ Footer**; select **Footer A** or **B**; click on **Create**. Type the text for the footer; justify the footer text; click on **Placement** and select the appropriate placement; click on **OK**; click on **Close**
Change Left and Right margins	Show the ruler, place the insertion point where you want to change the margins, drag the left margin marker to a new position, drag the right margin marker to a new position

Desired Result	How to Do It
Use the Margins dialog box to change margins	Place the insertion point where you want to change the margins; type in the appropriate margin settings in the Left, Right, Top, and Bottom text boxes; click on **OK**
Center text vertically on the current page	Place the insertion point on the page to be centered; choose **Layout, Page, Center Page**; click on **Current**; click on **OK**

In the next chapter, you will learn how to further enhance your documents by using the Speller, the Thesaurus, the Columns option, and hyphenation.

IF YOU'RE STOPPING HERE

If you need to break off here, please exit WordPerfect for Windows. If you want to proceed directly to the next chapter, please do so now.

CHAPTER 7: ENHANCING YOUR DOCUMENTS

Misspellings and poor word choice can severely undermine the credibility of your documents. In this chapter, we'll introduce you to tools that allow you to *proof* (check) your documents for potential spelling errors. Wording is also a critical factor in determining the effectiveness of a document; using inappropriate words may alienate or confuse your readers. We'll explore the WordPerfect for Windows electronic thesaurus and see how easy it is to find vocabulary alternatives in your documents.

In addition, you can enhance the appearance of your documents by placing the text in newspaper-style columns and hyphenating words at the end of lines.

When you're done working through this chapter, you will know

- How to check the spelling of your documents
- How to use the thesaurus to find alternative words
- How to create and modify newspaper-style columns
- How to hyphenate your document

CHECKING THE SPELLING OF YOUR DOCUMENTS

WordPerfect provides a spelling checker (called *Speller*) that you can use to proof the spelling of your documents. The Speller checks each word in a document against the words in its dictionary and highlights words it does not recognize. The Speller also checks for such common typing mistakes as repeated words (such as *the the*) and irregular capitalization (such as *tHe*).

Many documents contain properly spelled words that are not in the Speller dictionary, such as proper names and acronyms. You can instruct the Speller to continue the spell-check without correcting these words. You can add words to Speller—for example, company names—either to a *supplemental* dictionary (when you use those words in future documents, they will be considered correct); or to a *document* dictionary (the words will be considered correct only for the active document).

Whether you are checking the spelling of an entire document or just one word, you can do so through the Speller dialog box (see Figure 7.1).

There are two ways to access the Speller dialog box:

- Choose *Tools, Speller.*

OR

- Click on the *Speller* button on the power bar.

The first menu on the Speller menu bar (Check) provides you with the options of checking the spelling of

- A single word (at the location of the insertion point)
- A sentence (at the location of the insertion point)
- A paragraph (at the location of the insertion point)
- A single page

Figure 7.1 **The Speller dialog box**

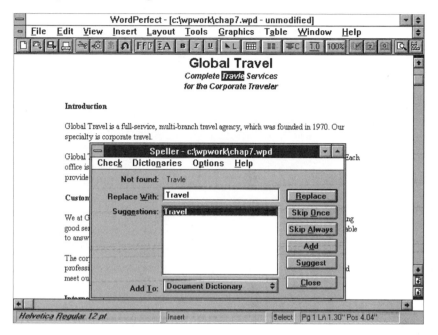

- The entire document
- The document, from the location of the insertion point to the end
- Selected text
- A specified number of pages

When the Speller finds a potential spelling error (a word not included in its internal dictionary), this word appears following "Not found," at the top of the Speller dialog box (see Figure 7.1). A list of suggested spelling corrections appears in the Suggestions list box. The first of these suggested spellings is placed in the Replace With text box. At this point, you can choose from the options described in Table 7.1.

Note: It's a good idea to save your document before and after using the Speller. Saving it before using the Speller ensures that you have a copy of the latest version of the document prior to spell-checking, while saving it after spell-checking saves any spelling changes you have made. This hint is particularly useful in case of disk failure, for example.

Table 7.1   **Speller Options**

Desired Result	Action Required
Leave the word unchanged	If you want to leave the word as it is and continue the spelling check, click on Skip Once. To skip all further occurrences of the word, click on Skip Always.
Correct the spelling	If the correction that you want is in the Replace With text box, click on Replace. If the correction that you want is in the Suggestions list box, click on that correction and then click on Replace. (Or, as a shortcut, simply double-click on the desired correction.) If the correction that you want is not suggested, type the correction in the Replace With text box and then click on Replace.
Add the word to a dictionary	WordPerfect allows you to build a supplemental dictionary (wpspelus.sup) that contains words not found in the Speller's dictionary. This is particularly useful for proper names (such as *Deanna*), abbreviations (such as *ACCTDEPT*), and acronyms (such as *UNICEF*) that you use frequently in your documents. If you want to add the word to a supplemental dictionary, click on Add. In addition, you can save words to a document dictionary, which is used to check only the current document.
Delete the word	If you want to delete the highlighted word from the document, select the word in the Replace With text box, press Del, and then click on the Replace button.
Undo the last correction	If you want to undo the last correction, choose Edit, Undo from the Document menu bar. WordPerfect allows you to undo your last correction. Click on Resume to restart the Speller.
Stop the spelling check	If you want to cancel the spelling-check procedure at any point, click on Close. All changes made up to that point will be preserved.

Table 7.1   **Speller Options (Continued)**

Desired Result   Action Required

Find a spelling   If you are unsure how to spell the highlighted
                     word and WordPerfect cannot find the correct
                     spelling, then type part of the word in the
                     Replace With text box, followed by wildcard
                     characters—for example, **?** (question mark) and
                     * (asterisk). For instance, to find the correct
                     spelling of *itinerary*, you might type *iti** in the
                     Replace With text box, and then click on Sug-
                     gest. Use a ? wildcard character to represent
                     one letter. Use an * wildcard character to repre-
                     sent an unknown number of letters.

 ## CHECKING THE SPELLING OF SELECTED TEXT

Here's the general procedure to spell-check a portion of a document:

- Select the text you wish to check (you can select a single word).
- Choose *Tools, Speller* or click on the *Speller* button.
- Click on *Start* to begin spell-checking the selected text.
- Follow the dialog box prompts to spell-check the selected text.

If you are not running WordPerfect on your computer, please start it now. Close all open documents except for the start-up document—Document1.

Let's begin by opening a document and spell-checking a selected portion of it:

1. Open **chap7.wpd** from your WPWORK directory.
2. Select the heading of the document (the first 3 lines).
3. Choose **Tools, Speller** to open the Speller dialog box.
4. Click on **Check** to display the Check menu options.
5. Observe the Check menu. The Selected Text option is checked. Speller will check only the selected text.
6. Click on **Check** again to close the menu without making any changes.

7. Click on **Start** to start spell-checking the selected text.

8. Observe the dialog box. Above the Replace With box, Speller displays the first word it found that was not in its internal dictionary (*Travle*, which appears in the second line of the heading). In the Suggestions list box, Speller displays a suggested spelling correction (*Travel*). The suggested correction (*Travel*) is also placed in the Replace With box.

9. Click on **Replace** to replace *Travle* with *Travel* and to search for the next potential spelling error in your text selection. In this case, no further errors are found. Speller prompts

        Spell check completed. Close Speller?

10. Click on **Yes** to end the spelling check and return to the document. Note that *Travle* has been corrected to *Travel* (see Figure 7.2).

11. Save the file as **mychap7**.

Figure 7.2   **A corrected spelling error**

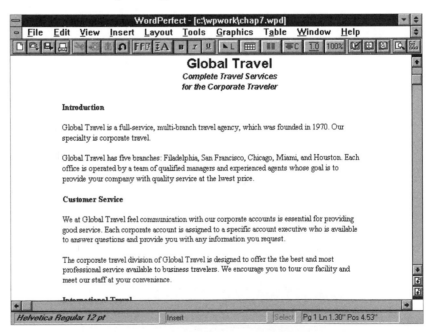

LOOKING UP THE SPELLING OF A WORD

You can also use the Speller to check the spelling of an individual word while you are typing.

Here's the general procedure to look up the spelling of a word:

- Place the insertion point anywhere within the word you want to check.

- Choose *Tools, Speller*.

- Choose *Check, Word*.

- Click on *Start*.

- Select the word you want from those listed in the Suggestions box.

- Click on *Replace*.

- Click on *Close*.

Let's check the spelling of a single word:

1. Scroll to place the heading *International Travel* (near the middle of page 1) at the top of your screen.

2. In the last sentence of the paragraph below *International Travel*, click anywhere on the misspelled word *garantees*.

3. Choose **Tools, Speller** to open the Speller dialog box.

4. Choose **Check, Word** to check the spelling of *garantees* only. Above the Replace With text box, Speller displays the spell-check information (*Spell check: Word*).

5. Click on **Start**. Four suggestions are listed in the Suggestion box.

6. Double-click on the second word in the Suggestions list, **guarantees** (or select **guarantees** and click on **Replace**). You can double-click on a word in the Suggestions list box to use it to replace the misspelled word.

7. Click on **Close** to close the Speller.

8. Save the file.

SPELL-CHECKING THE ENTIRE DOCUMENT

Here is the general procedure to spell-check the entire document:

- Press *Ctrl+Home* to move the insertion point to the top of the document.

- Choose *Tools, Speller* or click on the *Speller* button, located on the power bar (it displays a check mark on a dictionary), to open the Spelling dialog box.

- Click on *Start* to begin the spelling check.

- Follow the dialog box prompts to spell-check the document.

Now let's check the spelling of the entire document:

1. Press **Ctrl+Home** to deselect and move the insertion point to the top of the document.

2. Click on the power bar **Speller** button (the one with the check mark on a dictionary) to open the Speller dialog box.

3. Click on **Start**. Speller displays the first word it finds that is not in its dictionary (*Filadelphia*).

4. Click on **Replace** to replace *Filadelphia* with *Philadelphia* (the entry in the Replace With box) and to search for the next potential spelling error. Speller displays *lwest*. Note that *lowest* is listed as a suggestion, but is not displayed in the Replace With text box (see Figure 7.3).

5. Select (click on) **lowest** to place it in the Replace With text box. Click on **Replace** to replace *lwest* with *lowest* and to search for the next potential spelling error. Speller displays *the the* with the message *Duplicate words* above the Replace With text box. The Replace With text box displays one *the*.

6. Click on **Replace** to replace *the the* with *the* and to search for the next potential spelling error. Speller displays *faxed* with the message "Not found" above the Replace With box. This is a good example of a word that is correct as it appears in the document, but is not included in Speller's dictionary.

7. Click on **Skip Always** to skip *faxed* throughout the document. Speller prompts

```
Spell check completed. Close Speller?
```

Figure 7.3 **Using the Replace With text box**

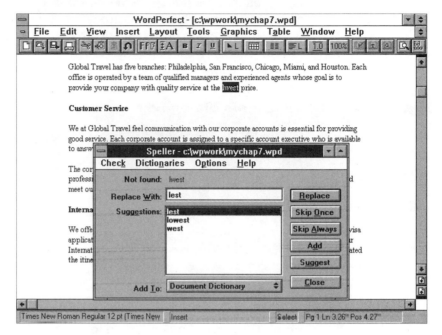

8. Click on **Yes** (or press **Enter**) to close the message box and end the spell-check.

9. Save the disk file.

THE WORDPERFECT THESAURUS

You can use WordPerfect's thesaurus to look up vocabulary alternatives in your documents. The thesaurus provides both *synonyms* (words with similar meanings) and *antonyms* (words with opposite meanings). Having a powerful and lightning-fast electronic thesaurus at your fingertips can greatly enhance the quality of the writing in your documents.

When you choose *Tools, Thesaurus* from the menu, the Thesaurus dialog box is opened in the lower part of the application window. The central area of the dialog box contains three columns, as shown in Figure 7.4. The *headword*, the word you are looking up, appears at the top of the first column. Word references appear underneath the headword. In this list, additional *headwords* (that is, words that are entries in the WordPerfect thesaurus) are preceded by bullets. References are divided into as many as four subgroups underneath each headword: nouns, verbs, adjectives, and antonyms. Not all headwords have all four subgroups.

Figure 7.4   **Thesaurus dialog box**

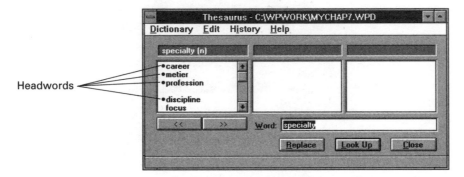

Here's the general procedure to look up synonyms and antonyms for a word in your document:

- Place the insertion point in the word you want to look up.

- Choose *Tools, Thesaurus* to open the Thesaurus dialog box and display a list of alternatives (including other headwords) related to the selected word.

- To see a longer list of alternatives, double-click on one of the headwords. To replace your original word, select a new word by clicking on it.

- Click on *Replace*.

- To look up another synonym, type a word in the Word text box.

- Click on *Look Up*. If you select a word that is not found in the WordPerfect Thesaurus, then the message "Word not found" appears at the bottom of the Thesaurus dialog box.

- Click on *Close* to close the Thesaurus.

Let's practice using the WordPerfect thesaurus to find synonyms:

1. Move to the top of the document, if necessary (press **Ctrl+Home**).

2. Place the insertion point in the word *specialty* (located in the second sentence of the paragraph beginning *Global Travel is a full-service*).

3. Choose **Tools, Thesaurus** to open the Thesaurus dialog box (see Figure 7.4).

4. Observe the left column: A list is displayed with several synonyms for the word specialty.

5. Use the scroll arrows to view the list. Any word preceded by a bullet is a headword (you can double-click on it to display its synonyms and antonyms).

6. Double-click on **forte** to select it. The center column displays a list of synonyms for *forte*.

7. Use the scroll arrows to view the list of words in the center column. It displays a list of synonyms and antonyms for *forte*. The antonyms appear at the end of the list. (In this case, there is only one antonym—*weakness*—listed.)

8. In the center column, select **strength**. The word *strength* now appears in the Word text box. Compare your screen to Figure 7.5.

Figure 7.5   **Selected synonym**

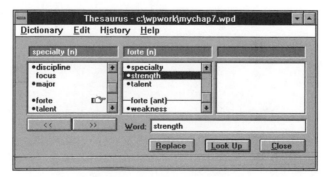

9. Click on **Replace** to replace *specialty* with *strength*.

10. Save the file.

Now let's use the thesaurus to find antonyms:

1. Place the insertion point anywhere in the word *qualified* (located in the paragraph beginning with *Global Travel has five branches*).

2. Click on the power bar **Thesaurus** button (next to the Speller button, it displays an open book with a *T*).

3. Scroll to view the list of alternatives. Antonyms are located at the end of the list (see Figure 7.6). Let's say that you found none of these antonyms appealing and decided to cancel the thesaurus look-up procedure.

4. Click on **Close** to close the Thesaurus dialog box and return to your document.

Figure 7.6   **Displaying antonyms**

Antonym list

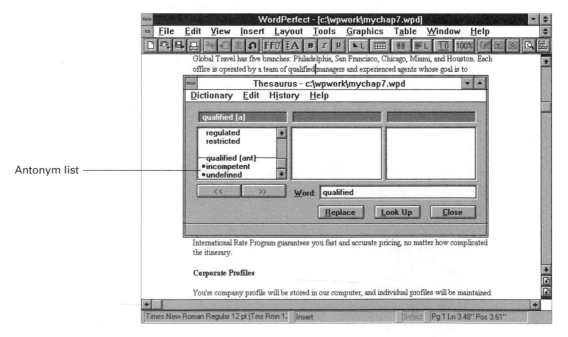

CREATING NEWSPAPER-STYLE COLUMNS

Once you're sure everything in your document is spelled correctly and you've gone to the trouble to look up synonyms and find the perfect word, you might want to enhance the appearance of your document by placing the text in columns.

You can define your columns before typing the text, or you can reformat existing text into newspaper-style columns.

Here's the general procedure to create newspaper-style columns:

* Place the insertion point where you want the columns to begin.

* Choose *Layout, Columns, Define*, or double-click on the *Columns* button in the power bar to open the Columns dialog box.

* Specify the desired number of columns in the Number of Columns text box (2 is the default).

* Click on *OK*.

Note: You can specify up to 24 columns of text per page.

Let's create a newspaper-style column format:

1. Click on the **Page Zoom Full** button (the second power bar button from the right) to view the entire page. Notice that all of the text is currently in a standard, single-column format.

2. Click on the **Page Zoom Full** button again to return to 100 percent magnification.

3. Place the insertion point to the left of the *I* in the *Introduction* heading, near the top of the page.

4. Choose **Layout, Columns, Define** to open the Columns dialog box (see Figure 7.7).

5. Observe the dialog box. In the Number of Columns text box, 2 is the default setting. The Sample box displays a sample of the two-column format. We want to place the text in two columns.

6. Click on **OK** to close the dialog box and return to the document.

7. Observe the text. All of the text from *Introduction* to the end of the document is formatted as two columns.

Figure 7.7   **The Columns dialog box**

Sample box ———

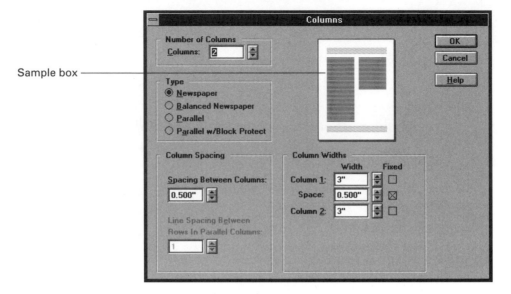

8. Choose **View, Two Page** to view the entire document.

9. Return to Page view (choose **View, Page**).

10. Save the file.

MODIFYING MULTICOLUMN TEXT FORMATS

When you create multiple columns, WordPerfect automatically apportions even amounts of space within each column and between columns, based on your document's margins. However, you can modify these values. For example, by default, WordPerfect places half an inch of space between each column. Depending on the effect you desire, as well as how many columns appear on the page, you might want to increase or reduce this amount.

Here's the general procedure to change the space between columns:

• Place the insertion point in the section containing the columns.

• Choose *Layout, Columns, Define*, or double-click on the *Columns Define* button in the power bar.

- In the Spacing Between Columns box, specify the desired width.
- Click on *OK*.

You can also insert a vertical dividing line between adjacent columns, which can produce a visually pleasing effect and further help the eye separate the columns. This is particularly true of columns that are by necessity spaced closely together.

Here's the general procedure to add a vertical line between columns:

- Place the insertion point in the section containing the columns.
- Choose *Layout, Columns, Border/Fill*.
- Place the mouse pointer on the *Border* button.
- Press and hold the *left mouse* button.
- Drag to select the *Vertical Line Between Columns* option.
- Release the mouse button.
- Click on *OK*.

Let's change the space between our columns, and then add a vertical line between them:

1. Place the insertion point to the left of the *I* in *Introduction*.

2. Observe the space between the columns. It is large enough to be reduced slightly to make more room within the columns for text. Notice also that a few lines of text have wrapped up to the second column, above the *Corporate Profiles* heading.

3. Double-click on the **Columns Define** button (the ninth button from the right on the power bar) to open the Columns dialog box.

4. Click twice on the Spacing Between Columns down increment indicator to decrease the amount of space between the columns of text to **0.3** inch or as close to this value as your configuration will allow.

5. Click on **OK**. The text columns now appear closer together. Notice that the text that earlier wrapped to the second column has now moved to the bottom of the first column, placing the

Corporate Profiles heading neatly at the top of the second column.

6. Verify that the insertion point is located before the *I* in *Introduction*.

7. Choose **Layout, Columns, Border/Fill** to open the Column Border dialog box (see Figure 7.8).

Figure 7.8   **The Column Border dialog box**

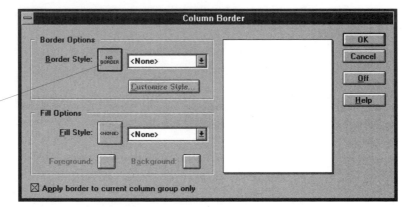

8. Place the mouse pointer on the **Border Style** button (currently it displays *No Border*).

9. Press and hold the **left mouse** button to display the Border options; then drag down to select the Vertical Line Between Columns option (it is the second choice in the last row of border options).

10. Click on **OK** and compare your screen to Figure 7.9.

11. Save the disk file.

Note: Remember that, if you prefer, you may use the Layout, Columns menu option to add a vertical line rather than clicking on the Columns button.

Figure 7.9   **Inserting a vertical line between columns**

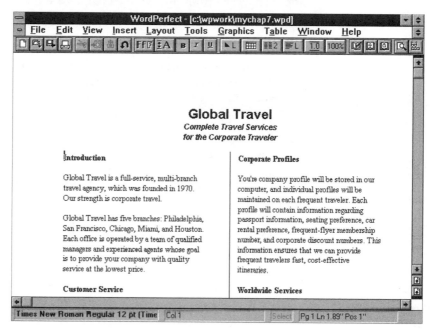

HYPHENATION

In Chapter 5, you learned that text that is left-justified has a ragged—or uneven—right margin. With a two-column document, the right margin is particularly uneven. To maintain the ragged margin but reduce raggedness, you can hyphenate the text. Fully justified text has smooth margins, but tends to also have rivers of space running through the columns. In either case, to fill in the gaps and improve the text fit, you can, again, hyphenate the text.

Here's the general procedure to hyphenate text in a document:

- Place the insertion point at the top of the document (or wher- ever you'd like hyphenation to begin).

- Choose *Layout, Line, Hyphenation* to open the Line Hyphen- ation dialog box.

- Click on *Hyphenation On*.

- Click on *OK*.

To turn off hyphenation, open the Line Hyphenation dialog box, and click on Hyphenation On to remove the *X* from the box.

Let's hyphenate a document, and then examine the effects of hyphenation:

1. Observe the document: It is left-justified, so it has a ragged-right margin. Because we changed to a two-column format, there is less room for text on each line; thus, the right margin is more uneven than usual.

2. Move the insertion point to the top of the document (press **Ctrl+Home**).

3. Choose **Layout, Line, Hyphenation** to open the Line Hyphenation dialog box.

4. Click on **Hyphenation On**, located toward the top of the dialog box. An X appears in the box to the left. Compare your screen to Figure 7.10.

Figure 7.10 **Turning on hyphenation**

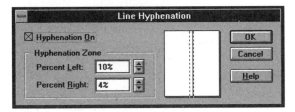

5. Click on **OK** to begin the hyphenation.

6. Click on **Insert Hyphen** to hyphenate *includes*. (**Note:** Depending upon the printer and font you have installed and selected, you either may not need to perform this step, or you may need to insert hyphens for different words.)

7. Observe the document; it is now hyphenated.

8. Save the document.

9. Close the file.

SUMMARY

In this chapter, you learned how to use WordPerfect for Windows's Speller and Thesaurus to help you write more efficiently and accurately. You also learned how to use newspaper-style columns and hyphenation to improve the appearance of documents.

Here's a quick reference guide to the WordPerfect features introduced in this chapter:

Desired Result	How to Do It
Spell-check selected text	Select the text you want to spell-check; choose **Tools, Speller**; click on **Start**; select the word you want from those listed in the Suggestions box; click on **Replace** to replace the word, click on **Skip Once** to leave the word unchanged one time, click on **Skip Always** to leave the word unchanged throughout the document, click on **Add** to add the word to the Document dictionary; click on **Close**
Spell-check an entire document	Place the insertion point at the top of the document; choose **Tools, Speller**; click on **Start**; select the word you want from those listed in the Suggestions box; click on **Replace** to replace the word, click on **Skip Once** to leave the word unchanged one time, click on **Skip Always** to leave the word unchanged throughout the document, click on **Add** to add the word to the Document dictionary; click on **Close**
Look up the spelling of a word	Place the insertion point anywhere within the word you want to check; choose **Tools, Speller**; choose **Check, Word**; click on **Start**; select the word you want from those listed in the Suggestions box; click on **Replace**; click on **Close**

Desired Result	How to Do It
Look up synonyms and antonyms for a word in your document	Place the insertion point in the word you want to look up; choose **Tools, Thesaurus** to open the Thesaurus dialog box and display a list of alternatives (including other headwords) related to the selected word. To see a longer list of alternatives, double-click on one of the headwords. To replace your original word, select a new word by clicking on it; click on **Replace**. To look up another synonym, type a word in the Word text box; click on **Lookup**; click on **Close**
Create newspaper-style columns	Place the insertion point where you want the columns to begin; choose **Layout, Columns, Define**; or, double-click on the **Columns** button in the power bar; specify the desired number of columns in the Number of Columns text box; click on **OK**
Change the space between columns	Place the insertion point in the section containing the columns; choose **Layout, Columns, Define**, or double-click on the **Columns Define** button in the power bar; in the Spacing Between Columns box, specify the desired width; click on **OK**
Add a vertical line between columns	Place the insertion point in the section containing the columns; choose **Layout, Columns, Border/Fill**; place the mouse pointer on the **Border** button; press and hold the **left mouse** button; drag to select the **Vertical Line Between Columns** option; release the mouse button; click on **OK**
Hyphenate text in a document	Place the insertion point at the top of the document (or wherever you'd like hyphenation to begin); choose **Layout, Line, Hyphenation**; click on **Hyphenation On**; click on **OK**

Desired Result	How to Do It
Turn off hyphenation	Open the Line Hyphenation dialog box; click on **Hyphenation On** to remove the X from the box

In the next chapter, you will learn to use and customize the Word-Perfect for Windows button bar, an area which allows you to perform many of the functions you've learned about without having to use the menu or press keys on the keyboard.

IF YOU'RE STOPPING HERE

If you need to break off here, please exit WordPerfect. If you want to proceed directly to the next chapter, please do so now.

CHAPTER 8: INTRODUCTION TO THE BUTTON BAR

Displaying and
Using the Default
Button Bar

Creating a New
Button Bar

Customizing the
Button Bar

Changing the
Button Bar
Options

Deleting a Button
Bar

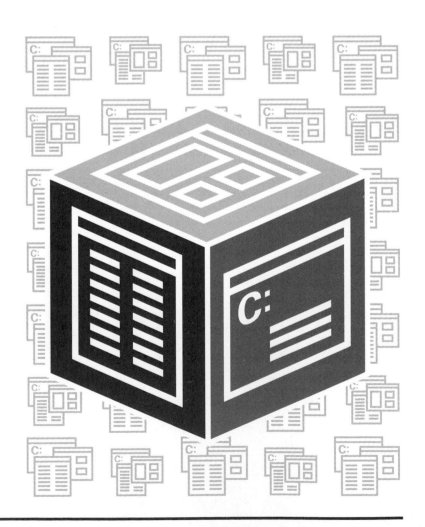

You've learned that you can use the menu, the power bar, and shortcut keys to issue commands. WordPerfect for Windows provides you with one more option for accessing many of the program's features—an area known as the *button bar*. This chapter introduces the basics of using the button bar to perform some of WordPerfect's commands.

When you're done working through this chapter, you will know

- How to use the button bar
- How to create and customize your own button bars
- How to save a button bar
- How to delete a button from a button bar
- How to delete a button bar

DISPLAYING AND USING THE DEFAULT BUTTON BAR

The button bar is similar to the power bar in that it enables you to quickly access menu commands and features that you use frequently. However, while WordPerfect always displays the same power bar (allowing you access to many of WordPerfect's general commands—such as Cut, Copy, and Paste), the button bar is context-sensitive. Twelve button bars are automatically included when you install WordPerfect for Windows. Each button bar contains a set of related commands and features. So, if you are formatting the text of a document, you might have the Font button bar displayed. Then, when you need to apply a text attribute that is usually available only in the Font dialog box—Redline, for example—you can simply click on the Redline button in the Font button bar to apply Redline to the selected text. The default button bar (*WordPerfect*) contains buttons for some of the most common menu commands and WordPerfect features that you might need (that can't be accessed through the power bar) as you create and edit your document.

Here's the general procedure to view the WordPerfect button bar:

- Choose *View, Button Bar*. The default button bar appears above the power bar. The button bar stays on until you turn it off.

Here's the general procedure to turn the button bar off:

- Choose *View, Button Bar*. Or, place the mouse pointer on the button bar, click the *right mouse* button, and choose *Hide Button Bar*.

If you are not running WordPerfect on your computer, please start it now. Close all open documents except for the start-up document—Document1. Let's display the WordPerfect button bar, and then use it to access some of the program's features:

1. Open **chap8.wpd** from your WPWORK directory.

2. Choose **View, Button Bar** to display the button bar above the power bar, as shown in Figure 8.1.

Figure 8.1   WordPerfect for Windows button bar

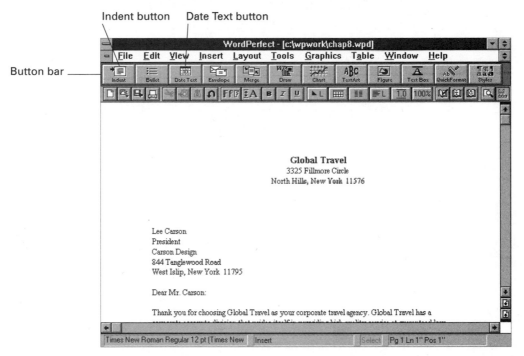

3. Observe the button bar: It contains buttons that will access a number of WordPerfect commands.

4. Place the mouse pointer on the third button from the left on the button bar (do not click the mouse button) and observe the long prompt in the title bar. This button inserts the current date in your document. If you don't remember what a particular button does, you can always place the mouse pointer on that button and read the prompt.

5. Place the mouse pointer on the first button on the button bar, and observe the long prompt in the title bar. The first button indents your paragraph. Let's indent a few paragraphs.

6. Scroll down to view the tabbed table in the body of the letter.

7. Place the insertion point to the left of the *M* in *March 3* (in the first row of the table).

8. Click on the **Indent** button on the button bar (the first button from the left). The first line of the tabbed table is indented (see Figure 8.2).

Figure 8.2   **Indenting the first line of the tabbed table**

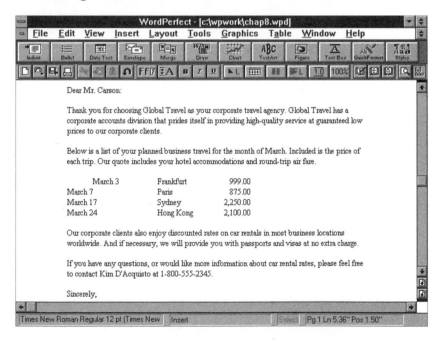

9. Place the insertion point to the left of the *M* in *March 7* (in the second line of the table) and click on the **Indent** button to indent the second line of the tabbed table.

PRACTICE YOUR SKILLS

Let's use the button bar to finish indenting the table paragraphs and to insert the current date in the letter:

1. Indent the third and fourth lines of the tabbed table. (**Hint:** You can only indent one line at a time.)

2. Place the insertion point at the top of the document.

3. Display the nonprinting symbols (**Hint:** Choose **View, Show ¶**.)

4. Place the insertion point to the left of the second paragraph mark below the *Global Travel* heading (see Figure 8.3 if you aren't sure where to place the insertion point).

Figure 8.3   **The letter with date inserted**

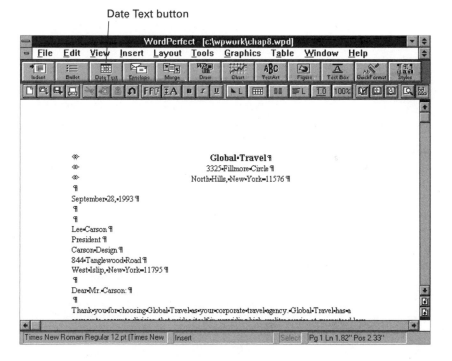

5. Click on the **Date Text** button. (**Hint:** It is the third button from the left on the button bar.)

6. Hide the nonprinting symbols. (**Hint:** Choose **View, Show ¶**.)

USING THE BUTTON BAR TO CREATE AN ENVELOPE

You can use the button bar to quickly and easily address envelopes for your business letters. Here's the general procedure to create an envelope for a letter:

- Place the insertion point at the top of the letter.

- Click on the *Envelope* button on the button bar.

- Click in the Return Address text box, if necessary.

- Type a return address; or, select an address from the Address drop-down list below the Return Address text box.

- Verify that the mailing address is correct.

- Click on *Print* to print the envelope; or, click on *Append to Doc* to close the Envelope dialog box and attach the envelope to the end of the letter.

Let's use the button bar to create an envelope for our letter:

1. Press **Ctrl+Home** to place the insertion point at the top of the document.

2. Click on the **Envelope** button (located on the button bar, it displays a miniature envelope) to open the Envelope dialog box (see Figure 8.4). WordPerfect reads the mailing address from your letter and places it in the Mailing Addresses text box.

3. Place the insertion point in the Return Addresses text box, if necessary.

4. Type **Global Travel** and press **Enter**.

5. Type **3325 Fillmore Circle** and press **Enter**.

6. Type **North Hills, New York 11576**.

7. Click on **Append to Doc** to exit from the Envelope dialog box without printing the envelope.

8. Scroll to the bottom of the document, if necessary. The envelope is attached to the end of the letter, but you can't really tell that it's an envelope.

9. Place the insertion point at the top of the document (press **Ctrl+Home**) and switch to Two Page view. Observe the letter and envelope (see Figure 8.5).

10. Return to Page view (choose **View, Page**).

Figure 8.4   **Envelope dialog box**

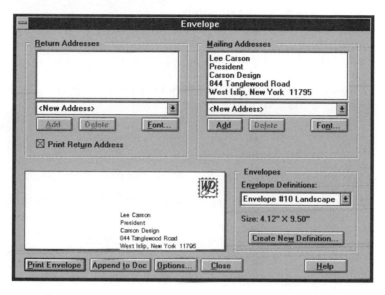

Figure 8.5   **The letter and envelope in Two Page view**

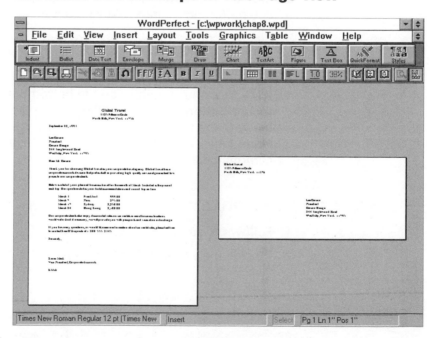

11. Save the file as **mychap8**.

12. Close the file.

 ## SWITCHING AMONG BUTTON BARS

You can quickly and easily move between the different button bars to find the one you want.

Here's the general procedure for switching among button bars:

- Display the button bar, if necessary.

- Place the mouse pointer anywhere on the button bar.

- Click the *right mouse* button to display the list of available button bars.

- Choose the appropriate button bar.

Let's take a look at some of the other button bars that are installed with WordPerfect for Windows:

1. Place the mouse pointer on the button bar.

2. Click the **right mouse** button to display the list of button bars and button bar features (see Figure 8.6).

3. Click on **Font** to display the Font button bar. It displays a set of buttons providing quick access to some of WordPerfect's text attribute commands.

4. Place the mouse pointer on the button bar, click the **right mouse** button, and choose **Page** to replace the Font button bar with the Page button bar. It displays a set of buttons providing quick access to some of WordPerfect's page layout commands.

PRACTICE YOUR SKILLS

1. Follow the steps above to display the Layout button bar.

2. Display the WordPerfect button bar.

Figure 8.6   **The button bar options**

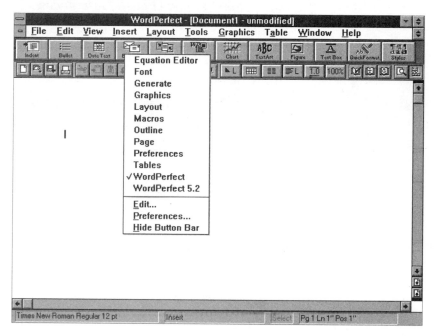

CREATING A NEW BUTTON BAR

WordPerfect's default button bar contains buttons that either perform commands, such as inserting the current date, or launch
some of WordPerfect's internal programs, such as *WPDraw* and
TextArt. (WPDraw and TextArt are not covered in this book. If you
want information about them, consult your WordPerfect user's
guide.) You might find that this button bar does not contain the
commands that you use most frequently. Although you can edit
the default button bar, you might want to create and save your
own custom button bars instead.

You can create button bars specifically designed for your type of
documents or work situation. You might want to design one button bar for working with graphics and another for working with
long documents. (You learned in the last section how to switch
among the button bars.)

Here's the general procedure to create a button bar:

•   Display the button bar, if necessary.

- Choose *File, Preferences*. Or, click the *right mouse* button on the button bar and choose *Preferences*.

- Double-click on the *Button Bar* icon to open the Button Bar Preferences dialog box. (**Note:** The Button Bar Preferences dialog box opens automatically when you choose Preferences from the button bar.)

- Click on *Create* to create a new button bar.

- Type a name for the button bar.

- Click on *OK*. The Button Bar Editor opens, and an empty button bar space is created.

- Select the appropriate options and click on *Add Button* to add the button to your button bar.

- Repeat the above step, as necessary.

- Click on *OK* to close the Button Bar Editor.

- Click on *Close* to close the Button Bar Preferences dialog box without selecting your new button bar. Or, click on *Select* to close the Button Bar Preferences dialog box and activate your new button bar.

- Click on *Close* to close the Preferences dialog box, if necessary.

Note: If you create a button bar with more buttons than can fit on one row, scroll arrows will appear to the right of the button bar. You can scroll the button bar by clicking on the up or down scroll arrows until you find the button you want.

Let's create a new button bar:

1. Choose **File, Preferences** to open the Preferences dialog box.

2. Double-click on the **Button Bar** icon to open the Button Bar Preferences dialog box (see Figure 8.7). It displays a list of available button bars along with the option to select, create, edit, copy, or delete a button bar.

3. Click on **Create** to create a new button bar. The Create Button Bar dialog box opens (see Figure 8.8).

4. Type **mybutton** to name the new button bar.

5. Click on **OK**. The Button Bar Editor opens and an empty button bar is displayed.

Figure 8.7   **The Button Bar Preferences dialog box**

Figure 8.8   **The Create Button Bar dialog box**

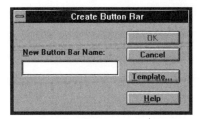

6. Observe the Button Bar Editor (see Figure 8.9). You can choose to have a button activate a feature (a menu command), play a keyboard script (typed text), launch another program (for example, *Paintbrush*), or play a macro (a series of commands and keystrokes). By default, Activate a Feature is selected.

Note: We do not cover macros in this book; if you would like to learn more about them, consult your WordPerfect user's guide.

7. Verify that the Feature Categories drop-down list displays *File*.

8. Scroll through the Features list. This is a list of all the commands you can access through the File menu.

9. In the Features list, click on **Close** to select it. A picture and description of the Close button are displayed at the bottom of the dialog box (see Figure 8.9).

Figure 8.9   **Button Bar Editor - mybutton dialog box**

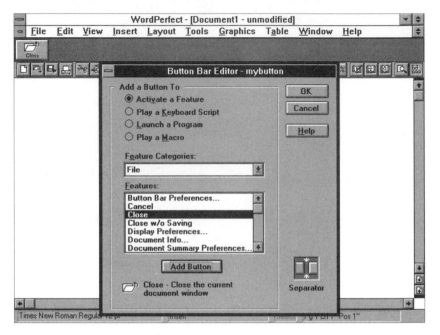

10. Click on **Add Button** to add the Close button to the empty button bar.

11. From the Feature Categories drop-down list, select **Edit** to display the Edit menu commands in the Features list.

12. Click on **Find** in the Features list and click on **Add Button** to add the Find button to the button bar.

You can also add a button to the button bar by selecting its corresponding command from the menu. Let's do this:

1. Choose **File, Save As** and observe the button bar. A Save As button is added to the button bar.

2. Choose **File, Exit** to add an Exit button.

3. Choose **Edit, Go To** to add a Go To button.

4. Choose **Edit, Replace** to add a Replace button.

5. Choose **View, Draft** to add a Draft view button.

6. Choose **View, Two Page** to add a Two Page view button.

7. Choose **View, Page** to add a Page view button.

8. Choose **View, Ruler Bar** to add a Ruler button.

9. Choose **View, Show ¶** to add a ShoSymbols button.

10. Choose **View, Reveal Codes** to add a RevCodes button.

11. Choose **Help, Contents** to add a Help button.

Now that we've finished adding buttons to the button bar, let's finish creating it:

1. Click on **OK** to close the Button Bar Editor and return to the Button Bar Preferences dialog box. Notice that *mybutton* is a choice in the Available Button Bars list.

2. Click on **Select** to close the Button Bar Preferences dialog box and activate the new button bar.

3. Click on **Close** to close the Preferences dialog box.

4. Observe the scroll arrows on the right side of the button bar: The button bar contains more buttons than can be displayed at one time. Notice that the last few buttons you created are not visible; you need to scroll down to display them.

5. Click on the down scroll arrow (the bottom arrow on the right of the button bar). The last few buttons are now visible.

CUSTOMIZING THE BUTTON BAR

You can rearrange, add, or delete buttons on any button bar. When you edit a button bar, your changes are visible immediately.

MOVING BUTTONS

One way to edit or customize a button bar is to change the order in which the buttons are displayed on it. Perhaps you would like to place often-used buttons at the beginning of the button bar.

Here's the general procedure to move a button:

- Open the Button Bar Preferences dialog box (click the *right mouse* button on the button bar and choose *Preferences*).

- Select the button bar you want to edit.

- Click on *Edit*.

- Place the mouse pointer on the button to be moved.

- Drag the button to the new location. When you release the mouse button, the button is repositioned on the button bar.

- Click on *OK.*

- Click on *Close.*

Note: To place a button at either end of the button bar, you need to drag the button as far toward that end as it will go. To place a button between two other buttons, drag it so that it is covering the border between the two buttons.

Let's change the positions of buttons on the button bar:

1. Place the mouse pointer on the button bar and click the **right mouse** button; then choose **Preferences** to open the Button Bar Preferences dialog box.

2. Verify that *mybutton* is selected in the button bar list.

3. Click on **Edit** to open the Button Bar Editor and edit *mybutton.*

4. Point to the **Close** button.

5. Drag the **Close** button between the *Save As* and *Exit* buttons; then release the mouse button. The *Save As* button moves to the left, and the *Close* button is moved between the *Save As* and *Exit* buttons.

PRACTICE YOUR SKILLS

Drag the **Find** button between the *Exit* and *Go To* buttons to place it before the Go To button.

ADDING BUTTONS

In addition to moving buttons, you can add buttons to your button bar. And, your buttons aren't limited to menu choices. You can add buttons that will type keystrokes for you. For example, you can create a button that types your mailing address.

Here's the general procedure to add buttons to the button bar:

- Open the Button Bar Preferences dialog box (click the *right mouse* button on the button bar and choose *Preferences*).

- Select the button bar you want to add a button to and click on *Edit.*

- Add the appropriate button.
- Click on *OK*.
- Click on *Close*.

Let's add a button that types the Global Travel mailing address:

1. Verify that the Button Bar Editor is still open.
2. Click on **Play a Keyboard Script**.
3. Place the insertion point in the text box, if necessary.
4. Type the following mailing address:

   Global Travel

   3325 Fillmore Circle

   North Hills, New York 11576

   (Press **Enter** at the end of each line.) Figure 8.10 displays the complete button script.

Figure 8.10   **Creating a button to play a keyboard script**

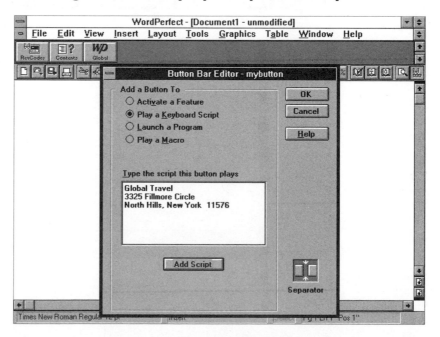

5. Click on **Add Script** to add the Global Travel mailing address button to the button bar.

6. Observe the new button. When you add a button to play a keyboard script, WordPerfect uses the first word of the script to name the button.

7. Click on **OK**; then click on **Close** to close the Button Bar Editor and Button Bar Preferences dialog boxes.

Let's try the Global Travel mailing address button:

8. Click on the **Global** button (you might need to click on the button bar's down scroll arrow to see the new button). The Global Travel mailing address is typed at the insertion point (see Figure 8.11).

Figure 8.11   **The Global Travel mailing address**

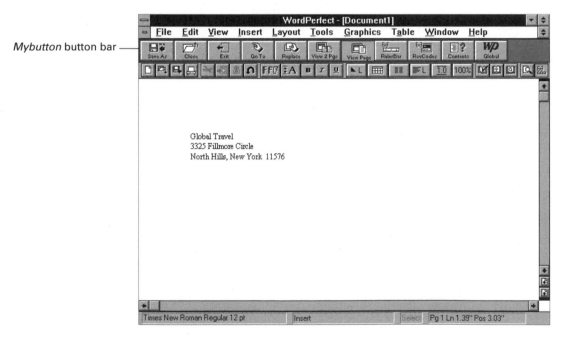

DELETING BUTTONS

You can further edit the button bar by removing buttons that you no longer need. Here's the general procedure to delete a button:

- Open the Button Bar Preferences dialog box.
- Select the appropriate button bar.
- Click on *Edit*.
- Place the mouse pointer on the button to be deleted.
- Drag the button down and off the button bar. When you release the mouse button, the button is deleted.
- Click on *OK*.
- Click on *Close*.

Let's delete some buttons from the button bar:

1. Open the Button Bar Preferences dialog box (click the **right mouse** button on the button bar and choose **Preferences**).

2. Verify that *mybutton* is selected in the Button Bar list; then click on **Edit** to open the Button Bar Editor.

3. Point to the **ShoSymbols** button (you might need to scroll to display it).

4. Drag the **ShoSymbols** button down off the button bar. Do not release the mouse button. When you drag a button off the button bar, the title bar of the dialog box reads *Delete this item* and the mouse pointer displays a button being thrown in a trash can.

5. Release the mouse button. The ShoSymbols button is removed from the button bar.

6. Point to the **View Draft** button (you might need to scroll to see it) and drag it down off the button bar.

7. Drag the **Find** button down off the button bar. The entire button bar now is visible, and the scroll arrows are gone.

8. Click on **OK**; then click on **Close** to close the Button Bar Editor and Button Bar Preferences dialog boxes. Compare your button bar to that shown in Figure 8.11.

CHANGING THE BUTTON BAR OPTIONS

WordPerfect gives you the option of changing the position of the button bar. You can place it vertically down the left or right side of the WordPerfect window, or horizontally along the top or bottom of the document window, or as a floating palette as shown in Figure 8.12. You can display the buttons with both text and icons, with text only, or with icons only.

Figure 8.12   **The button bar as a palette**

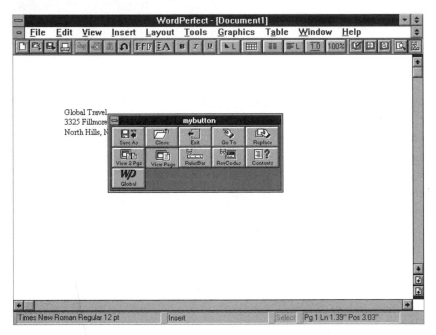

Note: Where you display the button bar, whether the buttons contain icons, and the type of monitor you are using will determine how many buttons can be displayed at one time.

Here's the general procedure to change the position and appearance of the button bar:

- Open the Button Bar Preferences dialog box.

- Select the appropriate button bar.

- Click on *Options*.

- Select the appropriate options.

- Click on *OK*.

- Click on *Close*.

Let's change the position and appearance of the button bar:

1. Open the Button Bar Preferences dialog box (click the **right mouse** button on the button bar and choose **Preferences**).

2. Verify that *mybutton* is selected in the Button Bar list and click on **Options** to open the Button Bar Options dialog box (see Figure 8.13). You can change the appearance and position of the button bar here.

Figure 8.13　　**Button Bar Options dialog box with changed options**

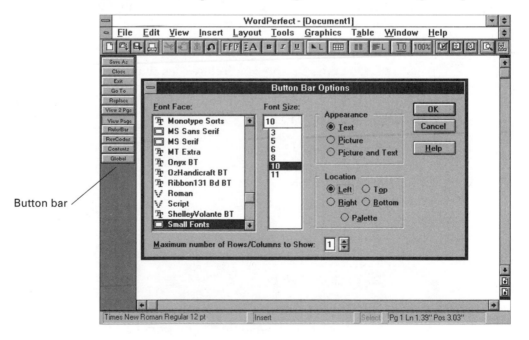

Button bar

3. In the Location box, click on **Left** to move the button bar to the left side of the window.

4. In the Appearance box, click on **Text** to display the buttons as text only. Compare your screen to Figure 8.13.

5. Click on **OK** and click on **Close**. The button bar is displayed on the left side of the window, with the buttons containing only text.

PRACTICE YOUR SKILLS

1. Change the location of the mybutton button bar to **Top**. (**Hint:** Use the Button Bar Options dialog box.)

2. Change the appearance of the buttons to **Picture and Text**.

3. Display the WordPerfect button bar.

DELETING A BUTTON BAR

If you no longer need a button bar, you can delete it in the Button Bar Preferences dialog box.

Here's the general procedure to delete a button bar:

- Open the Button Bar Preferences dialog box.

- Highlight the button bar you want to delete.

- Click on *Delete*.

- Click on *OK*.

Note: Before you delete a button bar, make sure it is not the active button bar.

Let's delete the button bar we created in this chapter:

1. Open the Button Bar Preferences dialog box.

2. Select **mybutton** from the Button Bar list.

3. Click on **Delete**.

4. Click on **Yes** to delete the button bar.

5. Observe the Available Button Bars list. Mybutton is not listed.

6. Click on **Close**. The mybutton button bar has been annihilated.

7. Close **Document1** without saving changes.

SUMMARY

In this chapter, you learned how to display and use the WordPerfect for Windows button bar as a quick alternative to using the menu. You also learned how to create and edit button bars to suit your own needs and how to delete button bars.

Here is a quick reference guide to the WordPerfect for Windows features introduced in this chapter:

Desired Result	How to Do It
Display the button bar	Choose **View, Button Bar**
Hide the button bar	Choose **View, Button Bar**
Switch among button bars	Place the mouse pointer on the button bar; click the **right mouse** button; select the appropriate button bar
Create an envelope	Click on the **Envelope** button; type the return address, if necessary; type the mailing address, If necessary; click on **Print** to print the envelope, or click on **Append to Doc** to attach the envelope to the document
Create a button bar	Choose **File, Preferences**; double-click on the **Button Bar** icon; click on **Create**; name the button bar; click on **OK**; choose the commands you want from the menu bar or the Button Bar Editor (if you use the Button Bar Editor, click on **Add Button** to add the buttons to the button bar); click on OK; click on **Close**; click on **Close** again, if necessary.

Desired Result	How to Do It
Move a button	Choose **File, Preferences**; double-click on the **Button Bar** icon; select the button bar; click on **Edit**; place the mouse pointer on the button you want to move; drag the button to the new position; release the mouse button; click on **OK**; click on **Close**; click on **Close** again, if necessary
Open the Button Bar Preferences dialog box	Place the mouse pointer on the button bar; click the **right mouse** button; choose **Preferences**
Add a button	Open the Button Bar Preferences dialog box; select the button bar you want to add a button to; click on **Edit**; add the button; click on **OK**; click on **Close**
Delete a button	Open the Button Bar Preferences dialog box; select the button bar you want to delete a button from; click on **Edit**; drag the button down off the button bar; click on **OK**; click on **Close**
Change the position and appearance of the button bar	Open the Button Bar Preferences dialog box; select the button bar you want to change; click on **Options**; select the appropriate options; click on **OK**; click on **Close**
Delete a button bar	Open the Button Bar Preferences dialog box; select the button bar you want to delete; click on **Delete**; click on **Close**

In the next chapter, you will learn how to create, modify, and enhance tables.

IF YOU'RE STOPPING HERE

If you need to break off here, please exit WordPerfect. If you want to proceed directly to the next chapter, please do so now.

CHAPTER 9: WORKING WITH TABLES

Creating Tables

Modifying Tables

Enhancing Tables

Converting Tabbed
Text to a Table

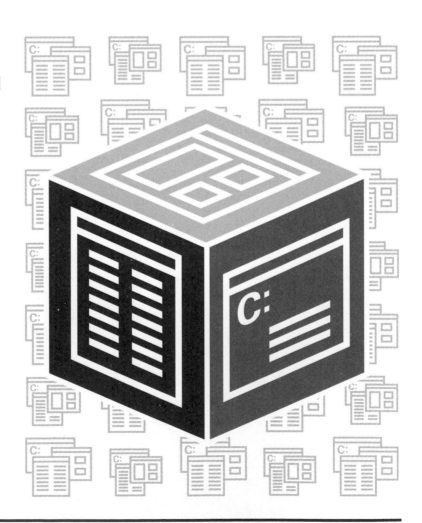

If you want to arrange information in a table, you can do so by setting tabs. However, creating tabbed tables is a slow and tricky process; you must figure out exactly how the table should look, measure the width of each column, and then set tabs that correspond to each measurement. (You've already seen an example of a tabbed table in Chapter 5.) You can also run into problems if your text does not fit between your tabs.

The WordPerfect for Windows Table feature allows you to create rows and columns of information without having to set tabs. You can even convert tabbed text to a table. A table can be useful for enhancing the presentation of data in your document, for creating side-by-side paragraphs, and for organizing information used in form letters.

When you're done working through this chapter, you will know

- How to create a table
- How to modify a table
- How to enhance a table
- How to convert tabbed text to a table

CREATING TABLES

Here's the general procedure to insert a table into your document:

- Place the insertion point where you want to insert the table.
- Choose *Table, Create* or click on the *Table* button in the power bar.

When you create tables by using the Menu command, you specify the number of columns and rows in the Create Table dialog box. You can also specify the width of the columns. When you use the Table button to create tables, you drag on the Table button grid to specify the number of columns and rows. (You'll learn how to use the Table button grid later in this section.) WordPerfect creates a table that fills the area inside the margins. The width of the columns adjusts automatically according to the amount of space available between the left and right margins.

A *table* consists of vertical columns and horizontal rows (see Figure 9.1). The intersection of a column and a row is called a *cell*. *Column borders* are vertical lines that separate the columns.

The ruler displays column markers (shown later) at the position of the column borders. When the ruler is showing, you can drag column markers to adjust the width of the table columns.

If you are not running WordPerfect on your computer, please start it now. Close all open documents except for the start-up document—Document1. Let's create and examine a table:

1. Open **chap9.wpd** from your WPWORK directory.

2. Go to page 2 and scroll to place the paragraph that begins *Global Travel guarantees* near the top of the document window. Place the insertion point in the blank line directly above the paragraph that begins *Our quality control.* (**Note:** If you aren't sure where the blank line is, use the View, Show ¶ command to display non-printing symbols.)

Figure 9.1   **Table components**

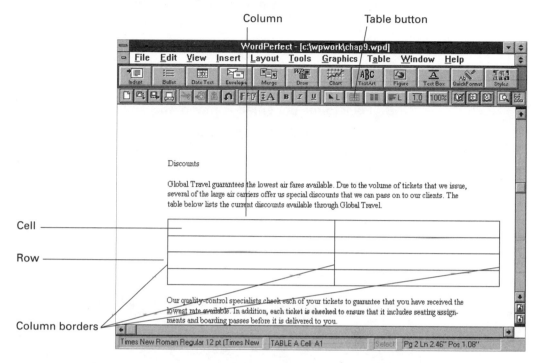

3. Choose **Table, Create** to open the Create Table dialog box, shown in Figure 9.2.

4. Observe the Columns text box. You can change the number of columns by typing a number in the text box or by clicking on the increment indicators.

Figure 9.2   **The Create Table dialog box**

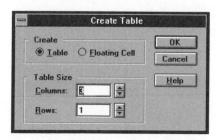

5. Observe the Rows text box. You can change the number of rows by typing a number in the text box or by clicking on the increment indicators.

6. Press **Esc** to close the dialog box without creating a table.

7. Click on the power bar **Table** button (the tenth button from the right) to display the Table button grid.

8. Point to the upper-left corner of the Table button grid.

9. Press and hold the **left mouse** button and drag down to select four rows of the grid. Then drag to the right to select two columns of the grid. The top of the grid displays *2x4* (see Figure 9.3).

10. Release the mouse button to display the table at the insertion point.

Figure 9.3   **Table button grid**

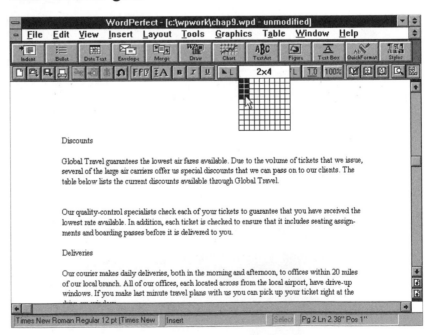

11. Observe the columns, which are displayed vertically on the page (see Figure 9.1).

12. Observe the rows, which are displayed horizontally on the page.

13. Observe the cells, which are the intersections of columns and rows.

14. Observe the column borders, which are the vertical lines.

15. Choose **View, Ruler Bar** to display the ruler.

16. Observe the column marker in the ruler (see Figure 9.4).

Figure 9.4   **Ruler displayed**

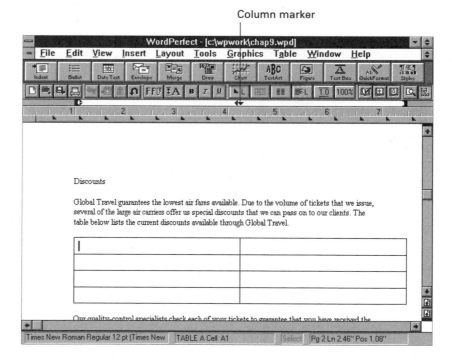

MOVING IN A TABLE

You can use the mouse to move to a table cell, or you can use the keyboard.

Here's the general procedure to move to a specific cell by using the mouse:

- Place the I-beam anywhere on the desired cell.

- Click the *left mouse* button.

Table 9.1 lists the keystrokes used for moving within a table.

Table 9.1

Moving in a Table by Using the Keyboard

Desired Result	How to Do It
Move one cell to the right	Press Tab
Move one cell to the left	Press Shift+Tab
Move up one row	Press up arrow
Move down one row	Press down arrow

If the insertion point is in the last cell of a row when you press Tab, the insertion point will move to the first cell in the next row. (**Note:** If the insertion point is in the last cell of the table, pressing Tab will create a new row.) Likewise, if the insertion point is in the first cell of a row when you press Shift+Tab, it will move to the last cell in the previous row.

Note: If you use the arrow keys on the numeric keypad, Num Lock must be off.

Let's practice moving in the table we've created:

1. Press **Tab** to move the insertion point to the second column of the first row.

2. Press **Tab** to move the insertion point to the first column in the second row.

3. Press **Shift+Tab** to move back to the second column of the first row.

4. Press **down arrow** to move down one row.

5. Press **up arrow** to move up one row.

6. Place the I-beam on the last cell of the table.

7. Click the **left mouse** button to place the insertion point in the last cell.

PRACTICE YOUR SKILLS

Place the insertion point in the first cell of the table.

SELECTING TABLE COMPONENTS

You can select a cell, a row, a column, or the entire table. Table 9.2 lists the methods used for making these selections.

Table 9.2　　　**Selecting Table Elements**

Desired Selection	How to Do It
Cell	Place the insertion point in the cell.
Row	Place the insertion point in any cell in the desired row and drag right or left to select the entire row.
Column	Place the insertion point in any cell in the desired column and drag up or down to select the entire column.
Multiple cells	Place the insertion point in the first cell, press Shift, and click in the last cell of the desired selection. You can use this method to select cells, rows, columns, or the entire table.

Let's try various selection techniques within our table:

1. Place the I-beam on the first cell.

2. Click to select the cell. Compare your screen to Figure 9.4.

3. Press and hold **Shift**.

4. Place the I-beam on the last cell in the first row and click the **left mouse** button to select the entire row (see Figure 9.5). Release Shift.

5. Place the insertion point in the first cell of the first column.

6. Press and hold **Shift** and click in the last cell of the first column to select the entire column (see Figure 9.6). Release Shift.

7. Place the insertion point in the first cell of the table.

8. Press **Shift** and click in the last cell of the table; then release Shift to select the entire table (see Figure 9.7).

9. Deselect the table (click outside the table).

10. Choose **Table**. Notice that when the insertion point is not in the table, only a few Table menu commands are available.

11. Choose **Table** to close the Table menu.

Figure 9.5   **Selected row**

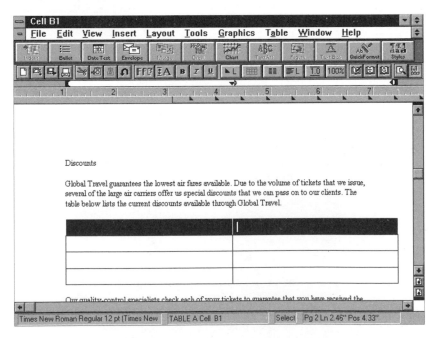

Figure 9.6   **Selected column**

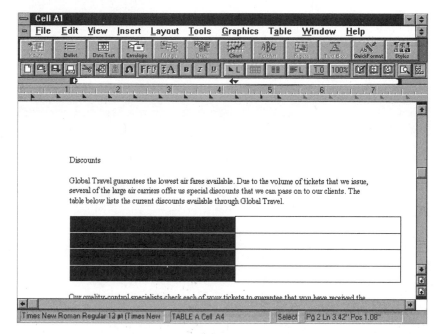

Figure 9.7   **Selected table**

Column marker

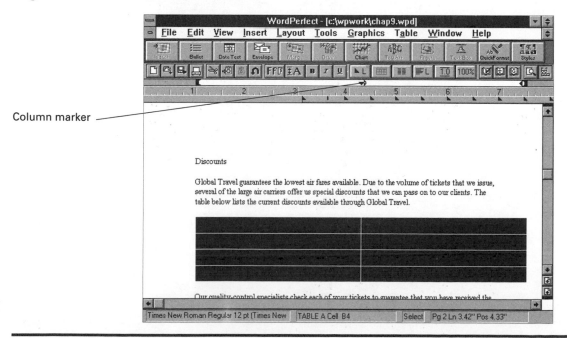

ENTERING TEXT IN A TABLE

Here's the general procedure to enter text in a table:

- Place the insertion point in the cell.

- Begin typing.

Let's enter text in our table:

1. Place the I-beam on the first cell and click.

2. Type **Destination**.

3. Press **Tab** to move to the next cell.

4. Type **Your Price** and press **Tab**.

PRACTICE YOUR SKILLS

1. Complete the table shown in Figure 9.8.

2. Save the disk file as **mychap9**.

Figure 9.8   **Completed table**

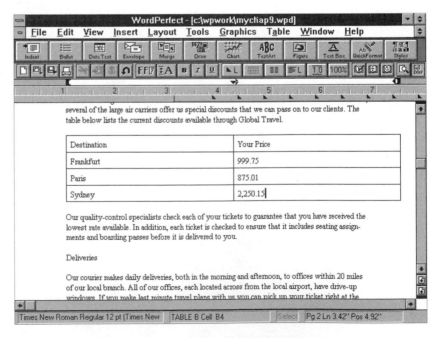

MODIFYING TABLES

After you have created your table—even after you have entered all the desired data—you can still change its structure. You can insert rows and columns within the table, add rows to the bottom or columns to the right side of the table, change the width of the columns, and delete rows and columns.

INSERTING ROWS AND COLUMNS

Here's the general procedure to insert a row at the end of the table:

- Place the insertion point in the last cell of the table.

- Press *Tab*.

Here's the general procedure to insert a row within a table:

- Select the row where you want to insert the new row

- Choose *Table, Insert*.

- Click on *Rows*, if necessary.

- Click on the *up* or *down increment arrow* next to the Rows box to indicate the number of rows you want to insert.

- Choose *Before* to insert the new row(s) before the selected row; or, choose *After* to insert the new row(s) after the selected row.

- Click on *OK*.

Here's the general procedure to insert a column within a table:

- Select the column where you want to insert a new column.

- Choose *Table, Insert*.

- Click on *Columns*.

- Click on the *up* or *down increment arrow* next to the Columns box to indicate the number of rows you want to insert.

- Choose *Before* to insert the new column(s) before the selected column; or, choose *After* to insert the new column(s) after the selected column.

- Click on *OK*.

Let's insert rows and columns in our table:

1. Verify that the insertion point is in the last cell of the table.

2. Press **Tab** to create a new row at the end of the table.

3. Type **Hong Kong** and press **Tab**.

4. Type **2,100.01**.

5. Place the insertion point to the left of the *F* in *Frankfurt* (in the second row of the table).

6. Choose **Table, Insert** to open the Insert Columns/Rows dialog box (see Figure 9.9).

Figure 9.9   **Insert Columns/Rows dialog box**

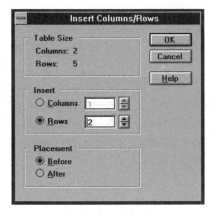

7. In the Insert box, verify that Rows is selected and click on the **up increment** arrow next to the Rows box to insert two rows.

8. Verify that Before is selected in the Placement box to insert the new rows before the Frankfurt row.

9. Click on **OK** to insert the rows. Compare your screen to Figure 9.10.

10. Place the insertion point to the left of the *Y* in *Your Price* (in the second cell of the first row).

11. Choose **Table, Insert** and click on **Columns** and verify that Before is selected in the Placement box.

Figure 9.10   **Inserted rows**

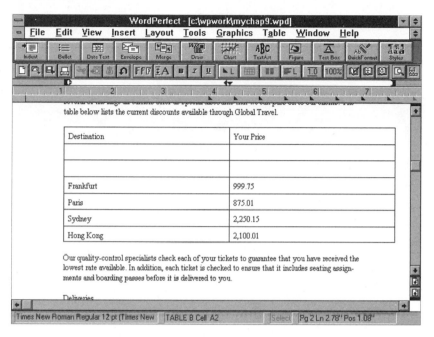

12. Click on **OK** to insert a column between the two existing columns. Compare your screen to Figure 9.11.

13. Place the insertion point in the *Your Price* cell, if necessary.

14. Choose **Table, Insert** and click on **Columns** to insert a column.

15. Click on **After** in the Placement box to insert the column after the selected column (*Your Price*).

16. Click on **OK** and compare your screen to Figure 9.12.

DELETING ROWS, COLUMNS, AND ENTIRE TABLES

Here's the general procedure to delete one or more contiguous rows or columns in a table:

• Select the row or rows that you want to delete.

• Choose *Table, Delete.*

• Check *Columns* or *Rows*.

Figure 9.11　　**Inserted column**

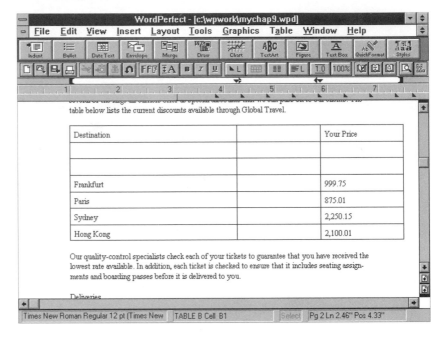

Figure 9.12　　**Table with inserted columns and rows**

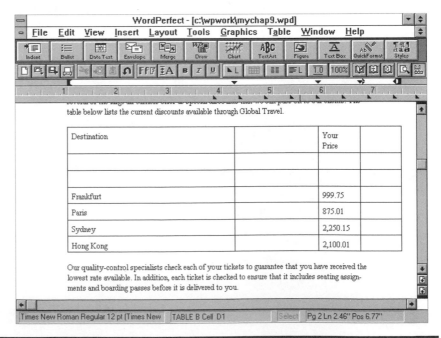

- Click on the *up* or *down increment arrow* to indicate the number of rows or columns you want to delete.

- Click on *OK*.

Here's the general procedure to delete an entire table:

- Place the insertion point in the first cell of the table.

- Choose *View, Reveal Codes.*

- Place the insertion point to the left of the Table code at the beginning of the table.

- Press *Del* to open the Delete Table dialog box.

- Click on *Entire Table*, if necessary.

- Click on *OK*.

Let's delete a row in our table:

1. Select the second row (click in any cell in the second row).

2. Choose **Table, Delete** to open the Delete dialog box (see Figure 9.13).

3. Verify that Rows is selected in the Delete box; then click on **OK** to delete the selected row.

Figure 9.13   **Delete dialog box**

CHANGING COLUMN WIDTH

Here's the general procedure to change the column width by dragging column borders:

- Point to the column border that you want to move; the mouse pointer will become a horizontal, double-headed arrow.
- Press and hold the *left mouse* button.
- Drag the column border to the desired location.
- Release the mouse button.

Here's the general procedure to change column width by using the ruler:

- Choose *View, Ruler Bar* to display the ruler.
- On the ruler, point to the column marker that you want to move.
- Press and hold the *left mouse* button.
- Drag the column marker to the desired location.
- Release the mouse button.

Here's the general procedure to change column width by using the menu:

- Select the desired column.
- Choose *Table, Format*.
- Click on *Column* to display the column format options.
- Type the desired width in the Width of Columns text box.
- Click on *OK*.

When you change the column width by using the menu, the width of the entire table changes to accommodate the adjusted width of its columns. If you decrease the width of a column, the width of the entire table decreases. If you increase the width of a column, the width of the entire table increases. However, when you change column width by dragging the column borders or by using the ruler, only the *column* width changes; the table width stays the same. Therefore, to affect the table width, you must change the width of all columns.

Note: Before you print a document that contains a table, use the Page Zoom Full button to make sure that the entire table fits on the page.

Let's try using all three methods to change the width of columns in our table:

1. Point to the column border between *Destination* and the empty cell. The mouse becomes a double-headed arrow.

2. Press and hold the **left mouse** button and observe the lower-right corner of the status bar. It displays the current position of the column border (4.25).

3. Drag the **column border** to the left until the Position in the status bar reads *2.25"* (see Figure 9.14).

Figure 9.14   **Dragging a column border to a new position**

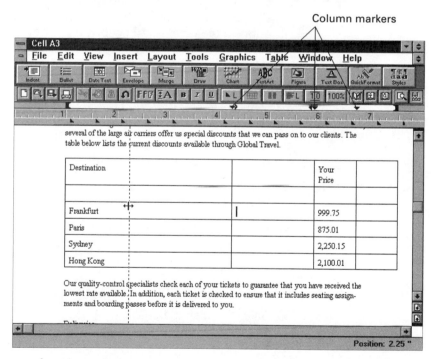

4. Release the mouse button. The width of the first column has been decreased, and the second column has been increased.

5. In the ruler, point to the column marker near the 6-inch mark.

6. Press and hold the **left mouse** button. Next, drag the **column marker** to the 3.5-inch mark on the ruler to decrease the width of the second column.

7. Release the mouse button. Notice that the width of the third column has increased while the second column decreased.

8. Place the insertion point in the third column of the table and choose **Table, Format** to open the Format dialog box.

9. Click on **Column** to display the column format options.

10. Double-click in the **Width** text box (in the Column Width box) to select it.

11. Type **1.25** and click on **OK** to change the width of the third column to 1.25 inches. Notice that when you use the Format dialog box to change the column width, the width of the entire table is affected accordingly, not just the column.

PRACTICE YOUR SKILLS

1. Use any of the methods above to change the width of the fourth column to 1.25 inches.

2. Compare your screen to Figure 9.15. Notice that all four columns are now equal in width.

3. In the first row of the second column, enter the heading **Standard Price**.

4. Complete the second column as shown in Figure 9.16.

5. In the first row of the fourth column, enter the heading **Savings**.

6. Complete the fourth column as shown in Figure 9.16.

7. Save the disk file.

ENHANCING TABLES

You already know how to enhance text in your document; doing so can improve its appearance and readability. Accentuating important text helps the eye to locate these reference points. The same text enhancements that are available in standard document text are also available when working in tables, including, for example,

Figure 9.15   **Table with columns of equal width**

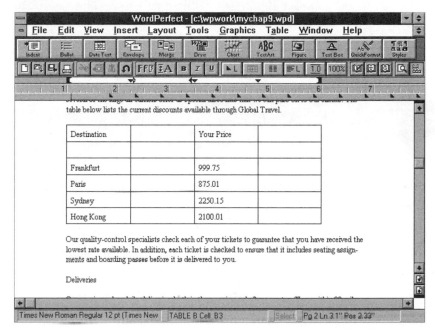

Figure 9.16   **Data entered in second and fourth columns**

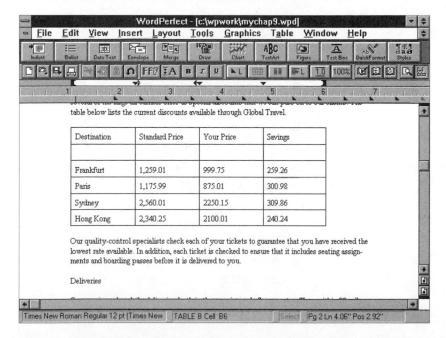

bold and italic text attributes, changes in font and font size, and text alignment within a cell. In addition, you can alter the alignment of the entire table relative to the margins you're using. You can apply character formats to text within a table. You can also enhance a table by adding a border or a gridline that will appear when the document is printed.

ALIGNING A TABLE

Here's the general procedure to align a table between the left and right margins:

- Place the insertion point in the table.
- Choose *Table, Format*.
- Click on *Table* to display the Table format options.
- In the Table Position box, select the desired alignment.
- Click on *OK*.

Let's format and align text in our table, and then center the table between the left and right margins:

1. Select the first row, which contains the column headings. (Drag to select all of the text in the first row.)

2. Choose **Table, Format** and click on **Cell**, if necessary.

3. Check **Bold** in the Appearance box; then click on **OK** to bold all of the text in the first row of the table.

4. Place the I-beam on the second cell in the Frankfurt row (1,259.01).

5. Press and hold the **left mouse** button and drag to select the second through the fourth columns of prices.

6. Choose **Table, Format** to open the Format dialog box. Verify that *Cell* is selected.

7. In the Alignment box, open the Justification drop-down list and choose **Right** (see Figure 9.17); then click on **OK**. All of the text in the selected columns is now right-aligned.

8. Switch to Two Page view. The table is currently aligned along the left margin.

9. Return to Page view.

Figure 9.17   **Format dialog box with cell justification options displayed**

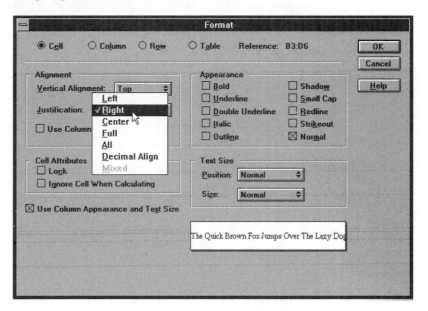

10. Click inside the table.

11. Choose **Table, Format** and click on **Table** to display the table format options.

12. In the Table Position box, select **Center** to center the table between the margins.

13. Click on **OK**. Notice that the table is centered between the left and right margins (see Figure 9.18).

14. Save the disk file.

CHANGING BORDERS

By default, WordPerfect creates a single-line border around each cell of a table. You can change the line style, or you can add a border around a cell, a column, a row, or the whole table.

Here's the general procedure to *change* the line style:

• Select the table, column, row, or cell around which you want to change the line style.

Figure 9.18   **Centered table**

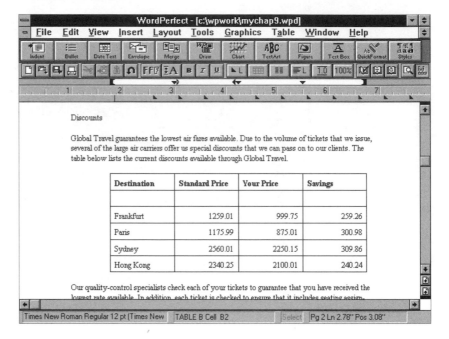

- Choose *Table, Lines/Fill*.
- Click on *Table*.
- Click on the *Line Style* button in the Default Line Style box.
- Click on the line style you want.
- Click on *OK*.

Here's the general procedure to *add* a border around the table:

- Select the table, column, row, or cell around which you want to add a border.
- Choose *Table, Lines/Fill*.
- Click on *Table*.
- In the Border Lines box, click on the *Border* button.
- Click on the border style you want.
- Click on *OK*.

Before closing the dialog box, you can observe the sample diagram in the Border box to see the effect of the border and line style that you selected.

Let's change the border style of our table:

1. Place the insertion point in the table, if necessary.

2. Choose **Table, Lines/Fill** to open the Table Lines/Fill dialog box (see Figure 9.19).

Figure 9.19   **Table Lines/Fill dialog box**

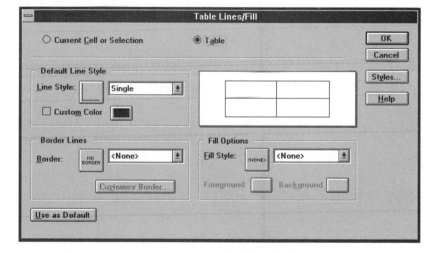

3. Click on **Table** to add a border around the outside of the table.

4. Click on the **Border** button to display the border styles palette.

5. Click on the thin double-line border (the first style in the third row of the border styles palette).

6. Click on **OK**.

7. Deselect the table.

8. Observe the table. Double lines are displayed around the outside of the table (see Figure 9.20).

Figure 9.20   **Completed table with border**

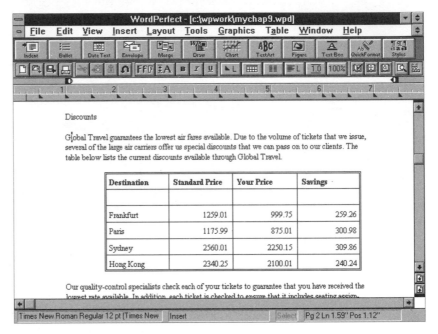

CONVERTING TABBED TEXT TO A TABLE

WordPerfect enables you to convert a tabbed table created by inserting tabs between columns of text into an actual table consisting of cells, rows, and columns.

Here's the general procedure to convert tabbed text to a table:

- Select the text that you want to convert to a table.
- Choose *Table, Create*.
- Click on *OK*.

Note: Occasionally, tables that have been created from tabbed text will require some modifications.

Let's convert tabbed text to a table:

1. Scroll to place the *Hotel Accommodations* heading, at the top of page 3, at the top of the screen.

2. Observe the tabbed text on page 3.

3. Select all of the lines in the tabbed table, from *Location* to *Hong Kong*, that you want to place in the table.

4. Choose **Table, Create**. The Convert Table dialog box opens (see Figure 9.21).

5. Verify that **Tabular Column** is selected and click on **OK**. The tabbed text is placed in a table like that shown in Figure 9.22.

Figure 9.21   **Convert Table dialog box**

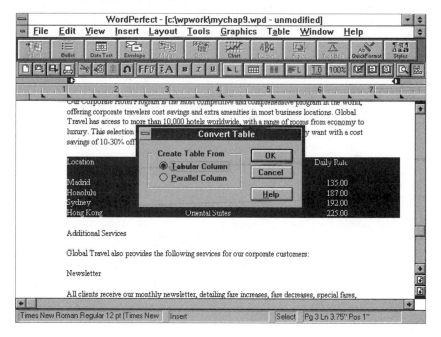

PRACTICE YOUR SKILLS

1. Set the width of all three columns to 1.5 inches.

2. Place a thick-line border around the table.

3. Center the table between the left and right margins.

4. Deselect the table.

5. Save the disk file.

6. Close the document.

Figure 9.22 **Converted table**

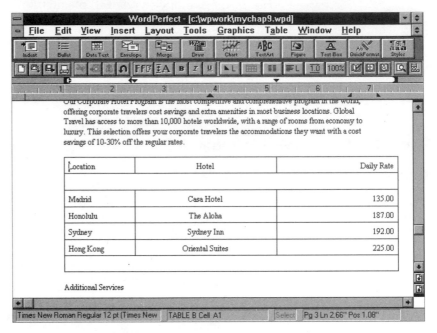

PRACTICE YOUR SKILLS

This exercise gives you the opportunity to practice the skills you just learned. The following instructions lead you through the steps necessary to edit the disk file PRAC9A.WPD to produce the document in Figure 9.23.

Follow these steps at your computer:

1. Open **prac9a.wpd** (Chapter 2).

2. Type the following information into your table:

(Row 3)	Trader Tom's	2300	1.49
(Row 4)	Aunt Emily's Market	4900	1.29
(Row 5)	Hamlet Farms	6500	1.29

3. Delete the row that contains information for *Price Farms* (this chapter).

Figure 9.23   **Completed MYPRAC9A.WPD document**

The Garden Patch
Product Line Announcement

Introduction

The Garden Patch is pleased to announce the unveiling of a new food line in the Garden Patch series: the Fruit Patch. The Fruit Patch product line was developed after two years of intense work through the cooperation and dedication of Dr. Faye Shad and her staff. The FDA recently approved the food, and it will be released for public sale in three weeks.

The Fruit Patch includes a variety of organically grown fruit: berries (cherries, strawberries, raspberries, blackberries, and blueberries), apricots, peaches, grapes, and plums.

Projected Quarterly Sales

Our finance department has been hard at work, determining sales projections for the next quarter. The results are shown in the following table.

Projected Quarterly Sales Table

Vendors	Boxes Sold	Profit (per box)
Trader Tom's	2300	1.49
Aunt Emily's Market	4900	1.29
Hamlet Farms	6500	1.29
B and J's	10000	0.79
Hout and Wallace Inc.	11500	0.79

4. Right-align the second and third columns (this chapter). (**Hint:** Select the columns, choose **Table, Format**, and click on **Cell** to align the text in the cells.)

5. Change the column width for the *Boxes Sold* column to 1.25 inches (this chapter).

6. Change the column width for *Profit (per box)* to 1.25 inches (this chapter).

7. Center the table on the page (this chapter).

8. Save the disk file as **myprac9a** (Chapter 1).

9. Print the document and compare it to Figure 9.23 (Chapter 1).

10. Close the document (Chapter 1).

If you have finished this activity, you might like to try a more challenging one requiring similar skills. In the next activity, you will edit PRAC9B.WPD to create the document shown in Figure 9.24.

Figure 9.24   **Completed MYPRAC9B.WPD document**

**The Garden Patch
Product Line Announcement**

Introduction

The Garden Patch is pleased to announce the unveiling of a new food line in the Garden Patch series: the Fruit Patch. The Fruit Patch product line was developed after two years of intense work through the cooperation and dedication of Dr. Faye Shad and her staff. The FDA recently approved the food, and it will be released for public sale in three weeks.

The Fruit Patch includes a variety of organically grown fruit: berries (cherries, strawberries, raspberries, blackberries, and blueberries), apricots, peaches, grapes, and plums.

Projected Quarterly Sales

Our finance department has been hard at work, determining sales projections for the next quarter. The results are shown in the following table.

Projected Quarterly Sales Table

Vendors	Boxes Sold	Total Profit
Trader Tom's	2300	3427.37
Aunt Emily's Market	4900	6321.25
Hamlet Farms	6500	7085.98

Follow these steps at your computer:

1. Open **prac9b.wpd** (Chapter 2).

2. Below the *Projected Quarterly Sales Table* heading, create a table that contains three columns and five rows (this chapter).

3. Enter the data as shown in Figure 9.24 (this chapter).

4. Right-align the second and third columns (this chapter).

5. Decrease the column width for the second and third columns to 1.5 inches (this chapter).

6. Center the table on the page (this chapter).

7. Place a double-line border around the table (this chapter).

8. Save the disk file as **myprac9b** (Chapter 2).

9. Print the document and compare it to Figure 9.24 (Chapter 1).

10. Close the document (Chapter 1).

SUMMARY

In this chapter, you learned how to create tables using the Table button in the power bar or using the Table, Create command from the menu. You learned how to move within a table; how to select cells, rows, columns, and the entire table; and how to enter data in a table. You also learned how to insert and delete rows and columns, how to change column width, how to change the alignment of a table between the left and right margins, and how to enhance the appearance of a table by creating various types of borders. Finally, you learned how to convert tabbed text to a table.

Here is a quick reference guide to the WordPerfect features introduced in this chapter:

Desired Result	How to Do It
Create a table using the menu	Place the insertion point where you want to create the table; choose **Table, Create**; select the appropriate number of columns and rows; click on **OK**
Create a table using the power bar	Place the mouse pointer on the Table button; drag to select the appropriate number of columns and rows
Move within a table using the mouse	Place the I-beam on the desired cell; click the **left mouse** button
Move one cell to the right	Press **Tab**
Move one cell to the left	Press **Shift+Tab**

Desired Result	How to Do It
Move up one row	Press **up arrow**
Move down one row	Press **down arrow**
Select a cell	Place the insertion point in the cell
Select a row	Place the insertion point in any cell in the row; drag left or right to select the row
Select a column	Place the insertion point in any cell in the column; drag up or down to select the column
Select an entire table	Place the insertion point in the first cell of the table; press and hold **Shift**; click the **left mouse** button in the last cell of the table; release Shift
Add a row at the end of a table	Place the insertion point in the last cell of the table; press **Tab**
Insert a row within a table	Select the row where you want to insert the new row; choose **Table, Insert**; click on **Rows**; click on the **up** and **down increment** arrows to set the number of rows you want to insert; click on **Before** to insert the row(s) before the selected row, or click on **After** to insert the row(s) after the selected row; click on **OK**
Insert a column within a table	Select the column where you want to insert the new column; choose **Table, Insert**; click on **Columns**; click on the **up** and **down increment** arrows to set the number of columns you want to insert; click on **Before** to insert the column(s) before the selected row, or click on **After** to insert the column(s) after the selected row; click on **OK**

Desired Result	How to Do It
Delete one or more rows	Select the row that you want to delete; choose **Table, Delete**; click on **Rows**; set the number of rows to delete; click on **OK**
Delete one or more columns	Select the column that you want to delete; choose **Table, Delete**; click on **Columns**; set the number of columns to delete; click on **OK**
Delete an entire table	Place the insertion point in the table; choose **View, Reveal Codes**; place the insertion point to the left of the table code; press **Del**; verify that **Entire Table** is selected; click on **OK**
Change column width by dragging column borders	Place the mouse pointer on the column border (it turns into a double-headed arrow); drag the column border to its new position
Change column width by using the ruler	Choose **View, Ruler Bar** to display the ruler; place the mouse pointer on the column marker for the column you want to change; drag the column marker to its new position
Change column width by using the menu	Place the insertion point in the column whose width you want to change; choose **Table, Format**; click on **Column**; double-click in the **Width** text box; type the new column width; click on **OK**
Align a table between the left and right margins	Place the insertion point anywhere in the table; choose **Table, Format**; click on **Table**; in the Table Position box, select the appropriate position; click on **OK**

Desired Result	How to Do It
Create a table border	Place the insertion point anywhere in the table; choose **Table, Lines/Fill**; click on **Table**; click on the **Border** button; click on a border style; click on **OK**
Convert tabbed text to a table	Select the tabbed text that you want to convert to a table; choose **Table, Create**; click on **OK**

In the next chapter, you will learn how to create form letters.

IF YOU'RE STOPPING HERE

If you need to break off here, please exit WordPerfect. If you want to proceed directly to the next chapter, please do so now.

CHAPTER 10: CREATING FORM LETTERS

In word processing, *merging* or *mail-merge* is the process of transferring selected information from one document to another document. For example, you can write a form letter and instantly merge it with your mailing list to produce a customized letter for everyone on the mailing list. Other common mail-merge documents include mailing labels, interoffice memos, and reports.

The WordPerfect for Windows Merge command enables you to take information from two documents—for example, a form letter and a list of names and addresses—and combine them into a single document. Equally important is the ability to sort the information in the mailing list (for example, in alphabetical order by last name) by using the Sort command available through the Merge feature bar or the Tools menu.

When you're done working through this chapter, you will know

- How to create and associate the components of form letters
- How to generate form letters
- How to sort data in a data file

COMPONENTS OF A FORM LETTER

Before using WordPerfect's Merge feature, you should be familiar with three important terms that correspond to the three main components of the merge process: the form file, the data file, and the merged document.

THE FORM FILE

The *form file* contains normal text plus *field names*, which contain the instructions for carrying out the merge. The basic information in the form file remains the same during the merge. For example, a letter of invitation could be prepared as a form letter. The form file would contain the invitation text and various field names that would cause WordPerfect to retrieve names and addresses from a data file (discussed after the next section). WordPerfect would then insert the names and addresses in specific places in the merged document. However, before you can instruct WordPerfect to merge documents, you must have inserted field names in your form file.

FIELD NAMES

In the form file, field names are used to indicate where variable information is to be inserted. In the data file (discussed next), field names indicate the category of information—for example, last names. The field names inserted in the form file must match the field names in the data file. You can insert field names in your document before the data file is associated; however, then you would have to enter field names twice. It is easier to insert the field names once—*after* the two files have been associated (you'll learn how to attach files later in this chapter).

THE DATA FILE

The *data file* stores information to be brought into the form file. You can think of the data file as a name-and-address list from which the program gets the information you want to include in the form file. However, not only can you store names and addresses in the data file, but you can also use it to store sentences, whole paragraphs, and any text or data you expect to use repeatedly. You can set up the data file as ordinary paragraphs or as a table. In this chapter, we use a table to compile data file information. In Chapter 9, you saw how compiling data in a table is an efficient way to keep the data organized. For this reason, we recommend that you set up your data files as tables.

The data file consists of a *header record*, which is a group of field names; *data records*; and *fields*. The header record is the first row of the table. It contains field names, which indicate the type of information in each column. Except for the header record, each additional row of the table contains a set of related information, known as a record. Each record includes all of the information for one person in the name-and-address list. The various types of information in each record are known as fields, which are the equivalent of cells in a standard table.

There are several important guidelines for naming fields in data files:

- Each field name must be unique.
- It can contain up to 40 characters.
- It can contain letters, numbers, and spaces.
- If you do not specify field names, WordPerfect gives each field a reference number.

Here's the general procedure to create a data file:

- Choose *Tools, Merge* (or click on the *Merge* button on the button bar).
- Check the *Place Records in a Table* check box.
- Click on *Data*.
- Type a field name and click on *Add*.
- Repeat the above step until all fields for the data file have been named.

- Click on *OK*.

- Enter the appropriate information for the first record in the Quick Data Entry dialog box (press *Tab* or click on *Next Field* to move to the next field text box).

- Click on *New Record* to move to the next record.

- Repeat the above two steps until all the data records are completed.

- Click on *Close*.

If you are not running WordPerfect on your computer, please start it now. Close all open documents except for the start-up document—Document1. Let's create a data file:

1. Choose **Tools, Merge** to open the Merge dialog box. (**Note:** You can also access the Merge dialog box by clicking on the button bar Merge button.)

2. Check the **Place Records in a Table** check box. Because it is easier to work with records in table format, we recommend that you place records in a table when you create a data file.

3. Click on **Data** to open the Create Data File dialog box. Before you can create data records, you need to name the fields (categories) for each record.

4. Type **First** and click on **Add** to add First to the Field Name List. This field will contain first names.

5. Type **Last** and click on **Add** to add Last to the Field Name List. This field will consist of last names.

6. Type **Address** and click on **Add** to add Address to the Field Name List.

7. Type **Destination** and click on **Add** to add Destination to the Field Name List. Compare your screen to Figure 10.1.

8. Click on **OK** to close the Create Data File dialog box. The data file is created and the Quick Data Entry dialog box opens (see Figure 10.2).

9. Observe the Quick Data Entry dialog box. The Record box displays a text box for each field name you defined in the Create Data File dialog box. You can enter the data records here.

10. In the First text box, type **Karrie**.

Figure 10.1   **Create Data File dialog box with defined field names**

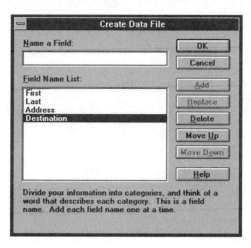

Figure 10.2   **The Quick Data Entry dialog box**

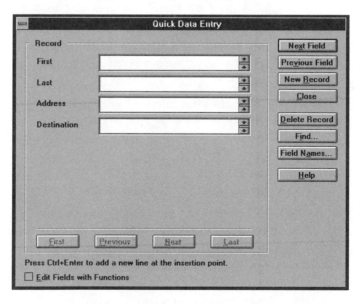

11. Click on **Next Field** (or press **Tab**) to move the insertion point to the field name Last.

12. Type **Utter** and click on **Next Field** (or press **Tab**).

13. Type **1105 West 10th Street** and press **Ctrl+Enter**. Then type **Omaha, NE 68127**. You can press Ctrl+Enter to force information to a separate line in the record. The second line of information remains within the same record.

14. Click on **Next Field** (or press **Tab**) and type **Rome**.

15. Click on **New Record** to move to the second record in the data file.

PRACTICE YOUR SKILLS

1. Complete the new record with the following information:

   James   Zaepfel   119 Culver Avenue   Paris
                        La Jolla, CA 93108

   (**Hint:** To place two lines in a field in the Quick Data Entry dialog box, press **Ctrl+Enter** at the end of the first line.)

2. Click on **Close** to close the Quick Data Entry dialog box.

3. Click on **Yes** to save the data as a disk file.

4. Choose **File, Save As** to save the file as **mychap10.dat**. (**Hint:** WordPerfect doesn't automatically add the .DAT extension to data files; therefore, you must type`.dat` when you name the file.)

5. Compare your screen to Figure 10.3. Note that each data record has its own row in the table.

ADDING RECORDS TO THE DATA FILE

You can add records to the data file or edit existing records at any time.

Here's the general procedure to add records to the data file:

- Open the data file.
- Place the insertion point in the last line of the table, if necessary.
- Press *Tab* to add a new line to the table.
- Enter the new information.
- Save the data file.

Figure 10.3 **The data file**

Merge feature box

Field names

Header record

Data records

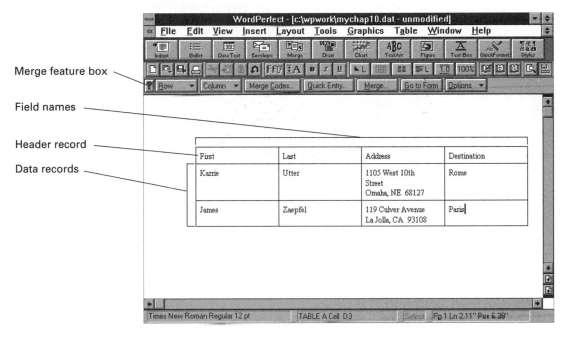

Let's add two new records to MYCHAP10.DAT:

1. Observe the header record, located in the top row of the table—it lists the field names.

2. Observe the data records, located in the rows below the header record; they contain the data for each field and record.

3. Place the insertion point at the end of the last field in the last record of the data file (after *Paris*).

4. Press **Tab** to add a row to the bottom of the table.

5. Type **Chris** and press **Tab**.

6. Type **Phillips** and press **Tab**.

7. Type **125 North Road** and press **Enter**. Then type **Yuma, AZ 85365**. Earlier, you learned that you can press Ctrl+Enter in a field text box to create a two-line field entry. When you add a data record directly to the table, you can press Enter to force

information to a separate line in the record. The second line of information remains within the same record.

8. Press **Tab** and type **Dallas**.

PRACTICE YOUR SKILLS

1. Add a new record to the data file. (**Hint:** With the insertion point at the end of the last record, press **Tab**.)

2. Complete the record with the following information:

   Pam   Smith   246 Eastman Street   Berlin
                       Chicago, IL 60604

3. Save the disk file and compare your screen to Figure 10.4.

4. Close the document.

Figure 10.4   **Completed MYCHAP10.DAT document**

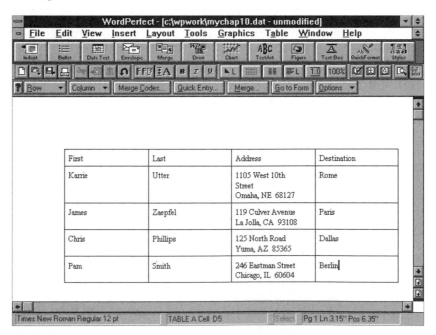

ASSOCIATING THE DATA FILE WITH THE FORM FILE

Associating the data file with the form file identifies the data file as the one to be used for the variable information when the two documents are merged. You can associate the data file either when you create the form file or after you finish the form file. We recommend that whenever possible, you associate the data file when you create the form file. (**Note:** When you associate the data file after the form file is complete, make sure the form file is open.)

Here's the general procedure to create a form file:

- Choose *Tools, Merge* (or click on *Merge* in the button bar).
- Click on *Form*.
- Indicate a data file to associate, or click on *None*.
- Click on *OK*.
- Type the form file text.
- Insert the fields.
- Save the form file with the extension .FRM.

Here's the general procedure to associate a data file with a form file after the form file has been completed:

- Make the form file the active document.
- Click on the *Insert Field* button in the Merge feature bar.
- Click on *OK*.
- Click on *Data File*.
- Specify the location and the name of the data file.
- Click on *OK*.

Note: Once a form file and a data file are associated, you can move between them using the Merge feature bar. In addition, you have quick access—through the Merge feature bar—to all of the field names in the data file. You can quickly and accurately insert the field names in your form file.

Here's the general procedure to insert field names in the form file by using the Merge feature bar:

- Place the insertion point where you want to add a field name.

- Click on the *Insert Field* button.

- In the Insert Field Name or Number dialog box, select the desired field name.

- Click on *Insert*.

Once the field name is inserted in the form file, it is preceded by the word *FIELD* and enclosed by parentheses—for example, FIELD(First), which represents the first-name field.

Let's view the form file, attach the data file, and then complete the form file:

1. Open **chap10.frm**. Form files should carry the extension .FRM. As with data files, WordPerfect does not automatically add this extension. When you save the file, you must add the *.frm* extension yourself.

2. Observe the field names in the document.

3. Observe the Merge feature bar. When you open a form file, WordPefect automatically opens the Merge feature bar, allowing you quick access to WordPerfect's merge features.

4. Place the insertion point on the first blank line below the *FIELD(First) FIELD(Last)* line.

5. Click on **Insert Field**. Because this form file is not associated with a data file, WordPerfect can't find any field names or records.

6. Click on **OK** to open the Insert Field Name or Number dialog box. You can either type and insert your own field names here, or you can associate a data file.

7. Click on **Data File** to associate a data file, gaining access to its field names.

8. From the File Name list box, double-click on **mychap10.dat** to associate the data file. All of the fields in the data file are now available in the Insert Field Name or Number dialog box.

9. In the Field Names list box, select **Address** (see Figure 10.5) to place the information from the Address column in the completed form letter.

10. Click on **Insert**. The address field is inserted in the completed form file.

Figure 10.5   **Inserting the Address field in the form file**

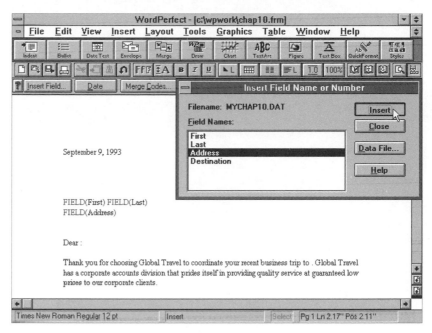

11. Place the insertion point to the left of the colon (:) in the form letter's greeting.

12. In the Insert Field Name or Number dialog box, double-click on **First** to place the information from the first-name column of the data file in the completed form letter.

PRACTICE YOUR SKILLS

1. Complete the form letter contained in the CHAP10.FRM disk file using Figure 10.6 as a guide. (**Hint:** The Destination field needs to be inserted at the end of the first sentence of the letter.)

2. Close the Insert Field Name or Number dialog box.

3. Save the disk file as **mychap10.frm**.

Figure 10.6   **Completed form file**

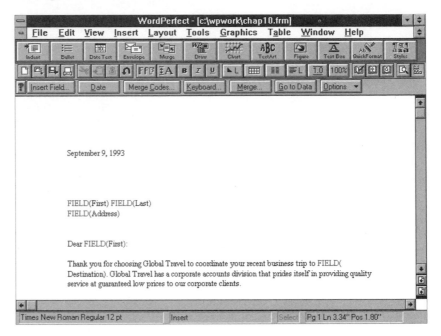

GENERATING FORM LETTERS

After you have completed and associated the data file and the form file, you can then merge the two documents.

Here's the general procedure to merge the data file and form file:

- With the form file open and active, click on the *Merge* button in the Merge feature bar.

- Click on the *Merge* button in the Perform Merge box.

- Select the appropriate Form, Data, and Output files in the Files to Merge box.

- Click on *OK*.

When you merge the documents, a new document is created. It contains a form letter created for each record in the data file. You can print the form letters just as you would print any other document. You can merge directly to the printer without creating a new document by choosing Printer in the Output File drop-down list of the Perform Merge dialog box.

Let's merge the form file and the data file to create our form letters:

1. Observe the name of the current document, *mychap10.frm*.

2. Click on the **Merge** button in the Merge feature bar to open the Merge dialog box.

3. In the Perform Merge box, click on **Merge** to open the Perform Merge dialog box (see Figure 10.7) and begin the merge process.

Figure 10.7 **The Perform Merge dialog box**

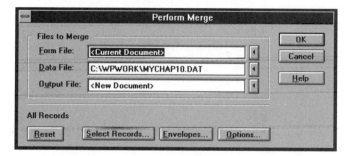

4. Verify that the Form File text box displays *<Current Document>*.

5. Verify that the Data File text box displays *C:\WPWORK\ MYCHAP10.DAT*.

6. Verify that the Output File text box displays *<New Document>*. You can merge directly to the printer by choosing Printer from the Output File drop-down list. However, it is a good idea to merge to a new document before you print, so you can check to make sure the merged documents are correct.

7. Click on **OK** to merge the data file and form file to a new document. Each letter is placed on a separate page within the document.

8. Scroll up to observe the form letters. A letter has been created for every data record in the MYCHAP10.DAT file.

9. Close all of the documents without saving them as disk files. It is not necessary to save the merged document because as long as you have both the data file and the form file, you can perform a merge at any time.

SORTING THE INFORMATION IN A DATA FILE

There will probably come a time when you will need to arrange a list of data, such as an address list, in alphabetical or numerical order. For example, you might want your data file records to appear in ascending alphabetical order by last name, or in descending numerical order by zip code.

You can use WordPerfect's Sort command to sort columns of text in data files alphabetically or numerically. If you want to sort by a column other than the first one, you need to specify the column number. Columns are numbered from left to right.

Here's the general procedure to sort data in a data file:

- Place the insertion point in the first cell of the table.

- Click on the *Merge* feature bar Options button.

- Click on *Sort*.

- In the Type drop-down list box, select the type of sort—*Alpha* or *Numeric.*

- In the Sort Order drop-down list box, select the desired order—*Ascending* or *Descending.*

- In the Cell box, select the number of the column by which to sort.

- Click on *OK.*

Let's experiment with sorting the records in a data file a couple of ways:

1. Open **ch10list.dat** from your WPWORK directory.

2. Observe the second column, which contains last names. The last names are not arranged alphabetically.

3. Place the insertion point in the first cell of the table (containing the text *First*).

4. Click on **Options** on the Merge feature bar (the first button from the right) to open the Options drop-down list.

5. Click on **Sort** to open the Sort dialog box.

6. In the Type drop-down list box, verify that **Alpha** is selected to sort alphabetically.

7. In the Sort Order drop-down list box, verify that **Ascending** is selected, in order to sort the last names from A through Z.

8. Double-click In the Cell box and type **2** to instruct WordPerfect to sort by the second column of the table. Compare your screen to Figure 10.8.

Figure 10.8   **Specified sort criteria**

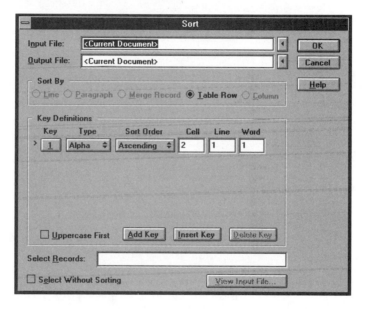

9. Click on **OK** to begin the sort.

10. Observe that the records have been sorted and that the last names in column 2 are listed in ascending alphabetical order (see Figure 10.9).

11. Observe that the zip-code data is not sorted in any particular order.

12. Click on the Merge feature bar **Options** button and click on **Sort** to open the Sort dialog box.

13. In the Type drop-down list, select **Numeric** to sort only numeric data.

Figure 10.9   **Records sorted by last name**

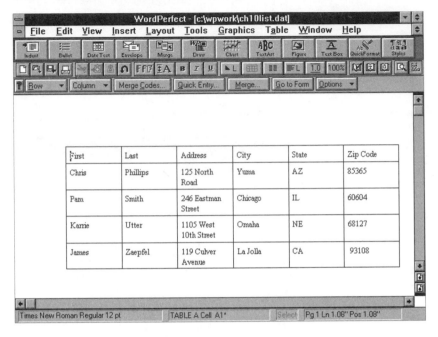

14. In the Sort Order drop-down list, select **Descending** to sort the zip codes from 9 through 0.

15. Double-click in the Cell box and type **6** to sort by the sixth column of the table. Compare your screen to Figure 10.10.

16. Click on **OK** to start the sort.

17. Observe that the zip code data is sorted in descending numeric order (see Figure 10.11).

PRACTICE YOUR SKILLS

1. Sort the table by zip code in ascending order.

2. Compare your screen to Figure 10.12.

3. Save the disk file as **mylist.dat**.

4. Close the document.

Figure 10.10   Specifying new sort criteria

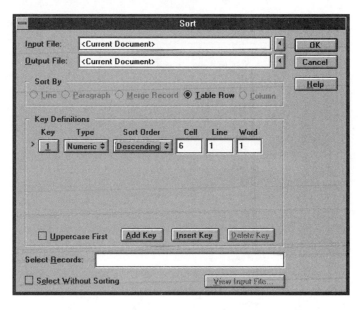

Figure 10.11   Records sorted by zip code

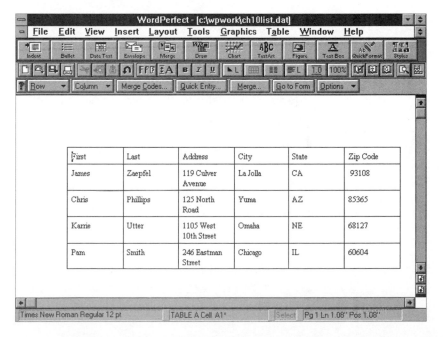

Figure 10.12   Completed MYLIST.DAT document

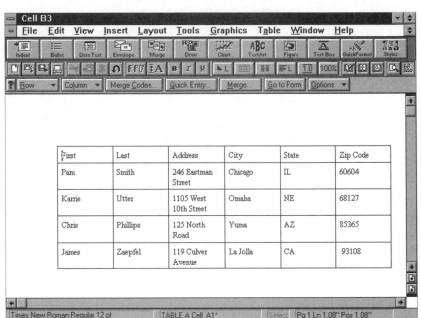

PRACTICE YOUR SKILLS

This exercise gives you the opportunity to practice the skills you just learned. The following instructions lead you through the steps necessary to complete and attach the components of a form letter (Figure 10.15 shows the merged form letters completed).

Follow these steps at your computer:

1. Open **prac10.dat** (Chapter 2).

2. Enter the data shown in Figure 10.13 (Chapter 9, and this chapter). Save the disk file as **myprac10.dat** (Chapter 1).

3. Open the disk file **prac10.frm** (Chapter 2).

4. Associate the data file MYPRAC10.DAT (this chapter).

5. Enter the field names shown in Figure 10.14 (this chapter). (**Note:** Figure 10.14 shows the PRAC10.FRM file with nonprinting characters displayed to aid you in placing field names in their correct places. You might want to choose View, Show ¶ to display the nonprinting characters on your screen, too.)

Figure 10.13   Completed data file

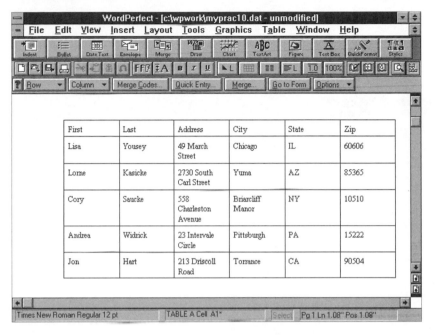

Figure 10.14   Entered fields

Figure 10.15   Merged form letters

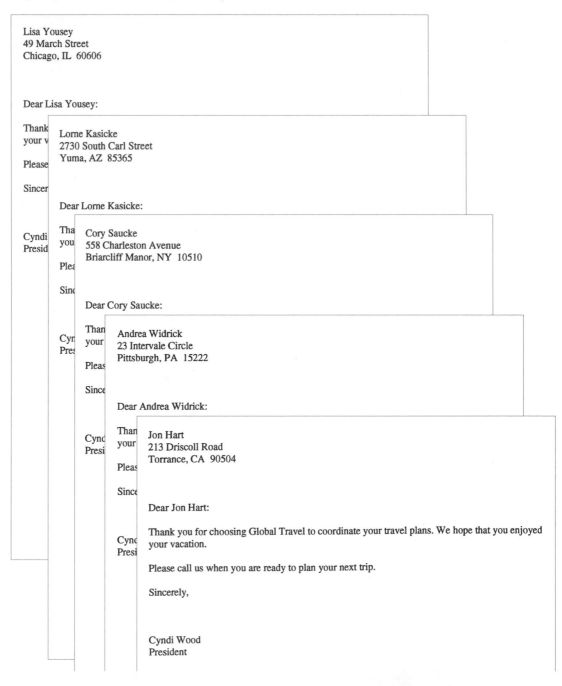

Lisa Yousey
49 March Street
Chicago, IL 60606

Dear Lisa Yousey:

Thank
your v

Please

Sincer

Cyndi
Presid

Lorne Kasicke
2730 South Carl Street
Yuma, AZ 85365

Dear Lorne Kasicke:

Tha
you

Plea

Sin

Cyr
Pres

Cory Saucke
558 Charleston Avenue
Briarcliff Manor, NY 10510

Dear Cory Saucke:

Than
your

Pleas

Since

Cynd
Presi

Andrea Widrick
23 Intervale Circle
Pittsburgh, PA 15222

Dear Andrea Widrick:

Than
your

Pleas

Since

Cynd
Presi

Jon Hart
213 Driscoll Road
Torrance, CA 90504

Dear Jon Hart:

Thank you for choosing Global Travel to coordinate your travel plans. We hope that you enjoyed your vacation.

Please call us when you are ready to plan your next trip.

Sincerely,

Cyndi Wood
President

6. Save the disk file as **myprac10.frm** (Chapter 2).

7. Merge the files to create a new document (this chapter).

8. Print the merged form letters (Chapter 1) and compare them to Figure 10.15.

9. Close all of the documents (Chapter 1) without saving them as disk files.

SUMMARY

In this chapter, you learned how to create form letters by merging the form file and the data file. You learned how to create a data file and add data records. You learned how to insert merge fields in a form file, and then associate the corresponding data file. You also learned how to sort a list of data in alphabetical and numerical order.

Here is a quick reference guide to the WordPerfect features introduced in this chapter:

Desired Result	How to Do It
Create a data file	Choose **Tools, Merge** (or click on the **Merge** button on the button bar); check the **Place Records in a Table** check box; click on **Data**; type a field name and click on **Add**; repeat the above step until all fields for the data file have been named; click on **OK**; enter the appropriate information for the first record in the Quick Data Entry dialog box (press **Tab** or click on **Next Field** to move to the next field text box); click on **New Record** to move to the next record; repeat the two steps above until all the data records are completed; click on **Close**
Add records to the data file	Open the data file; place the insertion point in the last line of the table, if necessary; press **Tab** to add a new line to the table; enter the new information; save the data file

Desired Result	How to Do It
Create a form file	Choose **Tools, Merge** (or click on the button bar **Merge** button); click on **Form**; indicate a data file to associate, or click on **None**; click on **OK**; type the form file text; insert the fields; save the form file with the extension .FRM
Associate a data file with a form file	Make the form file the active document; click on the **Insert Field** button in the Merge feature bar; click on **OK**; click on **Data File**; specify the location and the name of the data file; click on **OK**
Insert field names in the form file	Place the insertion point where you want to add a field name; click on the **Insert Field** button; in the Insert Field Name or Number dialog box, select the desired field name; click on **Insert**
Merge the data file and form file	With the form file open and active, click on the **Merge** button in the Merge feature bar; click on the **Merge** button in the Perform Merge box; select the appropriate Form, Data, and Output files in the Files to Merge box; click on **OK**
Sort data in a data file	Place the insertion point in the first cell of the table; click on the Merge feature bar **Options** button; click on **Sort**; in the Type drop-down box, select the type of sort—**Alpha** or **Numeric**; in the Sort Order drop-down box, select the desired order—**Ascending** or **Descending**; in the Cell box, select the number of the column by which to sort; click on **OK**

In the next chapter, you will work with templates and styles.

IF YOU'RE STOPPING HERE

If you need to break off here, please exit WordPerfect. If you want to proceed directly to the next chapter, please do so now.

CHAPTER 11: USING TEMPLATES AND STYLES TO AUTOMATE YOUR WORK

Using the Standard Template

Using the Memo2 Template

Creating and Using Styles

Each time you instruct WordPerfect for Windows to create a document, the program does so according to a template. A *template* is a stored file that contains boilerplate text and/or special formatting information. It serves as a kind of skeleton, providing your documents with an underlying structure. Templates also include styles, which contain special text attributes and paragraph formats. (You were introduced to text attributes and paragraph formats in Chapters 4 and 5, respectively.) Each style is stored under a specific name—for example, heading 1. WordPerfect comes with a number of useful templates, each designed for a specific kind of document. For example, the STANDARD template is used to create a standard document, while the MEMO templates can be used to create business memos.

The primary benefit of using a template is that all, or at least some, of the document's characteristics have been defined in advance. This enables you to create documents that have similar text attributes and paragraph formats, as well as similar page setups, without having to specify each parameter for each individual document.

When you're done working through this chapter, you will know

- How to create a document using the STANDARD template
- How to create a document using the MEMO template
- How to create and use styles

USING THE STANDARD TEMPLATE

Every document that you create in WordPerfect uses a template. By default, WordPerfect uses the STANDARD template for each new document. You can select a different template for a new document by choosing File, Template to open the Template dialog box and selecting a template in the Document Template to Use list box.

Here's the general procedure to attach a different template to a document:

- Choose *File, Template*.
- From the Document Template to Use list, select the desired template.
- Click on *OK*.

If you are not running WordPerfect on your computer, please start it now. Close all open documents except for the start-up document—Document1. Let's create a memo using the STANDARD template:

1. Choose **File, Template** to open the Templates dialog box, shown in Figure 11.1.

2. Observe the Document Template to Use list box. The STANDARD template is selected by default. All new documents are based on this template.

3. Click on **OK**.

4. Type **Interoffice Memo** and press **Enter** twice.

5. Type **To:** and press **Tab**.

6. Type **Dawn Smith** and press **Enter**.

7. Type **From:** and press **Tab**.

8. Type **Camille Mancuso** and press **Enter**.

Figure 11.1   **The Templates dialog box**

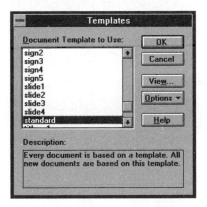

9. Type **Date:** and press **Tab**.

10. Click on the **Date Text** button on the button bar (the third button from the left) to insert the current date in your document.

11. Press **Enter**.

12. Type **Subject:** and press **Tab**.

13. Type **Change in Additional Services**.

14. Press **Enter** twice.

 INSERTING A FILE

In Chapter 3 you learned how to use the Edit, Copy and the Edit, Paste commands to copy and move selected text from one location to another. You can use this method to copy text from one document to another document. However, the easiest way to insert the entire contents of one document in another document is to use the Insert, File command.

Here's the general procedure to insert an entire file:

• Place the insertion point where you want the document to appear.

• Choose *Insert, File*.

• Select the desired disk file.

• Click on *OK*.

Note: If you have more than one window open, remember to activate the window of the document receiving the inserted disk file before you choose Insert, File. The inserted file is always placed in the active window.

Let's insert the contents of the CHAP11A.WPD disk file in our memo:

1. Choose **Insert, File** to open the File dialog box.

2. Double-click on **chap11a.wpd** in the WPWORK directory and click on **Yes**, if necessary, to place the contents of the file in the current document.

3. Move the insertion point to the end of the document, if necessary (press **Ctrl+End**).

4. Type **cc:** and press **Tab**.

5. Type **Barb Stork,** (including the comma) and press the **spacebar**.

6. Type **Marcie Forrest**.

7. Save the disk file as **mych11a.wpd**.

8. At the top of the document, select **Interoffice Memo**.

9. Apply the **bold** character style and change the point size to **14**.

10. Choose **View, Ruler Bar** to display the ruler.

11. Select the four paragraphs beginning with *To:* and ending with *Subject:* (see Figure 11.2).

12. Select and delete the default tab stops at the 1-inch and 1.5-inch marks on the ruler (press **Shift** and drag to select the tab stops; then drag the selected tab stops off the ruler).

13. Set a left-aligned tab at the 2-inch mark, if necessary.

14. Deselect the text.

15. Select **To:** (do not select the entire line) and apply the bold text attribute.

16. Apply the bold text attribute to **From:**, **Date:**, and **Subject:**.

17. Select **Additional Services**, below the Subject line, and apply the bold text attribute.

18. Select **Newsletter** and apply the bold text attribute. Compare your screen to Figure 11.3.

Figure 11.2   **Deleting default tabs for selected paragraphs**

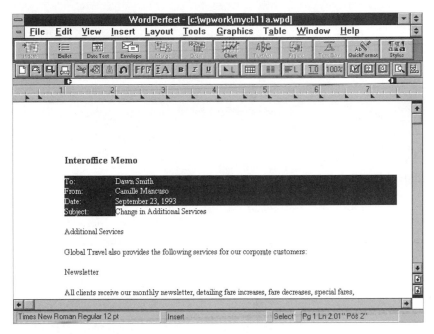

Figure 11.3   **Formatting the memo**

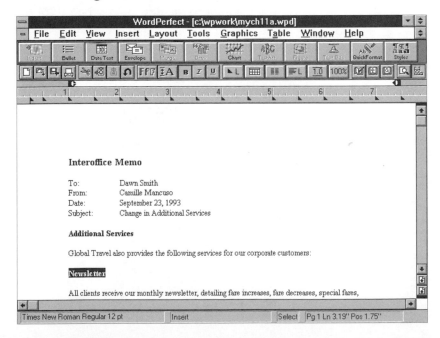

PRACTICE YOUR SKILLS

1. Apply the bold text attribute to the **Telex**, **Personal Vacations**, **Flight Insurance**, and **Fax** headings.

2. Click on the **Page Zoom Full** button (on the power bar) to preview the document.

3. Return to 100 percent magnification. (**Hint:** Click on the **Page Zoom Full** button again.)

4. Save the disk file and close the document.

USING THE MEMO2 TEMPLATE

Earlier, you learned how to create a memo using the STANDARD template. However, you can also create a business-style memo by using WordPerfect's MEMO2 template, which is a special template created specifically for this purpose.

Let's create a memo using the MEMO2 template:

1. Choose **File, Template** to open the Templates dialog box.

2. In the Document Template to Use list box, select **memo2** (see Figure 11.4).

3. Click on **OK** to display text at the top of the document. The Template Information dialog box is displayed (see Figure 11.5).

Figure 11.4   **Choosing the memo2 template**

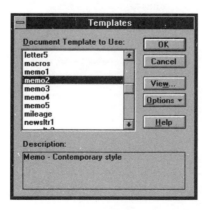

Figure 11.5   **The Template Information dialog box**

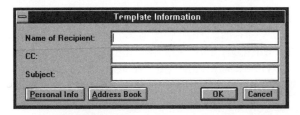

Note: The first time you use a template other than STAN-DARD, the Personalize Your Templates dialog box opens. If this happens to you, click on **OK**, type the appropriate information, then click on **OK** when you are finished. Now you should see the Template Information dialog box.

4. In the Name of Recipient text box, type **Dawn Smith**.

5. Press **Tab** to move to the CC text box; then type **Barb Stork, Marcie Forrest**.

6. Press **Tab** to move to the Subject text box; then type **Change in Additional Services**.

7. Click on the **Personal Info** button to open the Your Personal Information dialog box (see Figure 11.6). (**Note:** Your dialog box may already contain your information.)

Figure 11.6   **Your Personal Information dialog box**

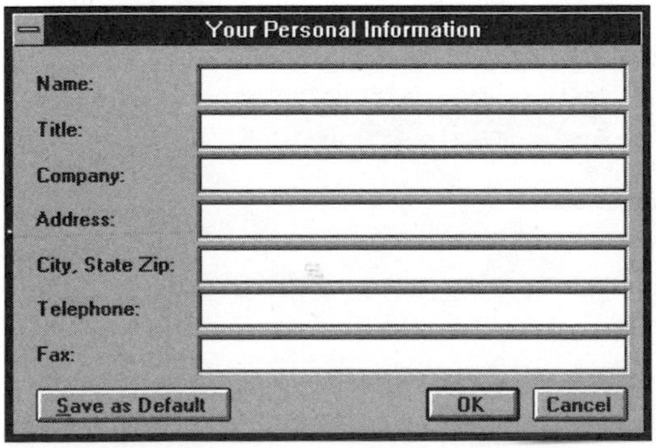

8. Select any text in the Name text box, if necessary, and type **Camille Mancuso.**

9. Click on **OK** to close the Your Personal Information dialog box and return to the Template Information dialog box. **Note:** You can use the Personal Info button to edit your personal information whenever you open a template. In addition, you can save the information in the Your Personal Information dialog box as the default simply by clicking on Save as Default.

10. Click on **OK** to close the Template Information dialog box and insert the names and subject into the memo.

11. Place the insertion point at the end of the document, if necessary.

12. Insert the file **chap11a.wpd** at the end of the document.

13. Compare your screen to Figure 11.7.

Figure 11.7   **The completed memo**

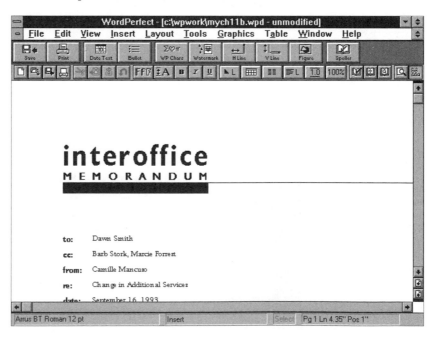

14. Save the disk file as **mych11b.wpd**.

15. Close the file.

CREATING AND USING STYLES

In Chapters 4 and 5 you learned how to format text and paragraphs. If you wanted to apply bold and italics to a selected paragraph and then right-align the paragraph, you had to apply each attribute separately. There is a faster way. *Styles* are named sets of formatting instructions. They enable you to quickly and easily format the paragraphs in a document. You can create your own styles.

Note: These styles differ from the ones you learned about in Chapter 4 in that here each style might contain a set of instructions, as opposed to a single instruction. For example, in Chapter 4 you saw how a word can have the bold text attribute (style) applied to it. As it is used here, a style might refer to bold, 10 point, Times Roman, and underline. Furthermore, these styles are applied to whole paragraphs. All of the paragraphs using the same style will contain the same formatting.

WordPerfect allows you to create your own customized styles. The first step is to apply the desired formatting to text, or place the insertion point in text that already has the desired formatting applied to it. Then choose Layout, Styles from the menu or press Alt+F8. We recommend using the shortcut key, as it is simpler and faster.

Here's the general procedure to create a style based on a formatted paragraph:

- Place the insertion point in the formatted paragraph.

- Choose *Layout, Styles*.

- Click on *Quick Create*.

- Type a style name.

- Press *Tab*.

- Type a description for the style.

- Click on *OK*.

- Click on *Apply* to apply the style to the selected paragraph; or, click on *Close* to close the Styles dialog box without applying the style to the selected paragraph.

Style names can contain up to 12 characters. They can include any combination of characters and spaces.

When you create a new style for a document, it is saved whenever you save the disk file. You can create up to 220 styles for a single document. The styles created in a document can be used only in that document. If you create a style in a template, it can be used in any new documents that are based on that template.

Once you have created a style, it is easy to apply it to any paragraph in your document. If you use styles to format your documents, they will have a more consistent look throughout.

Here's the general procedure to apply a style to a paragraph:

- Place the insertion point in the paragraph you want to apply the style to.
- Choose *Layout, Styles* (or press *Alt+F8*).
- From the Style List dialog box, select the style you want to apply.
- Click on *Apply.*

Let's create and apply some styles:

1. Open **chap11c.wpd** from your WPWORK directory.

2. Observe the *Global Travel* heading at the top of the document. It is formatted the way we want all our headings to look.

3. Place the insertion point in the *Global Travel* heading, if necessary.

4. Choose **Layout, Styles** to open the Style List dialog box (see Figure 11.8).

5. Click on **Quick Create** to open the Styles Quick Create dialog box (see Figure 11.9). You can use the Quick Create option to create a style based on a formatted paragraph.

6. Type **Title** in the Style Name text box.

Figure 11.8   The Style List dialog box

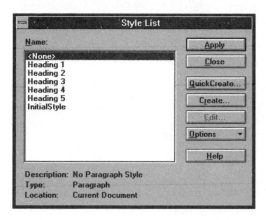

Figure 11.9   The Styles Quick Create dialog box

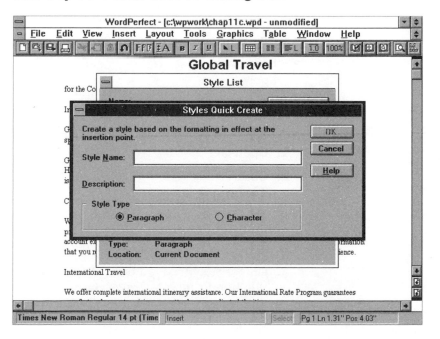

7. Press **Tab** to move the insertion point to the Description text box. It is important to type a description of your style. Then, if you forget what a style does, you have something to jog your memory.

8. Type **Formats report titles**.

9. Click on **OK** to close the Styles Quick Create dialog box and add the Title style to the Style List.

10. Click on **Apply** to close the Style List dialog box and apply the Title style to *Global Travel*.

11. Go to the top of page 2 (use **Ctrl+G**).

12. Place the insertion point in the *Global Travel* heading at the top of the page.

13. Open the Layout menu (click on **Layout**) and observe the shortcut key next to Styles. It is Alt+F8.

14. Close the Layout menu (click on **Layout** again).

15. Press **Alt+F8** to open the Style List dialog box.

16. Select **Title** from the Style list.

17. Click on **Apply** to apply the Title style to the selected paragraph.

18. Observe the heading. It is now Helvetica, 24 point, bold, and centered.

19. Save the disk file as **mych11c.wpd**.

PRACTICE YOUR SKILLS

1. Move to the top of the document. (**Hint:** Press **Ctrl+Home**.)

2. Create a style called **Subtitle** based on the formatted sub-title line *Complete Travel Services*. (**Hint:** Place the insertion point in the paragraph before you open the Style List dialog box.)

3. Give Subtitle style the following description:

   Formats report subtitles.

4. Apply Subtitle style to *For the Corporate Traveler* (the second line of the subtitle on page 1).

5. Apply Subtitle style to both lines of the subtitle (*Complete Travel Services* and *For the Corporate Traveler*) on page 2.

6. Apply Bold, Underline, and 13-point formats to *Introduction* (the first heading on page 1).(**Hint:** Select *Introduction* and then apply the text attributes.)

7. Create a style called **Sectionhding** based on *Introduction*.

8. Give Sectionhding style the following description:

    Formats section headings for reports.

9. Apply Sectionhding style to the following paragraphs:

Customer Service	Deliveries
International Travel	Auto Rentals
Corporate Profiles	Hotel Accomodations
Worldwide Services	Additional Services
Discounts	

10. Save the disk file.

11. Compare your screen to Figure 11.10.

12. Close the document.

SUMMARY

In this chapter, you learned how to create documents using the templates provided with WordPerfect. You also learned how to create styles and apply them to your documents. Finally, you learned how to modify styles.

Figure 11.10   **Completed MYCH11C.WPD document**

Global Travel
Complete Travel Services
for the Corporate Traveler

Introduction

Global Travel is a full-service multi-branch travel agency, which was founded in 1970. Our specialty is corporate travel.

Global Travel has branches in five major cities: Philadelphia, San Francisco, Chicago, Miami, and Houston. Each of these offices is operated by a team of qualified managers and agents whose goal is to provide your company with quality service at the lowest price.

Customer Service

We at Global Travel feel that communication with our corporate accounts is essential for providing good service. Each corporate account is assigned to a specific account executive. Your account executive will be available to answer any questions and provide you with any information that you request. We encourage you to tour our facility and meet our staff at your convenience.

International Travel

We offer complete international itinerary assistance. Our International Rate Program guarantees you fast and accurate pricing, no matter how complicated the itinerary.

Corporate Profiles

Your company profile is stored in our computer. In addition, individual profiles are maintained on each of your frequent travelers. Each profile contains passport information, seating and car rental preference, frequent-flyer membership number, and corporate discount numbers. This information ensures that we can provide frequent travelers fast, cost-effective service.

Worldwide Services

Global Travel's Reservation Center handles all of your weekend and after-hour reservations and changes. The reservation center can be reached toll-free, 24 hours a day. The worldwide service emergency numbers will be clearly marked on your travel itineraries.

Discounts

Global Travel guarantees the lowest air fares available. Due to the number of tickets that we issue, several large air carriers offer us special discounts that we can pass on to our clients. Our quality-control specialists check each of your tickets to guarantee that you have received the lowest rate available.

Figure 11.10   Completed MYCH11C.WPD document (Continued)

Global Travel
Complete Travel Services
for the Corporate Traveler

Deliveries

Our courier makes daily deliveries twice a day to offices within 20 miles of our local branch. Each one of our offices is located across from the local airport and has a drive-up window. If you make last minute travel plans with us, you can pick up your ticket at the drive-up window on your way to the airport.

Auto Rentals

We guarantee the lowest prices on all car rentals. We will match the type of car with the information provided in the profile for each of your frequent travelers. Each car that is rented through Global Travel carries an extra $50,000 worth of liability insurance.

Hotel Accommodations

Our Corporate Hotel Program is the most competitive and comprehensive program in the world. We offer cost savings and extra amenities in most business locations. Global Travel has access to more than 10,000 hotels worldwide, with a range of rooms from economy to luxury. Your corporate travelers get the accommodations they want with a savings of 20-30% off regular rates.

Additional Services

Global Travel also provides the following services for our corporate customers:

Newsletter

All clients receive our montly newsletter covering a variety of travel topics.

Personal Vacations

Our corporate clients are invited to discuss their vacation and personal travel plans with an agent from Global Travel's Vacation division.

Flight Insurance

We supply all clients with $250,000 worth of flight insurance.

Here is a quick reference guide to the WordPerfect for Windows features introduced in this chapter:

Desired Result	How to Do It
Attach the STANDARD template to a file	Choose **File, New**
Insert a file	Activate the destination document window; place the insertion point at the desired destination; choose **Insert, File**; select the name of the file to be inserted; click on **OK**
Attach the MEMO2 template to a file	Choose **File, Template**; select **memo2**; click on **OK**; type the name of the recipient; press **Tab**; type the name(s) of any persons you want to carbon copy the memo to; press **Tab**; type the subject of the memo; click on **Personal Info**; type the name of the sender; click on **OK**; click on **OK** again; type the memo text
Create a style based on a formatted paragraph	Place the insertion point in the formatted paragraph; choose **Layout, Styles** (or press **Alt+F8**); click on **Quick Create**; type a name for the style; press **Tab**; type a description; click on **OK**; click on **Apply** to close the Style List dialog box and apply the style to the selected paragraph, or click on **Close** to close the Style List dialog box without applying the style
Applying a style	Place the insertion point in the paragraph you want to apply the style to; choose **Layout, Styles** (or press **Alt+F8**); from the Style List dialog box, select the appropriate style; click on **Apply**
Deleting a style	Choose **Layout, Styles**; select the style you want to delete; click on the **Options** button; click on **Delete**; click on **OK**; click on **Close**

Congratulations! You have now learned how to use many of WordPerfect for Windows's features. You are now prepared to take all that you've learned and apply it to your own documents. Remember, to master the skills that you've acquired, you must supply the most important ingredient—practice. With practice you will learn to use WordPerfect for Windows to its fullest potential. Good luck!

APPENDIX A: INSTALLATION

Before You Begin
Installing

Installing
WordPerfect on
Your Computer

Selecting a Printer

This appendix contains instructions for installing WordPerfect 6.0 for Windows on your computer and for selecting a printer for use with WordPerfect.

BEFORE YOU BEGIN INSTALLING

Please read through the following two sections before beginning the installation procedure.

PROTECTING YOUR ORIGINAL INSTALLATION DISKS

WordPerfect comes with several floppy disks that you'll need to install the program on your computer. Before you begin, you should protect your original installation disks from accidental erasure. When a disk is protected, its data can be read, but not modified.

Here's the general procedure to protect a 3½-inch disk

- Slide the plastic locking button in the corner of the disk to its uppermost position.

Here's the general procedure to protect a 5¼-inch disk:

- Place a write-protect tab over the notch on the edge of the disk.

REQUIRED HARD-DISK SPACE

You need to have at least 33MB (33,000,000 bytes) of free hard-disk space to completely install WordPerfect 6.0. If you do not have at least 33MB of free hard-disk space, you must delete enough files from your hard disk to bring the total free space up to 33MB. For help in doing this, please refer to your DOS or Windows manuals.

Note: Remember to back up (copy to a floppy disk) any files that you wish to preserve before deleting them from your hard disk.

In addition, WordPerfect recommends that you have 6–8MB of RAM (random access memory).

INSTALLING WORDPERFECT ON YOUR COMPUTER

Follow these steps to install WordPerfect 6.0 for Windows:

1. Turn on your computer and start Windows. (If you have not already installed Windows on your system, please do so now; for help, see your Windows reference manuals.)

2. Insert the installation disk labeled *Install 1* in the appropriately sized disk drive.

3. Choose **File, Run** from the Windows Program Manager menu.

4. Type **a:install** (for drive A) or **b:install** (for drive B), and then press **Enter** to start the WordPerfect installation program.

5. If you are prompted to enter your name and license number, follow the on-screen directions to do so. Click on **Continue** when you are done.

6. A dialog box appears showing the available types of installation (see Figure A.1).

Figure A.1   **Installation Type dialog box**

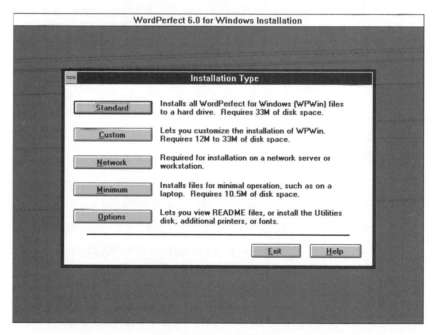

To complete the hands-on activities in this book, you must select the standard installation option; the other installations do not provide the necessary WordPerfect options.

7. Click on the **Standard** button.

8. When you are prompted to specify the hard-disk drive where you want to install WordPerfect, click on **OK** to accept the

default drive, *c:*. (**Note:** If you want to install WordPerfect on a different hard-disk drive, type the drive letter and click on **OK**.)

9. A dialog box appears, informing you of the installation procedure's progress for the current disk as well as the program: 100% in the top bar means the current floppy disk installation is complete; 100% in the bottom bar means the WordPerfect installation is complete. When you are asked to insert a new Installation or Program disk, please do so.

   Note: You can click on **Cancel** at any time to cancel the entire installation.

10. After all the program files are installed, a Read Me Files dialog box appears. This dialog box provides access to documentation not available in the WordPerfect reference guide. Click on **Yes** to access the files, or **No** to complete the installation without accessing the files.

11. When the installation procedure is complete, you are returned to Windows. To start WordPerfect, simply double-click on the newly created WordPerfect icon located in the newly created group *WPWin 6.0*.

SELECTING A PRINTER

Before you can print from WordPerfect, you must select a printer. To do so, follow these steps:

1. Start WordPerfect 6.0 for Windows.

2. Choose **File, Select Printer** to open the Select Printer dialog box. The dialog box displays a list of the printers that are currently installed on your system.

3. If your printer appears on the list (you may have to scroll), select it and click on **Select**. You can now use this printer with WordPerfect.

4. If your printer does not appear on the list (even after scrolling), install the printer on your system (for instructions, refer to your Windows or WordPerfect documentation), and then repeat this printer selection procedure from step 1.

Note: The printed examples shown in this book were all printed on a PostScript laser printer. Your printouts may differ somewhat, depending on which printer you are using. Printer choice also affects how text appears on your screen. If you are using a non-PostScript printer, your screen typestyles and sizes may differ from those shown in this book's figures.

APPENDIX B: KEYSTROKE REFERENCE

Insertion Pointer Movement

Text Selection

Text Entry

Text Editing

Character Formatting

Paragraph Formatting

File and Window Management

Miscellaneous

This appendix lists the keystrokes that you can use to issue WordPerfect commands.

INSERTION POINTER MOVEMENT

Move	Key/Key Combination
One character to the left	Left Arrow
One character to the right	Right Arrow
One line up	Up Arrow
One line down	Down Arrow
One word to the left	Ctrl+Left Arrow
One word to the right	Ctrl+Right Arrow
To the end of a line	End
To the start of a line	Home
Down one screen	PgDn
Up one screen	PgUp
To the start of a document	Ctrl+Home
To the end of a document	Ctrl+End
To any page of a document	Ctrl+G

TEXT SELECTION

Select	Key/Key Combination
Left character	Shift+Left Arrow
Right character	Shift+Right Arrow
Previous line	Shift+Up Arrow
Next line	Shift+Down Arrow
Select text	F8
Select cell	Shift+F8

TEXT ENTRY

Format	Key/Key Combination
Start new paragraph	Enter
Insert hard page break	Ctrl+Enter
Insert normal hyphen	Hyphen
Insert hard space	Ctrl+Spacebar
Insert current date	Ctrl+D

TEXT EDITING

Edit	Key/Key Combination
Cut selected text	Ctrl+X
Copy selected text	Ctrl+C
Paste text	Ctrl+V
Delete character to the right	Del
Delete character to the left	Backspace
Undo	Ctrl+Z
Undelete	Ctrl+Shift+Z

CHARACTER FORMATTING

Format	Key/Key Combination
Change font	Ctrl+F
Change point size	F9
Case toggle	Ctrl+K
Bold	Ctrl+B

Format	Key/Key Combination
Underline	Ctrl+U
Italic	Ctrl+I

PARAGRAPH FORMATTING

Format	Key/Key Combination
Center lines	Shift+F7
Left-justify paragraphs	Ctrl+L
Right-justify paragraphs	Ctrl+R
Center-justify paragraphs	Ctrl+E
Full-justify paragraphs	Ctrl+J
Indent	F7
Hanging indent	Ctrl+F7
Double indent	Ctrl+Shift+F7
Flush right	Alt+F7
Styles	Alt+F8
Change margins	Ctrl+F8
Insert bullet	Ctrl+Shift+B

FILE AND WINDOW MANAGEMENT

Format	Key/Key Combination
New document	Ctrl+N
Save As	F3
Save	Ctrl+S
Open	Ctrl+O

Format	Key/Key Combination
Open a template	Ctrl+T
Print document	Ctrl+P
Close document	Ctrl+F4
Close without saving	Ctrl+Shift+F4
Next open document	Ctrl+F6
Previous open document	Ctrl+Shift+F6
Next pane	F6
Previous pane	Shift+F6
Next window	Alt+F6
Previous window	Alt+Shift+F6
Page Zoom Full	Shift+F5
Draft view	Ctrl+F5
Page view	Alt+F5
Hide bars	Alt+Shift+F5
Exit WordPerfect	Alt+F4

MISCELLANEOUS

Function	Key/Key Combination
Help	F1
Help pointer	Shift+F1
Print	Ctrl+P
Speller	Ctrl+F1
Thesaurus	Alt+F1
Find	F2

Function	Key/Key Combination
Find Next	Shift+F2
Find Previous	Alt+F2
Replace	Ctrl+F2
Refresh screen	Ctrl+F3
Show nonprinting characters	Ctrl+Shift+F3
Reveal codes	Alt+F3

APPENDIX C:/ EXCHANGING DOCUMENTS WITH OTHER PROGRAMS

Opening Non–
WordPerfect 6.0
Files

Saving Non–
WordPerfect 6.0
Files

WordPerfect 6.0 for Windows is compatible with many popular word processing and spreadsheet programs. You can open a non–WordPerfect 6.0 document (disk file), edit and print it, and then save it in its original file format or as a WordPerfect 6.0 file. Or, you can open a WordPerfect 6.0 document and then save it in a file format that can be used with a non–WordPerfect 6.0 program. This appendix lists the various formats in which WordPerfect can open and save files, and shows you how to make your desired file conversions.

OPENING NON–WORDPERFECT 6.0 FILES

Here's the general procedure to open a non–WordPerfect 6.0 file:

- Choose *File, Open* (or click on the power bar *Open* button) to display the File Open dialog box.

- Select the desired drive in the Drives list box.

- Select the desired directory in the Directories list box.

- Select the desired file in the Filename list box. Or, type the desired file name (with extension) in the Filename text box.

- Click on *OK* (or press *Enter*). The Conversion File Format dialog box appears, listing the file formats that WordPerfect 6.0 can convert from (that is, the file types that it can open). The format of the file you specified in the previous step is highlighted. (**Note:** If the file format of your specified file does not appear in this box, but does appear in Table C.1, exit this procedure, run the WordPerfect installation program to add the missing file-format converter, and then repeat this procedure.)

- Click on *OK* (or press *Enter*) to convert your file from the highlighted format to WordPerfect 6.0 format.

Once you've opened a non–WordPerfect 6.0 file, you can edit, print, save, or close it exactly as you would any standard WordPerfect 6.0 file. If you want to save the file in WordPerfect 6.0 format, use Save (to keep the same name and location) or Save As (to change the name and/or location). If you want to save the file in its original format (for example, as a Word for Windows 2.0 file), please refer to the procedure presented in the next section, "Saving Non–WordPerfect 6.0 Files." Table C.1 lists the types of non–WordPerfect 6.0 files that can be opened.

SAVING NON–WORDPERFECT 6.0 FILES

Here's the general procedure to save a file in a non–WordPerfect 6.0 file format:

- Choose *File, Save As* to display the Save As dialog box.

- Select the desired drive in the Drives list box.

- Select the desired directory in the Directories list box.

Table C.1   **File Types You Can Open from WordPerfect 6.0**

File Format	Type of File
.sam	AmiPro
.	ANSI
.	ASCI
.DOC	DisplayWrite 4.0, 4.2, 5.0
.FFT	IBM DCA FFT
.RFT	IBM DCA RFT
.	Kermit (7-Bit Transfer)
.DOC	Microsoft Word 4.0, 5.0, 5.5
.DOC	Microsoft Word for Windows 1.0, 1.1, 1.1a, 2.0, 2.0a, 2.0b
.	WordStar 2000 1.0, 2.0, 3.0
.	WordStar 3.3, 3.31, 3.4, 4.0, 5.0, 5.5, 6.0
.DOC	MultiMate 3.3, 3.6, 4.0
.DOC	MultiMate Advantage II 1.0
.DIF	Navy DIF Standard
.WP	Office Writer 6.0, 6.1, 6.11, 6.2
.RTF	Rich Text Format
.DOC, .WP	WordPerfect 4.2, 5.0, 5.1, 5.2, 6.0, and WordPerfect 2.0, 2.1 for Macintosh
.TXT	Windows Write

- Select the desired file format in the Format drop-down list box. (**Note:** If your desired file format does not appear in this box, but does appear in Table C.2, exit this procedure, run the Word-Perfect installation program to add the missing file-format converter, and then repeat this procedure.)

- Type the desired file name (without extension) in the Filename text box.

- Click on *OK* (or press *Enter*).

Once you've saved a file in a non–WordPerfect 6.0 file format, you can open it from the program that uses this file format (for example, Word for Windows 2.0) and then edit, print, save, or close it exactly as you would any standard file in that program.

You can save a file in a non–WordPerfect 6.0 file format listed in Table C.2.

Table C.2   **File Types You Can Save from WordPerfect 6.0**

File Format	File Type
.SAM	Ami Pro
.	ANSI
.	ASCII
.DOC	DisplayWrite 4.0, 4.2, 5.0
.FFT	IBM DCA FFT
.RFT	IBM DCA RFT
.	Kermit (7-Bit Transfer)
.DOC	Microsoft Word 4.0, 5.0, 5.5
.DOC	Microsoft Word for Windows 1.0, 1.1, 1.1a, 2.0, 2.0a, 2.0b
.	WordStar 2000 1.0, 2.0, 3.0
.	WordStar 3.3, 3.31, 3.4, 4.0, 5.0, 5.5, 6.0
.DOC	MultiMate 3.3, 3.6, 4.0

Table C.2 **File Types You Can Save from WordPerfect 6.0 (Continued)**

File Format	File Type
.DOC	MultiMate Advantage II 1.0
.DIF	Navy DIF Standard
.WP	Office Writer 6.0, 6.1, 6.11, 6.2
.RTF	Rich Text Format
.DOC, .WP	WordPerfect 4.2, 5.0, 5.1, 5.2, 6.0, and WordPerfect 2.0, 2.1 for Macintosh
.TXT	Windows Write

APPENDIX D: CUSTOMIZING WORDPERFECT 6.0 FOR WINDOWS

Customizing the
Screen

Setting File
Preferences

*O*ne of the wonderful features about WordPerfect 6.0 for Windows is its adaptability. WordPerfect is a fully customizable program, so you can give your WordPerfect for Windows application window the look you want. Also, the Preferences options let you customize other aspects of WordPerfect to suit your needs. Many of these options are preset to accommodate most users. If you are happy with the way WordPerfect is set up, you need not use Preferences. However, you can change any of the WordPerfect preferences. If, for example, you are responsible for sending letters to potential clients, you might want to have all of the print merge features on your default button bar.

In addition, you can tell WordPerfect exactly where you want to save files and how often to save an automatic backup of the file you are working on.

This appendix is only intended to introduce some of the more useful Preferences options. Feel free to play with any of the other Preferences options, or consult your WordPerfect User's Guide for more information about them.

CUSTOMIZING THE SCREEN

When you first install WordPerfect for Windows, the program opens with the default screen (the WordPerfect button bar, power bar, and status bar in graphics mode) displayed. You can create your own default button bar, add or delete buttons from the power bar, and add or delete options on the status bar.

MOVING THE BUTTON BAR

As you learned in Chapter 8, you can move the button bar in the Button Bar Preferences dialog box. However, you can also drag the button bar to a new location without the bother of opening the Preferences dialog box.

Here's the general procedure to drag the button bar to a new location:

- Place the mouse pointer on the border of the button bar (the mouse pointer turns into a hand when it is positioned on the border).

- Drag the button bar down into the text area to display it as a palette; or, drag it to the left, right, or bottom of the screen to display the button bar in the location you want.

Note: You can also reduce the size of the application window (place the mouse pointer on the bottom border of the window and drag up), and drag the button bar outside of the application window.

THE RIGHT MOUSE BUTTON

The right mouse button (secondary mouse button) makes it easier for you to customize your WordPerfect for Windows screen. Instead of using the menu, you can place the mouse pointer on any of the WordPerfect bars, click the right mouse button, and access the Preferences dialog box for that bar. Following this paragraph is a list of options you can access when you click the right mouse button on each of the WordPerfect bars.

Location	Access
Button bar	Defined button bars, Button Bar Preferences and Editor dialog boxes, hide button bar
Power bar	Power Bar Preferences dialog box, hide power bar
Status bar	Status Bar Preferences, hide status bar
Scroll bar	Go To, Bookmark, and Display Preferences dialog boxes
Menu bar	Menu Bar Preferences dialog box

Note: In addition, when you click the right mouse button on different areas of your screen, WordPerfect opens different QuickMenus, giving you instant access to several of the most common word processing commands based on the location of the mouse pointer when you click the right mouse button.

POWER BAR

The WordPerfect power bar has all of the general text-editing and layout features that you most often use. It is different from the button bar in that the button bar is context-sensitive (for example, you can create a special button bar for a document style you use frequently—such as a memo—and save it with the current document), but the power bar always displays the same buttons each time you start WordPerfect or open a new or existing document. In addition, while you can drag the button bar all over the screen, the power bar always displays in the same position on screen.

However, you're not stuck with the default power bar buttons—you can edit the power bar. If there are several buttons on the power bar that you rarely use, you can delete them. Then you can add buttons for the options that you do use. You can also move buttons.

Deleting Buttons from the Power Bar

Depending upon the size of your screen, WordPerfect for Windows can display only a certain number of buttons on the power bar. If you want to add buttons to the power bar, you'll probably first need to delete buttons you don't use.

Here's the general procedure to delete buttons from the power bar:

- Place the mouse pointer on the power bar and click the *right mouse* button.

- Click on *Preferences* to open the Power Bar Preferences dialog box (see Figure D.1). A check mark next to an item indicates that item is displayed as a button on the power bar.

Figure D.1   **The Power Bar Preferences dialog box**

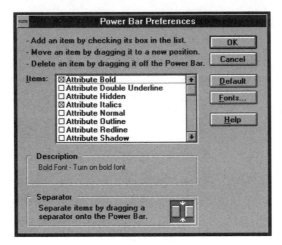

- Place the mouse pointer on the button you want to delete and drag the button off the power bar.

- Click on *OK* to close the Power Bar Preferences dialog box.

Note: Any changes you make to the power bar remain in effect for all future documents until you edit the power bar again.

Adding and Moving Buttons

Here's the general procedure to add a button to the button bar:

- Open the Power Bar Preferences dialog box.

- Click on the check box next to the item you want to add to the button bar.

- Click on *OK*.

Note: Separators allow you to space groups of similar items (such as the Cut, Copy, and Paste items) on the power bar, or to make frequently used items stand out from other items. You add a separator by dragging it from the Power Bar Preferences dialog box to the appropriate place on the power bar.

Here's the general procedure to move a button on the power bar:

- Open the Power Bar Preferences dialog box.

- Place the mouse pointer on the button you want to move.

- Drag the button to its new location.

- Click on *OK*.

Note: If, at any time, you wish to redisplay the default power bar, you need only click on Default in the Power Bar Preferences dialog box.

 STATUS BAR

The status bar allows you to quickly see information related to the document you are working on. By default, the status bar displays the font you are using as well as the position of the insertion point and whether you are in insert or typeover mode or have a style applied to the active paragraph.

Customizing the Status Bar

You can customize the status bar so that it contains the type of information you want to see as you create documents.

Here's the general procedure to customize the status bar:

- Place the mouse pointer on the status bar and click the *right mouse* button.

- Choose *Preferences*.

- Select any of the options you want to appear on the status bar.

- Move items by dragging them to a new position on the status bar.

- Delete items by dragging them off the status bar.

- Resize items by placing the mouse pointer on either end of an item until the pointer becomes a two-headed arrow, and then dragging to resize.

- Click on *OK* to close the dialog box and accept the changes to the status bar.

Note: You can usually include five to seven items on the status bar. If you cannot see all of the items you choose, then delete, move, or resize the items.

If you decide you want to use the original default settings again, you can open the Status Bar Preferences dialog box and click on Default.

You can double-click on the various status bar options to open dialog boxes. Table D.1 lists the status bar options and what happens when you double-click on each option.

Table D.1   **Status Bar Options**

Status Bar Item	Double-click to
Alignment Char	Open the Tab Set dialog box
Caps Lock State	Turn Caps Lock on or off
Combined Position	Open the Go To dialog box
Date	Insert the current date at the insertion point
Font	Open the Font dialog box
Columns	Open the Columns dialog box
Tables	Open the Table Format dialog box
Merge	Open the Insert Merge Codes dialog box
Paragraph Style Name	Open the Style List dialog box
Insert Mode	Switch between insert and typeover modes
Keyboard	Open the Keyboard Preferences dialog box
Line	Open the Go To dialog box

Table D.1   **Status Bar Options (Continued)**

Status Bar Item	Double-click to
Num Lock State	Turn Num Lock on or off
Outline On/Off	Turn Outline on or off
Page	Open the Go To dialog box
Position	Open the Go To dialog box
Printer	Open the Select Printer dialog box
Scroll Lock State	Turn Scroll Lock on or off
Select On/Off	Turn Select on or off
Zoom	Open the Zoom dialog box

SETTING FILE PREFERENCES

You can set file preferences (for example, the directory where you always save WordPerfect documents) as well as change the Word-Perfect interface. For example, you can ask WordPerfect to auto-matically save your document to a particular directory every 15 minutes instead of every 10 minutes. Or, if you don't want Word-Perfect to save your document automatically, you can turn the option off.

You can set a different default directory for the following items:

- Documents
- Templates
- Spreadsheets
- Databases
- Printers/Labels
- Hyphenation
- Graphics
- Macros

Here's the general procedure to change file preferences:

- Choose *File, Preferences* to open the Preferences dialog box.

- Double-click on the *File* icon to open the File Preferences dialog box.

- Click on the file type (at the top of the dialog box) for which you want to change the default options.

- Select the text in the Default Directory box and type the new default directory path. Or, if you aren't where the directory is located, click on the *Directory* button to the right of the Default Directory box, select the appropriate directory, and click on *OK*.

- Change any other settings.

- Click on *OK*.

Note: By default, WordPerfect saves a backup of your document every 10 minutes. To turn this option off, uncheck the Timed Document Backup check box.

INDEX

Note: Italicized page numbers denote figures and tables.

A

a:install, 305

active document, 10, 26

Address field, inserting in form file, *271*

Add Script button in Button Bar Editor, 218

Alignment Char status bar item, *328*

alignment and tabs, 17–18, 34, 117

all justification, 138, 139

Alpha sort order, 274, 275

Alt+F8 (Styles feature), 293, 294, 296, 300

AmiPro files

opening, *319*

saving, *320*

ANSI files

opening, *319*

saving, *320*

antonyms, finding with Thesaurus, 189, *192,* 200

Appearance box (Font dialog box), 91, 94

Append to Doc button in Envelope dialog box, 208

applications, 1, 9

application windows, 7–11

reducing to icon, 9

shrinking and expanding, 11

arrow, mouse pointer as, 15

B

arrow with question mark, mouse pointer as, 56, 58

arrows on button bar, 212, 215

Ascending sort order, 274, 275, 282

ASCI files

opening, *319*

saving, *320*

asterisk (∗) wildcard character and spell checks, *185*

attributes

applying with power bar, 95–97, 111

applying to text, 90–92

copying with Quick Format feature, 97–99, 111

removing from text, 92, 94, 111

repeating, 97–99

automatic page breaks, 158–159

automatic page-numbering, 165

b:install, 305

Backspace key, deleting text with, 18–19, 34

backups, setting timing of, 330

blank lines, creating, 15–16, 34

blinking vertical bar, 14

blocks of text, 20–21

deleting, 22

selecting, 70

bold attribute, 90, 91, 95, 96, 246

Bold button, 95, 98, 104

[Bold] paired codes, 102, *103,* 104

borders

adding to tables, 248–249

changing in tables, 247–250, 258

Border Style button, 196

bulleted headwords in Thesaurus feature, 190, 191

bulleted procedures, 4

Button Bar command (View menu), 42

Button Bar Editor, 213, *214,* 215

Button Bar icon, 212

button bar options, *211,* 221

Ziff-Davis Press Survey of Readers

Please help us in our effort to produce the best books on personal computing.
For your assistance, we would be pleased to send you a FREE catalog
featuring the complete line of Ziff-Davis Press books.

1. How did you first learn about this book?

Recommended by a friend . . . . ☐ -1 (5)
Recommended by store personnel . . . . ☐ -2
Saw in Ziff-Davis Press catalog . . . . ☐ -3
Received advertisement in the mail . . . . ☐ -4
Saw the book on bookshelf at store . . . . ☐ -5
Read book review in: _____ ☐ -6
Saw an advertisement in: _____ ☐ -7
Other (Please specify): _____ ☐ -8

2. Which THREE of the following factors most influenced your decision to purchase this book? (Please check up to THREE.)

Front or back cover information on book . . . ☐ -1 (6)
Logo of magazine affiliated with book . . . . . . ☐ -2
Special approach to the content . . . . ☐ -3
Completeness of content . . . . ☐ -4
Author's reputation. . . . . ☐ -5
Publisher's reputation . . . . ☐ -6
Book cover design or layout . . . . ☐ -7
Index or table of contents of book . . . . ☐ -8
Price of book . . . . ☐ -9
Special effects, graphics, illustrations . . . . . . ☐ -0
Other (Please specify): _____ ☐ -x

3. How many computer books have you purchased in the last six months? _____ (7-10)

4. On a scale of 1 to 5, where 5 is excellent, 4 is above average, 3 is average, 2 is below average, and 1 is poor, please rate each of the following aspects of this book below. (Please circle your answer.)

Depth/completeness of coverage	5	4	3	2	1	(11)
Organization of material	5	4	3	2	1	(12)
Ease of finding topic	5	4	3	2	1	(13)
Special features/time saving tips	5	4	3	2	1	(14)
Appropriate level of writing	5	4	3	2	1	(15)
Usefulness of table of contents	5	4	3	2	1	(16)
Usefulness of index	5	4	3	2	1	(17)
Usefulness of accompanying disk	5	4	3	2	1	(18)
Usefulness of illustrations/graphics	5	4	3	2	1	(19)
Cover design and attractiveness	5	4	3	2	1	(20)
Overall design and layout of book	5	4	3	2	1	(21)
Overall satisfaction with book	5	4	3	2	1	(22)

5. Which of the following computer publications do you read regularly; that is, 3 out of 4 issues?

Byte . . . . ☐ -1 (23)
Computer Shopper . . . . ☐ -2
Corporate Computing . . . . ☐ -3
Dr. Dobb's Journal . . . . ☐ -4
LAN Magazine . . . . ☐ -5
MacWEEK . . . . ☐ -6
MacUser . . . . ☐ -7
PC Computing . . . . ☐ -8
PC Magazine . . . . ☐ -9
PC WEEK . . . . ☐ -0
Windows Sources . . . . ☐ -x
Other (Please specify): _____ ☐ -y

Please turn page.

6. What is your level of experience with personal computers? With the subject of this book?

	With PCs	With subject of book
Beginner...........	☐ -1 (24)	☐ -1 (25)
Intermediate.......	☐ -2	☐ -2
Advanced...........	☐ -3	☐ -3

7. Which of the following best describes your job title?

Officer (CEO/President/VP/owner)........ ☐ -1 (26)
Director/head......................... ☐ -2
Manager/supervisor.................... ☐ -3
Administration/staff................... ☐ -4
Teacher/educator/trainer.............. ☐ -5
Lawyer/doctor/medical professional....... ☐ -6
Engineer/technician................... ☐ -7
Consultant........................... ☐ -8
Not employed/student/retired........... ☐ -9
Other (Please specify): _____ ☐ -0

8. What is your age?

Under 20........................... ☐ -1 (27)
21-29............................. ☐ -2
30-39............................. ☐ -3
40-49............................. ☐ -4
50-59............................. ☐ -5
60 or over......................... ☐ -6

9. Are you:

Male.............................. ☐ -1 (28)
Female............................ ☐ -2

Thank you for your assistance with this important information! Please write your address below to receive our free catalog.

Name: _____

Address: _____

City/State/Zip: _____

Fold here to mail.

0203-01-01

_____

_____

_____

BUSINESS REPLY MAIL
FIRST CLASS MAIL   PERMIT NO. 1612   OAKLAND, CA

POSTAGE WILL BE PAID BY ADDRESSEE

Ziff-Davis Press
5903 Christie Avenue
Emeryville, CA 94608-1925
Attn: Marketing

■ TO RECEIVE 5¼-INCH DISK(S)

The Ziff-Davis Press software contained on the $3\frac{1}{2}$-inch disk included with this book is also available in $5\frac{1}{4}$-inch format. If you would like to receive the software in the $5\frac{1}{4}$-inch format, please return the $3\frac{1}{2}$-inch disk with your name and address to:

Disk Exchange
Ziff-Davis Press
5903 Christie Avenue
Emeryville, CA 94608